MEMORIES OF LIFE IN EAST GERMANY:

Snapshots

RICHARD A. ZIPSER

Memories of Life in East Germany: Snapshots

Copyright © 2022 Richard A. Zipser.

ISBN: 978-1-66784-243-1 (Paperback)

First printing edition 2022.

Printed by BookBaby Publishing
7905 North Crescent Boulevard
Pennsauken Township, NJ 08110

www.richardzipser.com

CONTENTS

I
ACKNOWLEDGMENTS

I want to express gratitude to several persons who assisted me as I was writing and preparing to publish this memoir. I am especially indebted to former East Germans Iris Busch and Heinz-Uwe Haus, who are now faculty members at the University of Delaware (UD) and good friends of mine, for their insightful commentaries on many of the prose texts in this book. Their remarks helped me make necessary revisions and add relevant factual information that only persons from the German Democratic Republic (GDR) would know. Many individuals—friends, colleagues, acquaintances—who are unable to read German became my readers along the way and also provided me with valuable feedback. These persons had little or no knowledge of East Germany, so their responses as 'naïve readers' of these pieces were immensely helpful. After all, my collection of GDR memories is aimed at an English-speaking audience, so I had to find out if the texts I had written were in fact connecting with those persons. Fortunately, they were!

Let me now thank some of the readers, almost all of whom had been my colleagues at the University of Delaware, whose candid comments were useful to me when revising my snapshots: Ulrike Diedenhofen, my wife, Mary Donaldson-Evans, Susan Goodman, Katharine Kerrane, Kevin Kerrane,

Bonnie Robb, whom I also thank for penning such an illuminating afterword, and Rae Stabosz, the person who maintains both of my websites and posts what I have written. As Project Manager Rae oversaw the production of this book and did outstanding work as tech editor, interior text formatter, and proofreader. Her contributions were truly invaluable.

Most of all, I deeply appreciate the ongoing support I receive from my wife, Ulrike Diedenhofen, who encouraged me to undertake this project. She provides much-needed encouragement, also an open ear whenever I need a listener, as she has done throughout my career for more than forty years. To her I once again say "thank you," knowing that these words are not a sufficient expression of my gratitude.

II
READER ORIENTATION

INTRODUCTION

Memories of Life in East Germany: Snapshots is a collection of short prose pieces on aspects of life in the former German Democratic Republic (GDR) as I experienced it directly in the 1960s, 1970s, and 1980s. This book is meant to be a companion piece to my documentary memoir, *Remembering East Germany. From Oberlin to East Berlin* (Pennsauken: BookBaby, 2021), which is based largely on the 396-page file the East German secret police (Stasi) compiled on me between 1973 and 1988, when I was travelling and working on a number of scholarly projects in that country. The original version of the memoir, written in German and entitled *Von Oberlin nach Ostberlin. Als Amerikaner unterwegs in der DDR-Literaturszene* (From Oberlin to East Berlin. An American Underway in the GDR Literary Scene), was published in 2013 by the Ch. Links Verlag in Berlin.

Large amounts of material from my top secret Stasi-file, reports primarily, have been incorporated into my memoir, along with appropriate commentary. The reports provide a kind of factual foundation for the memoir, as do various printed materials, letters I wrote and received, reports about me that were found in the files of ten Stasi informants, and some memories as well. The book does not have chapters, it has sections which are called parts—114 in all, some short, some long—that are devoted to all sorts of topics and events that I consider significant. For the most part, the narrative proceeds chronologically, starting in 1973 and moving forward in time to 2002, with the occasional flashback.

By comparison, *Memories of Life in East Germany: Snapshots* is rather impressionistic in nature, presenting the author's highly personal and admittedly somewhat subjective glimpses of people, events, experiences, etc., as seen through the lens of his mind's eye which—despite the passage of many years—is still focusable. Each of the vignettes that comprise this collection is a moment in time the author recalls and captures in words, hence snapshots. In contrast to the memoir, these sketches are presented without accompanying documentary evidence (such as a Stasi-file report), but they nevertheless reflect what life was really like in the GDR in a vivid and authentic way.

Perhaps one should think of these two closely related books as members of the same family—as twins, not identical twins of course, but rather two siblings who have certain attributes in common while being different in a number of significant ways. Apart from their general focus on the GDR, a country that no longer exists, what precisely do the two books have in common? Undoubtedly, the most important commonality is the author's insider/outsider perspective—i.e., his unique point of view as an American outsider who was able to acquire insider knowledge of the GDR and its literary scene while living there off and on. His knowledge of the GDR and his singular perspective on aspects of life in that country are on full display in both books, albeit in very different ways. Also, both books provide unusual insights into a totalitarian society and literary scene that no other Westerner was able to experience so intensely, reflecting on several levels how he experienced communist East Germany and how it experienced him. And finally, both books transport the reader back in time to the chilling Cold War days of yesteryear.

My hope is that interested persons will begin by reading this *Introduction* and then proceed to the next two prose pieces, the one on *Writing Snapshots* followed by *East Germany in Brief.* These three texts will provide readers with the background and other information they need to understand and appreciate the snapshots that follow. The snapshots are grouped in categories, such as PEOPLE, EXPERIENCES, SHOPPING, THINGS, etc. Most of the pieces could be posted in two or more categories, but I have elected to post each in one category only. Each snapshot can be read as a stand-alone text or as part of a cluster of texts that are closely or loosely related. For an example of the latter, read the following snapshots in this order: *Carlos and the Cockroaches, Vintage Photo Postcards,* and *Resistance and Solidarity.* These pieces are loosely connected by time period—the fall of 1977—, as well as by location—, the East Berlin apartment house I was living in at that time. The six snapshots listed within the IN RETROSPECT category are related in interesting ways and presented in chronological order. If read in this sequence, they are likely to be more revealing and meaningful. The catchy titles of some snapshots—e.g., *Soap and Bananas* (my favorite), *Bucket List,* and *Toilet Paper,* are intended to arouse the readers' curiosity.

Because each snapshot was written as a stand-alone text and not intended initially to become a chapter in a book, some basic background information was repeated almost verbatim in several of the pieces; this was necessary in order to provide a context for a particular event, experience, or situation. With elimination of repetition in mind, I carefully edited the individual texts after arranging them in appropriate categories, but now that they are presented together in book form some redundancy remains. I trust that my readers will not be disturbed by this.

WRITING SNAPSHOTS

Since I have written and posted on my website more than sixty short prose pieces about aspects of life in the former German Democratic Republic (GDR), everyday life as I experienced it in the 1960s, 1970s and 1980s, I am well prepared and eager to discuss the process of writing snapshots. How did I go about creating these vignettes, which are aimed chiefly at an English-speaking audience that knows very little or nothing whatever about the GDR?

Let me comment first on the snapshot topics. After obtaining my secret police file (*Stasi-Akte*) in 1999, I began making a list of topics I might want to write about; today there are 180 topics on that list. Many of them were added as I was working on my memoir, *Von Oberlin nach Ostberlin* (From Oberlin to East Berlin), which was published in April 2013. In almost every case, there are just a few key words that serve to trigger my memory of an experience, a person, a thing, an episode, a place—something I imagined I might eventually want to work up and develop into a short prose piece. Here are some examples: the Marlboro man, soap and bananas, antiques and artwork, bucket list, blue jeans, clothes and shoes, the inventor, secondhand smoke, resistance and solidarity, toilet paper, standing in line. Those key words, some of which now have become the titles of snapshots, were the triggers for my memory and the creative process that eventually would produce vignettes.

What are the components of a typical snapshot and what do these short prose pieces have in common? One very important component is the provision of factual information about some aspect of life in East Germany, which is meant not only to educate the reader but also to help create a framework for my story. I always proceed on the assumption that most readers in the English-speaking world have never visited the GDR and probably know nothing at all about the communistic Germany that came into being after World War II and ceased to exist in 1989. It is a world that vanished suddenly and unexpectedly, and my objective with the vignettes is to partially recreate this bygone world by recounting some unusual things I experienced while travelling and living there. The GDR was a harsh dictatorship, an unforgiving police state where many people suffered all sorts of injustices as well as physical and psychological abuse at the hands of the secret police and state authorities. What took place in East Germany while it was under Soviet occupation and communist rule (1945 to 1989) cannot be permitted to be quietly swept under the carpet and conveniently forgotten with the passage of time.

Indeed, this extraordinary chapter of German history must be chronicled painstakingly and preserved for future generations in various ways—via archives containing relevant documents such as secret police files, museum collections of art works and material objects, literary works, scholarly books, diaries, school books, memoirs and eye witness accounts, photographs, and films. It is not only important that we remember unvarnished East Germany, it is essential.

Many of my snapshots have what one might call "an unusual twist," a turn of events that is unforeseen and unexpected. The vignette entitled *Resistance and Solidarity* provides a splendid example. This piece opens with a historical perspective on three divided nations in the post-World War II era—Germany (East and West), Vietnam (North and South), and Korea (North and South), then moves to the personal as I relate my own story. The focal point of this snapshot is an incident that occurred in my East Berlin apartment house in November 1977, when I took a stand on a political issue that affected every resident of that building. I refused to be bullied, as others had been, into making a "solidarity" contribution to benefit communist Vietnam. After my act of resistance became widely known, it dissolved a boundary (like east and west) between my neighbors and me and unexpectedly produced a sense of solidarity.

Here is another good example. The vignette entitled *Soap and Bananas* focuses on what I experienced as a guest of honor at a number of dinner parties in the GDR. Readers will see how ironic it is that, on the one hand, I "consumed" something that was for display only at such parties (fine soap) and, on the other hand, I declined to consume something procured with considerable difficulty and that *was* intended to be consumed with great appreciation (the bananas). These minor social infractions revealed that I was unaware of the East German code of conduct and led my hosts and their guests to conclude that I was what I claimed to be, a visiting scholar from America. I never suspected that my hosts and others at these parties doubted that I was "for real," but they did. It was not the careful way I answered their questions or the information I gave them about my research and life in the

US that persuaded them, but rather my obvious ignorance of East German culture. I used the precious soap and refused the offer of bananas (a rare treat in the GDR) for dessert.

One of my readers, a former colleague who has read and commented on most of my snapshots, had the following to say about *Soap and Bananas*. "It is 'funny' that using fine soap and not eating bananas proved an unwitting means to dispel suspicion! But even more than that, this story was touching. The same themes I've seen in other snapshots return here and recombine in a slightly different way—friendship, generosity, art and literature (and in this snapshot, celebrity) in a society suffering scarcity, monotony, suspicion."

Before concluding, I want to offer a few comments on the subject of memory. All of the snapshots rely to a certain extent on my memory, which is at best a fickle friend and therefore not always a reliable source of information. But composing these stories is an amazing process that involves imagination as well as memory. As I sit at my computer and write about things I remember clearly, more memories press to the surface. It is as if I have peeled away a layer or two of an onion, and then more layers emerge. After all, the human brain keeps some memories in deep storage—that we know. Not everything can be on or near the surface, ready for instant recall. But one can recall so much more than one ever imagined during the actual process of writing; it is amazing how the mind works! As my friend Carl Dawson asserts in his masterful transatlantic memoir, *Living Backwards*: "Memories may fade or even die. Memories also endure as nothing else can, focusing the past and sustaining the present." (Charlottesville and London: The University Press of Virginia, 1995), 220. I am going to conclude this piece by sharing an observation an unusually perceptive reader made about my memoir: "This project about a seminal point in your intellectual and emotional development has been a conduit to the past that extends to the person you are today. It has given your friends—and I imagine will give countless other readers—much pleasure as well as much to consider." Comments like the ones above have given me valuable insight into the significance of my writing for my readers and for myself.

EAST GERMANY IN BRIEF

After World War II ended in 1945, Germany was occupied and divided into four zones that were administered by the main Allied Powers (the United States, Great Britain, France, and the Soviet Union). Initially, each of these countries was responsible for the administration of a single territorial zone. However, after tensions mounted between the Soviet Union and the three Western powers, the US, Great Britain, and France merged their zones and enabled the establishment of the Federal Republic of Germany (FRG, commonly known as West Germany) on September 21, 1949. The Soviets responded on October 7, 1949, by facilitating the creation of the communistic German Democratic Republic (GDR, commonly known as East Germany) within their occupation zone. The US maintained that the GDR was without any legal validity; it refused to recognize the GDR formally as a state and did not establish diplomatic relations until 1974. The US gave its full support to the government of the FRG located in Bonn, which was in the process of building a free and democratic Germany. In 1955, the US established formal diplomatic relations with the FRG. While the GDR and the FRG acknowledged each other's existence, they never had official diplomatic ties.

The status of Berlin was an especially problematic and contentious issue during the forty-five-year period that preceded the reunification of the two Germanys in 1990. In 1949, when the FRG was created in the West, the small Rhineland city of Bonn became its de facto capital. The government considered it to be a provisional capital because Berlin had become the symbol of resistance and the FRG never abandoned the idea of a re-unified Germany. Toward the end of 1949, the sectors of Berlin occupied by the Western Allies became "West Berlin," which aligned itself politically with the FRG. The Soviet occupation zone in the eastern part of Germany completely surrounded the city of Berlin. East Germany considered East Berlin to be its capital, and the Soviet Union as well as all the other Eastern Bloc countries recognized East Berlin as the GDR's capital. However, the Western Allies disputed this recognition, considering the entire city of Berlin to be occupied territory governed jointly by the four Allied Powers. Berlin was eventually divided into East Berlin and West Berlin, even though it was situated deep inside the area of Soviet occupation.

Emigration from the GDR to the West, and in particular to the FRG, was a major problem for the GDR, especially since many of the emigrants were well-educated young people. It weakened the state economically and prompted the government to fortify the western borders and ultimately, in 1961, to construct the massive Berlin Wall. From that point on, the East Germans were unable to travel to West Berlin or any Western country. For all practical purposes, they were all living under what one could call "homeland arrest," confinement within the borders of the GDR, a country about the size of Tennessee. Many citizens attempting to flee were killed by East German border guards, landmines, or other types of booby traps. Those who were caught received lengthy prison sentences for committing a crime known as "*Republikflucht*" (desertion from the republic).

I am concluding this concise overview of East Germany, the country that disappeared suddenly and unexpectedly, with a bit more basic information that my snapshot readers should find useful. The GDR was a country that existed from 1949 to 1990; it was part of the Soviet-ruled Eastern Bloc throughout the Cold War and also the Soviet Union's most powerful ally. Although it began to function as a sovereign state in October 1949, Soviet occupation forces were stationed in East Germany throughout its nearly forty-one years of existence. The GDR was governed by the communistic Socialist Unity Party (SED), which made the teaching of Marxism-Leninism and the Russian language compulsory in schools. It described itself as a socialist "workers' and peasants' state" (*Arbeiter- und Bauernstaat*). The economy was centrally planned, and most businesses were state-owned and operated by the government, which avidly confiscated land, private dwellings of every type, and valuable personal property such as antiques. Even though the GDR had to pay substantial war reparations to the Soviets, it nevertheless managed to develop the most successful economy in the Eastern Bloc. In 1989, numerous political, social, and economic forces in the GDR, the Soviet Union, and other Eastern European countries led to the collapse of the Berlin Wall and then in 1990 to the reunification of Germany. Snapshots on both of these important topics may be found in the section labelled IN RETROSPECT.

[Note: For the information presented above, I relied chiefly on three online sources: The Office of the Historian's "A Guide to the United States' History of Recognition, Diplomatic, and Consular Relations, by Country, since 1776: East Germany (German Democratic Republic)," "Wikipedia – History of East Germany," and "Wikipedia – East Germany."]

Addendum: Snapshot readers will surely be interested to know that Russian leader Vladimir Putin, when he was a young officer in the Soviet secret service (KGB), was stationed in the East German city of Dresden. He arrived there in the mid-1980s for his first posting as a KGB agent. In an article entitled "*Vladimir Putin's formative German years*" (March 27, 2015), BBC News correspondent Chris Bowlby describes the "devastating, life-changing shock" (p. 2) Putin received as he witnessed directly the implosion of the GDR in December 1989. The East German 'bloodless revolution' that swept away the GDR's political leaders, its communist ideology, and eventually the GDR itself left Putin with "a huge anxiety about the frailty of political elites, and how easily they can be overthrown by the people." (p. 3) "We would have another Putin and another Russia without his time in East Germany," his German biographer Boris Reitschuster is quoted as saying. The 11-page online version of Bowlby's fascinating article may be found at https://www.bbc.com/news/magazine-32066222

III
POLICE AND SECRET POLICE

POLICE STATE

There is no doubt about it: The GDR was a quintessential police state and this was especially evident in the center of East Berlin. There the police seemed to be everywhere, both in police cars and on foot, mostly in teams of two or more, never alone, always vigilant and often armed with automatic weapons. For many East Germans this highly visible police presence was threatening. I did not find it menacing, however. On the contrary, I always felt very safe walking around East Berlin and other cities in the GDR, even at night when I was by myself. There were no guns in the hands of private citizens and crime of every sort was low. As long as you played by the rules and obeyed the laws, the GDR police state was one of the safest places to live and visit. But if you stepped out of line, you would in all likelihood find yourself in trouble. I confess that I stepped out of line on a number of occasions, but luckily I never had to pay the piper.

The official name of the GDR's national police force was *Deutsche Volkspolizei* (German People's Police), abbreviated to *DVP* or *VP*, and colloquially known as the *VoPo*. The *Volkspolizei Agency* was formed on October

31, 1945 and dissolved in 1990. The Agency had its headquarters in East Berlin and was responsible for most law enforcement throughout the GDR. Because of its organization and structure it was also considered to be as much a paramilitary force as a civilian police force. In contrast to the police forces of most other countries, the *VP* was equipped with armored personnel carriers and artillery, and its recruits received military training. It also executed traditional police duties such as investigation and traffic control. People in the GDR made fun of the police because everyone knew, as a friend of mine who grew up in East Germany put it, that they were not the sharpest knives in the drawer. There were also agents of the *VP* working at the local level, the so-called Abschnittsbevollmächtigten (ABV), community policemen who were responsible for patrolling neighborhoods. They were at the bottom of the totem pole and commanded the least respect. At the top of the totem pole was the secret police agency, the *Stasi*, one of the most feared and hated institutions of East Germany's communist dictatorship.

THE STASI

The Stasi, an abbreviation for Staatssicherheit (literally: State Security), is what the secret police of East Germany were commonly called. The Ministry for State Security (MfS) was responsible for both domestic surveillance and espionage in the Soviet-occupied German Democratic Republic (GDR). At its peak, it employed 90,000 officers full-time. With the help of approximately 190,000 informants, it monitored and gathered intelligence on East German citizens. It also conducted covert operations in West Germany, West Berlin, and elsewhere in the West, including the United States. Headquartered in East Berlin, in the very building that today houses Berlin's Stasi Museum, the MfS was widely regarded as one of the most effective and repressive intelligence and secret police agencies in the world, comparable to the Soviet Union's KGB. East Germans hated and feared the Stasi which engaged in spying on the entire population, mainly through a vast network of citizens turned informants who were referred to as unofficial collaborators. Erich Mielke was the Stasi's longest-serving chief; he was head of the GDR's MfS from 1957 until shortly after the fall of the Berlin Wall in 1989. Markus Wolf was head of the Main Directorate for Reconnaissance, the foreign intelligence division of the MfS. He was the Stasi's second in charge for 34 years, which amounted to most of the Cold War period.

The Stasi was formed in 1950 and dissolved after German reunification in 1990. Numerous Stasi officials were prosecuted for their crimes after 1990, but neither Mielke nor Wolf was imprisoned. In 1991, the government of newly reunified Germany passed the Stasi Records Law, under which former GDR citizens and foreigners were granted the right to view their Stasi-files. By the early 21st century, more than 1.5 million individuals had done so. I, Richard Zipser, am one of those persons.

IN SEARCH OF MY STASI-FILE

With German reunification on October 3, 1990, a new government agency was established, The Federal Commissioner for the Records of the State Security Service of the former German Democratic Republic (Der Bundesbeauftragte für die Unterlagen des Staatssicherheitsdienstes der ehemaligen Deutschen Demokratischen Republik). This federal commission with the unwieldy name was informally called the Gauck Agency (Gauck-Behörde) for short, after anti-communist human rights activist and Lutheran minister Joachim Gauck, who served as the first Federal Commissioner from 1990 to 2000. Today the agency commonly refers to itself and is also known as the Stasi-Unterlagen-Behörde (Stasi Records Agency).

This office was responsible for preserving the records of the Ministry for State Security of the GDR, including files the secret police had compiled on individuals and stored in archives. There was a debate about what should happen to the files, whether they should be opened to the people or kept closed. The fate of the files was finally decided under the Unification Treaty between the German Democratic Republic and the Federal Republic of

Germany, which allowed access to and use of the files under certain circumstances. Along with the decision to keep the files in a central location in the eastern part of Berlin, they also decided who would be able to see and use the files, and to permit individuals to see their own files. Following a declassification ruling by the German government in 1992, the files of the Ministry for State Security of the GDR were opened, leading people to seek access to their files. Between 1992 and 2011, around 2.75 million individuals, mostly former GDR citizens, requested access to their own files. The declassification ruling also gave people the right to acquire copies of their documents after certain information had been blacked out by a case worker, in order to protect innocent third parties.

In March 1993, I decided to join the ranks of those seeking access to their Stasi-files and sent the Gauck Agency a letter expressing my desire to see any documents they might have related to my person. The letter described in detail my scholarly work on GDR literature, my professional and private contacts with prominent GDR authors, some of whom I had hosted as guest writers in residence at Oberlin College. It provided a list of my publications and editorial work on various aspects of GDR literature. I also mentioned my many trips to the GDR and stays there, as well as my contact with the Writers' Union and the Humboldt University. Finally, I inquired about the possible existence of a Stasi-file containing information on me and, if one did exist, how to go about gaining access to that file.

In April I received a response to my inquiry, indicating that I needed to submit two items to the Agency: a file inspection application on a special form and a proof-of-identity certificate. I dutifully completed the uncomplicated application form, dated it April 20, 1993, and returned it to the Agency along with a photocopy of my passport. In early May, I received a letter acknowledging receipt of the documents I had submitted and assigning a registry number for my application. The letter concluded with a vague and somewhat discouraging message indicating that, due to the large number of inquiries the Agency was receiving every day, the processing of my application would take some time. I did not expect that the processing of my application would take several years, but that is in fact what occurred.

In June I received another letter from the Gauck Agency, this time requesting a <u>notarized</u> proof-of-identity certificate. I was told that the search for documents containing information on my person could not be initiated until that certificate was on hand. According to my records, I sent a notarized photocopy of my passport to the Agency on August 9, 1993, and after that I received no more communications from them.

In 1996, former GDR author Joachim Walther published his landmark study, *Sicherungsbereich Literatur: Schriftsteller und Staatssicherheit in der Deutschen Demokratischen Republik* (Security Zone Literature: Writers and State Security in the German Democratic Republic, Berlin: Ch. Links). This 888-page book carefully documents and analyzes how the Stasi went about implementing and enforcing the SED Party's cultural policies in the realm of literature, how it monitored and tried to influence and control GDR writers. Walther, who worked as an editor for the publishing house Buchverlag Der Morgen Berlin from 1968 to 1983, had been forced to resign from that position due to his opposition to censorship and related issues. He began working on this meticulously researched documentary study shortly after the "Wende," the change in direction away from communism in 1989 and 1990, following the fall of the Berlin Wall. Walther, and only Walther, was given full access to the files of all former GDR writers. In brief, his assignment was to use those documents to determine the nature of the relationship and level of collaboration between GDR writers and the secret police agency.

In the introduction to *Sicherungsbereich Literatur*, Walther comments on the reasons why GDR writers and artists were willing to work with and for the Stasi: "A special factor in the readiness of writers and artists to collaborate with the Ministry for State Security was the belief in utopia, along with ignoble reasons like careerism, envy, craving for power, and need for recognition." (10) He also confirms my own conviction that high-level SED Party officials and Stasi officers overestimated by far the importance of literature in their society and the power of free speech; and that explains why they went to extraordinary lengths to suppress freedom of expression.

When *Sicherungsbereich Literatur* was published in 1996, I immediately purchased a copy and spent a couple of hours browsing through it. At one point, I skimmed through the index from A to Z, looking for the names of writers and other persons I knew. When I reached Z, I found "Zipser, Richard 533, 544, 546, 589, 598." Five references to me, incredible! I then proceeded to read the reports below from or about those informants, who were also referred to as unofficial collaborators (IM=*Inoffizieller Mitarbeiter*): Uwe Berger, Fritz Rudolf Fries, Anneliese Löffler, and Paul Wiens. The first of these is meant to illustrate the form and content of an informant's report.

[Uwe Berger: alias "Uwe"]

1) The lyric poet Uwe Berger, alias "Uwe," handwritten on August 11, 1976: "June 22, 1976. In accordance with instructions, I called Sarah Kirsch. I told her that Dr. Richard Zipser had mentioned her twice in his conversation with me. Specifically, he said she had recommended me, and that she and I are GDR authors of the literary genre that is his favorite. Sarah Kirsch answered cautiously. 'When he was at my place, I gave him a number of names; yours was also one of them. He had asked me whom else I might be able to recommend.' We then exchanged a few unimportant sentences. I tried to find out about her opinion of Zipser. But she only agreed with me when I said it might become a very valuable book. She thanked me for my call and waited for me to end the conversation. The motivation for my call was weak. Further initiatives of this sort could make Sarah Kirsch suspicious. My friendly rapport with her remained intact." (533)

[Fritz Rudolf Fries: alias "Pedro Hagen"]

In 1978 monthly meetings were held. [*Stasi officer Gerhard*] Hoffmann noted that the collaboration had become significantly more trustful; the IM would occasionally report "of his own accord," for example about Sarah Kirsch and the American literary scholar Richard Zipser. In 1979 "Pedro Hagen" was re-registered as an IMV [*a higher level of informant than IM and IME*]. Report on meeting of March 6, 1979: "The IM was open-minded, interested, also provided information unreservedly on the issues that were raised." (544)

At the next meeting on March 12, 1981, "Pedro Hagen"—who in the meantime was re-registered as an IMB [*a higher level of informant than IMV*]—received the cover address "Käthe Martin," to which he was supposed to send a postcard from every place he stayed in the USA. In addition, he was handed 500 West German marks in an EG-container and given instructions on how to go about opening and destroying the container. The IM acknowledged receipt of the 500 West German marks in writing. After his trip it says in the evaluation meeting report of May 19, 1981: "He initiated activities in the USA that enabled him to proceed as instructed and demonstrated perseverance, e.g., in the efforts he made to contact Dr. Zipser." (546)

[Anneliese Löffler: alias "Dölbl"]

After "Dölbl" had written reader's reports in the summer of 1978 on Günter Grass ("Der Butt" [*"The Flounder"*]) and Klaus Poche ("Atemnot" [*"Shortness of Breath"*]) and delivered reports on the USA Germanist Richard Zipser as well as Franz Fühmann and on some of her students, her report file breaks off abruptly with the reader's report dated August 13, 1978 on Poche's novel, without any reference to archiving or completing that piece of work. This would suggest that the remaining parts have been destroyed, so that it is not possible to make a reliable statement about the duration of IM "Dölbl's" informant activity beyond the year 1978. (589)

[Paul Wiens: alias "Dichter" / *"Poet"*]

According to the name index of his report file, he provided information from 1967 on about (among others) Bella Achmadulina, H.C. Artmann, Amfried Astel, Rudolf Augstein, Jurek Becker Wolf Biermann, Heinrich Böll, Nicolas Born, Volker Braun, Heinz Czechowski, Hilde Domin, Adolf Endler, Hans Magnus Enzensberger, Efim Etkind, Konrad Franke, Fritz Rudolf Fries, Barbara Frischmuth, Franz Fühmann, Lew Ginsburg, Peter Gosse, Peter Härtling, Stephan Hermlin, Stefan Heym, Walter Janka, Uwe Johnson, Gustav Just, Heinz Kahlau, Rainer Kirsch, Sarah Kirsch, Lew Kopelew, Ludvik Kundera, Günter Kunert, Reiner Kunze, Alain Lane, Jurij Ljubimow, Erich Loest, Frank-Wolf Matthies, Christoph Meckel, Karl Mickel, Irmtraud Morgner, Heiner Müller, A. W. Mytze, Bulat Okudshawa, Fritz Pleitgen, Ulrich Plenzdorf, Boris Polewoi, Hans Werner Richter, Andrej Sacharow, Klaus Schlesinger, Christoph Schlotterer, Peter Schneider, Hans Georg Soldat, Alexander Solshenizyn, Erwin Strittmatter, Klaus Wagenbach, Joachim Walther, Berta Waterstradt, Christa Wolf, Gerhard Wolf, Richard Zipser and other German, French, Hungarian, Yugoslavian and Soviet authors. Moreover, the poet was also an informant in his private life: In his IM-file there are private letters from the year 1972 to Irmtraud Morgner, to whom Paul Wiens was married from 1971 on, with the notation: "from 'Poet,' hand over at meeting." (598)

After reading the passages above, which made me more certain than ever that I had a Stasi-file, I decided to give Joachim Walther a call. I wanted to see if he could cast more light on my situation and also seek his advice on how best to proceed. While I had not met him, we had corresponded from time to time in connection with my GDR censorship projects, so I had his telephone number. I placed the call, we had a good conversation and I learned some things that were quite helpful. Walther told me it was very likely that I had a file, but he had not seen it. Furthermore, he said that my name appeared frequently in the files of GDR writers he had reviewed and he cautioned me about writing another book on GDR authors before I had gained access to my own file. As it turned out, that was excellent advice, as I realized when I read my file.

The last of these reports is about the poet Paul Wiens, who provided the Stasi with information on more than sixty German, French, Hungarian, Soviet, and Yugoslavian authors, literary critics, and human rights advocates. Included on the list of names provided in the report are three Nobel Prize winners: Heinrich Böll, Alexander Solzhenitsyn, and Andrei Sakharov. Moreover, we learn here that Wiens was also an informant in his private life. According to Walther, his IM-file contains private letters from the year 1972 to prominent GDR writer Irmtraud Morgner, to whom Wiens was married from 1971 on, with the notation: "from 'Poet', hand over at meeting." (598) That notation alone speaks volumes about Paul Wiens's unscrupulous character.

The informants' references to me in five sections of *Sicherungsbereich Literatur* gave me the excuse I needed to approach the Stasi Records Agency again, this time with evidence that I in all likelihood did have a Stasi-file. Since more than four years had elapsed since my initial inquiry in March 1993, I wrote a more forceful letter to which I attached photocopies of the relevant passages that appeared in Joachim Walther's book. In this letter, which is dated June 30, 1997, I asked about the status of my application to gain access to my Stasi-file, assuming that one existed. In the concluding paragraph I wrote:

> The mention of my name several times in Joachim Walther's book strengthens my suspicion that Ministry for State Security documents related to my person exist. I would therefore like to ask you, on the basis of the new information that has surfaced, to process my application as soon as possible and advise me as regards the existence of files containing personal information about me and, if applicable, grant me permission to inspect those documents. I would be grateful for a reply.

My letter had the desired effect; it got the process of locating the reports and other documents that comprise my file underway—at last! In September 1997, I received a letter from a case worker at the Agency, Ms. Eckert, indicating that the preliminary search for documents had met with success. In the letter Ms. Eckert stated that, due to the relatively small size of my file, they would be willing to make a photocopy of it and send that to me. She invited me to call her at the Agency and let her know how I wanted to proceed.

I was delighted to learn that I would not have to travel to Berlin, in order to inspect my file. I called Ms. Eckert and expressed interest in receiving a photocopy of the file and, when asked, affirmed that I was prepared to cover the expense of photocopying and shipping everything. She did not say when I could expect to receive the file, just that it would take a while to gather all the documents and then process and photocopy them.

After sixteen more months had gone by, my Stasi-file arrived in the mail on January 22, 1999, one day before my 56th birthday. That was a surprise as well as the most unusual birthday present I have ever received!

MY STASI-FILE

I remember vividly when the Stasi-file arrived at my home, in late January 1999, around the time of my 56th birthday. The bulky, innocent-looking package filled the mailbox; according to the label, the sender was Der Bundesbeauftragte für die Unterlagen des Staatssicherheitsdienstes der ehemaligen Deutschen Demokratischen Republik (The Federal Commissioner for the Records of the State Security Service of the former German Democratic Republic). The Gauck Agency had come through at last!

What an exciting surprise! After six years of waiting impatiently, after writing countless letters to the Stasi Records Agency, most of which went unanswered, there it was! And I was more than curious to see what was inside that package. Upon opening it, I found a cover letter explaining that research in the Stasi archives in Berlin and Leipzig had led to the discovery of my file.

Also, that as of December 3, 1982, my file had been labelled "KK-erfasst." Karteikartenerfassung" (recorded on index cards) was the designation the Stasi used for potential enemies of the state, "for persons who from the State Security Service's perspective had given indications of hostile activity." The letter went on to explain: "Main Department XX was responsible from 1964 on for securing and controlling the state apparatus, culture, and opposition. Department 7 of Main Department XX was responsible for securing and controlling culture, art, and literature." And finally, it stated that the names of innocent third parties had been blacked out to protect their privacy, in accordance with German law. I discovered that holding pages under a strong light so as to read the blacked-out names was a futile exercise, for the original document had first been photocopied by a case worker, then the names had been blacked out, and then a copy of that copy had been made for me. Still, using context and memory as my guides, I was able to fill in most of the blanks without difficulty.

My file is almost 400 pages long. It is filled with information the East German secret police compiled on me in the 1970s and 1980s. The file is not a chronological or linear narrative; it is a haphazard compilation of reports containing information about my personal life, my personality, my academic background, and the nature of my work and activities in the GDR and elsewhere. There is speculation about the "real" purpose of my visits to the GDR, how these visits were financed, and the damage my publications on East German literature might cause the GDR state. The most fascinating sections are the reports written by or based on debriefings of informants, all identified with code names, who were providing the Stasi with detailed information derived from their contacts and conversations with me. The file spans a period of fifteen years, beginning in the summer of 1973 and concluding in the spring of 1988. Most of the information and reports are from the period 1975 to 1978, when I was living off and on in the GDR and working on three book projects. My file is considered to be a victim's file ("Opferakte"), which means that only I and the case worker who read it have had access to it.

There are reports from five types of secret informants in my file; each has a code name preceded by one of the following acronyms: IM, IME, IMV, IMS, and IMB. The acronym IM stands for "Inoffizieller Mitarbeiter" (unofficial collaborator), the most common type of informant in the GDR. These persons usually were not on the Stasi payroll, but often received favors or privileges in exchange for the information they provided. IME stands for "Inoffizieller Mitarbeiter im besonderen Einsatz," i.e., collaborators with special assignments. IMV is short for "Inoffizieller Mitarbeiter, der unmittelbar an der Bearbeitung und Entlarvung im Verdacht stehender Personen mitarbeitet;" these were the upper echelon of informants, individuals the Stasi trusted and deployed to gather information directly from potential enemies of the state. IMS and IMB were the highest level of informants, individuals whose loyalty and trustworthiness had been tested and proven beyond a doubt. IMS is the acronym for "inoffizieller Mitarbeiter zur politisch-operativen Durchdringung und Sicherung des Verantwortungsbereichs." Informants so designated were assigned to gather information and report on suspicious activities in workplaces or areas considered important to state security, such as the cultural sphere. IMB is short for "inoffizieller Mitarbeiter der Abwehr mit Feindverbindung bzw. zur unmittelbaren Bearbeitung im Verdacht der Feindtätigkeit stehender Personen." These informants were often in direct contact with persons considered to be enemies of the state, not only in the GDR but occasionally in foreign countries as well.

The file reveals that there were at least nine unofficial collaborators of one sort or another who reported on my GDR-related activities and gathered information on me for the Stasi. Three were writers: IME "Dichter" (Poet), Paul Wiens, a well-known, well-connected poet and communist party loyalist; IMV "Pedro Hagen," the prominent prose writer and opportunist, Fritz Rudolf Fries; and IM "Uwe," the poet Uwe Berger, a cunning opportunist motivated more by careerism than ideology. Two informants were good acquaintances, a married couple I got to know while living in East Berlin: IMV "Kurt" and IMV "Julia." They were friends of the prose writer, Klaus Schlesinger, who introduced us. Another was a publisher, Konrad Reich, who until the 2013 publication in Germany of my book *Von Oberlin nach Ostberlin* (From Oberlin to East Berlin) had not been outed as an informant. There was also IM "Dölbl," Anneliese Löffler, a professor at the Humboldt University; she was assigned to keep tabs on me while I was working in Berlin as an IREX (International Research and Exchanges Board) scholar. Eberhard Scheibner, a functionary in charge of the international department of the GDR Writers' Union, submitted reports periodically on our meetings and communications. And finally, IM "Frieda," the housekeeper of the GDR's most famous writer, Stefan Heym. There is evidence that two American Germanists, "unofficial sources," informed the Stasi about my GDR-related activities in the United States. Although they are unnamed, I was able to identify them from the information provided. The file also contains four surveillance reports (one stretching over a three-day period), which were authorized by the Ministry for State Security and prepared by Stasi operatives. In these I have a code name: "Adler," eagle, the bird of prey.

Most of the reports are poorly written, worse than English 101 compositions. The language is bureaucratic and wooden, laden with Stasi-jargon, marred by misspellings and grammatical errors of all sorts. Since many of the reports were drafted by Stasi personnel, this is not surprising. Some were written by the informants themselves, others recorded on tape and transcribed by Stasi personnel, and others cobbled together from handwritten notes taken in meetings between Stasi officers and informants. A favorite word, one that recurs like a leitmotif throughout the document, is "operative."

READING MY STASI-FILE

As I previously stated, the package containing a copy of my 396-page Stasi-file arrived in the mail without any forewarning on January 22, 1999, one day before my 56th birthday. What an unexpected and unusual birthday present that was! I had been waiting patiently for almost six years, wondering all the while if I would ever see my file and, if so, what sort of information it would contain. I had no idea what to expect and, in truth, was somewhat apprehensive when I opened the package. I was eager to dive in and start reading and, at the same time, somewhat reluctant to start reading. It was a strange and uneasy feeling, this fear of the unknown.

Inside the package containing my file, I found a six-page cover letter from Ms. Jabs, a Stasi Records Agency case worker. The letter is dated January 15, 1999, and makes reference to my application to gain access to my file, which the Agency had received on April 20, 1993. Ms. Jabs addresses and explains a number of important matters in her letter, most of which have already been discussed in the snapshot entitled "My Stasi-File."

Ms. Jabs points out that the information she sent me comes from Stasi records that have been compiled to date. She says one cannot rule out the possibility that additional documents related to my person will be found as the ongoing organizational work continues at the Records Agency in Berlin and other repositories. But due to the large number of applications she has to process, she is unable to inform individual applicants when new documents have been discovered. Therefore, I should consider contacting her again in about two years with regard to supplemental information. Moreover, she also recommends that I submit a renewal application to the central Stasi Records Agency in Berlin, something I chose not to do.

In order to make sense of the material in my file, I needed to organize the individual reports. I began doing this in the fall of 2002 while I was on sabbatical leave and preparing to write a book based on my file. I decided to put the individual reports in chronological order, starting with the initial entry dated June 6, 1973, and concluding with the last entry dated March 17, 1988. Once I had completed that task, I removed redundant materials such as the second copy of duplicate reports and an irrelevant report on the activities of the US Peace Corps. I then went through the document again and numbered the pages, keeping them in chronological order. From beginning to end I now had a 300-page Stasi-file, something that would tell a coherent and intriguing Cold War story—my story. The Stasi Records Agency sent me 44 additional pages in November 2002, which also took me by surprise.

These were reports and information about me that had been found in the Stasi-file of GDR prose writer Fritz Rudolf Fries, who had collaborated with the secret police in the 1970s and 1980s. Some sections of my memoir, *Von Oberlin nach Ostberlin* (From Oberlin to East Berlin), are based on material from what I like to call the Fries/Zipser file. In April 2012, I received another communication from the Stasi Records Agency, this time a letter with six pages from the Stasi archives regarding my alleged efforts to create an "inner opposition" among persons from the cultural sphere and writers in the GDR. This supplemental material increased the length of my abridged Stasi-file to 344 pages. That is the document that would serve as the factual foundation for the memoir I published in 2013. (Note: The Records Agency sent me the additional reports because it was preparing to publish that information. It was required by law to contact persons named in such documents and give them an opportunity to object to their publication.)

As it turned out, the day when my Stasi-file showed up unexpectedly in my mailbox marked the beginning of a remarkable transformative journey for me. For, the file has enabled me to relive some important stages of my life and my academic career in ways that would not have been possible without such a document. It also enabled me to rediscover the person I was in the 1970s and 1980s, and I learned a great deal about myself through the eyes and observations of others. I also realized that my experiences in the GDR and interactions with East German writers, bureaucrats, and regular citizens—especially in the 1970s and 1980s—transformed me gradually into a different human being, into a more compassionate and politically-aware person with a more comprehensive and conservative world view. And, I think the process of reading my file and the Fries/Zipser file, assimilating and reflecting on the contents of those unusual documents, and then writing my memoir, was life-changing as well. As I now write my snapshots, each one based on a special memory, I am acutely aware that I have at an advanced age embarked on another important transformative journey.

By sharing much of my file with readers of *Remembering East Germany* and this collection of short prose pieces, I hope to provide them with unique insights into cultural-political, literary, and everyday life in the GDR. Few if any Americans have experienced the GDR as I did, and I am pleased to share some of my personal experiences and memories so others can gain a better understanding of what life was like in the actually existing GDR, "the other Germany," the nation with a forty-one-year history that no longer exists.

Reading my Stasi-file closely while writing *Von Oberlin nach Ostberlin* was a bitter-sweet, emotionally draining experience, painful at times—e.g., when I came across unexpected deception or outright lies about my person; reassuring at other times—e.g., when the file confirmed that none of my closest friends had informed on me, something I had come to fear. Much of what I read intrigued me, and it was particularly interesting to see how most of my informants tried to make themselves look good to their handlers by distorting or omitting certain facts or even fabricating things in their reports. In the end, I realized that none of them had done me any real harm, but that realization did not make me feel better about them. The file brought back many memories, good ones and bad ones; it also reacquainted me with Richard Zipser of yesteryear, a person I realized I no longer knew. One day, perhaps, I will find another package from the Stasi Records Agency in my mailbox, another surprise. But if that package never arrives, I will not be disappointed. Again, and especially after writing my memoir (*Von Oberlin nach Ostberlin*) and then translating it into English, I have a serious case of file fatigue and am eager for closure.

In his eloquent memoir, *The File* (New York: Vintage Books, 1998), Timothy Garton Ash tells us

> how a Stasi-file opens the door to a vast sunken labyrinth of the forgotten past, but how, too, the very act of opening the door itself changes the buried artifacts, like an archaeologist letting in fresh air to a sealed Egyptian tomb. For these are not simply past experiences rediscovered in their original state. Even without the fresh light from a new document or another's recollection—the opened door—our memories decay or sharpen, mellow or sour, with the passage of time and the change of circumstances... But

with the fresh light the memory changes irrevocably. A door opens, but another closes. There is no way back now to your own earlier memory of that person, that event. It is like a revelation made, years later, to a loved one. Or like a bad divorce, where today's bitterness transforms all the shared past, completely, miserably, seemingly forever. Except that the bitter memory, too, will fade and change with the further passage of time. (108-09)

TIMOTHY GARTON ASH'S BOOK, *THE FILE*, 1997

This eloquent memoir, which Timothy Garton Ash (hereafter Ash) calls "A Personal History," was first published in hardcover in the US by Random House, New York, in 1997. The first paperback edition was published in the US by Vintage Books on September 29, 1998. A friend of mine, a professor of German history who was aware that I was trying to gain access to my Stasi-file, alerted me to the publication of Ash's book, which I promptly purchased and eagerly read from cover to cover. I found it fascinating and discovered that he and I had had many similar experiences in East Germany (the GDR). At that time, in October 1998, I had no way of knowing that a copy of my own 400-page file would soon be coming my way and reach me at home in January 1999. The publication of Ash's personal history was a stroke of good fortune and came at just the right time for me.

The File reads much like a spy thriller; it is suspenseful, well written, and an enjoyable read. As the story unfolds, virtually all readers will come to realize that they have never read anything even remotely like it. On one level, it is a probing examination of domestic spying in East Germany during the Cold War period that fewer and fewer of us remember. On another level, it is about the author's file, but less so when the focus shifts to the work he had done while living in Berlin. More information on and from that secret police file would have been welcome, at least to this reader, but Ash is highly protective of his personal privacy.

What is Ash's book about? Let me quote directly from the book's back cover:

> In 1978 a romantic young Englishman took up residence in Berlin to see what that divided city could teach him about tyranny and freedom. Fifteen years later Timothy Garton Ash— who was by then famous for his reportage of the downfall of communism in Central Europe—returned. This time he had come to look at a file that bore the code-name "Romeo." The file had been compiled by the Stasi, the East German secret police, with the assistance of dozens of informers. And it contained a meticulous record of Garton Ash's earlier life in Berlin.
>
> In this memoir, Garton Ash describes what it was like to rediscover his younger self through the eyes of the Stasi, and then to go on to confront those who actually informed against him to the secret police. Moving from document to remembrance, from the offices of British intelligence to the living rooms of retired Stasi officers, *The File* is a personal narrative as gripping, as disquieting, and as morally provocative as any fiction by George Orwell or Graham Greene. And it is all true.

While I was reading *The File* for the first time, I began to think about writing something based on the contents of my own file, even though I had no idea what that might entail. Ash's book was immensely helpful to me; above all, it provided me with a model, a beautifully written one that in fact intimidated me at first. After my initial review of the documents in my 400-page Stasi-file in 1999, I realized that I would have to distance myself from Ash, take a completely different approach and write a very different sort of book. Easier said than done, as I would discover. Much of *The File* is a first person narrative, and of course Ash is both main character and narrator. I observed how masterfully he manages to drive the story forward as he pursues his goal. It was also very instructive to see how he presents himself in the narrative, at times stepping forward into the story he is telling and occasionally doing just the opposite, always in control. In the process we meet and get to know the version of Ash the author wishes to present to his readers, generally but not always in a positive light.

In the first chapter of his book, Ash tells us that the opening report in his 325-page Stasi-file dates from March 1981. Prepared by one Lieutenant Wendt, it provides his personal details, notes that he has been studying in Berlin since 1978 and that he lived for several months during 1980 in "the capital of the GDR." It also mentions that he travels frequently from West Berlin to East Germany and Poland, and that he has repeatedly "made contact with operationally interesting persons." As a result, "there are grounds for suspecting that G. [for Garton Ash] has deliberately exploited his official functions as research student and/or journalist to pursue intelligence activities." (*The File*, 13-14)

Ash permits more details about his person to become known via the Stasi-file. He indicates that Wendt's report pays special attention to information supplied by the Stasi's own informers, known as *Inoffizielle Mitarbeiter*—literally "unofficial collaborators"—or IM for short. And, he says that the opening report summarizes the information gathered by IM "Smith," IM "Schuldt," and especially by IM "Michaela" and her husband, KP (Contact Person) "Georg." "Outwardly G. makes a pretty casual impression and overall seems 'a typical British intellectual.'" Wendt notes that "G. works purposefully and with scholarly thoroughness" but displays "a bourgeois-liberal attitude and no commitment to the working-class." (15) G. is said to have sought contact with people who could be of interest for intelligence purposes. On his trips to Poland he almost certainly maintains connections with "antisocialist forces." Hence, the secret police need to find out more, with a view to possible prosecution under Article 97 of the Criminal Code. A four-point "plan of action" follows, setting forth how the Stasi would go about investigating G.

After revealing their "plan of action," Ash tells the reader how <u>he</u> intends to proceed. "My plan of action, now, is to investigate their investigation of me. I shall pursue their inquiry through this file, try to track down both the informers and the officers on my case, consult other files, compare the Stasi record with my own memories, with the diary and notes I kept at the time, and with the political history I have since written about this period. And I shall see what I find." (17-18) He is eager to see what the Stasi and their helpers had assembled on him and find out how reliable that information is. "After all," he declares, "I should know what I was really up to. And what did my officers and informers think they were doing? Can the files, and the men and women behind them, tell us anything more about communism, the Cold War and the sense or nonsense of spying?" (23)

Ash's investigation is motivated by more than curiosity or a desire for more information than his file contains. "The effect of reading a file can be terrible," (21) he asserts emphatically. "The experience may even teach us something about history and memory, about ourselves, about human nature. So if the form of this book seems self-indulgent, the purpose is not. I am but a window, a sample, a means to an end, the object in this experiment." (23)

He elucidates: "I must explore not just a file but a life: the life of the person I was then. This is not the same thing as 'my life.' What we usually call 'my life' is the mental autobiography with which and by which we all live. What really happened is quite another matter. Searching for a lost self, I am also searching for a lost time. And for answers to the question How did the one shape the other? Historical time and personal time, the public and private, great events and our own lives." (23)

As he begins his search for a lost self and a lost time, Ash recalls leaving for Germany during his early days as a graduate student at Oxford. He set off for Berlin on his twenty-third birthday, July 12, 1978, driving his new, dark blue Alfa Romeo (hence, the code name "Romeo"). He lived in West Berlin for a year and a half, before driving through Checkpoint Charlie on January 7, 1980 to his lodging in East Berlin. His original purpose was to write an Oxford doctoral thesis about Berlin under Hitler. For this year and a half, he says, the Stasi's intelligence is fragmentary because he was living in the West. At the end of 1979, he prepared to move to East Berlin, where he had been offered a place as a research student attached to the Humboldt

University, under a new cultural agreement recently signed between Britain and East Germany.

Ash reports that, while living and conducting research in East Germany, he appeared to have had the attention of five unofficial collaborators. Their evidence and operational potential are carefully weighed by Lieutenant Wendt. He elaborates:

> As I study their reports on me, and set out to identify, find and talk to them in person, I am drawn back not just into my own past life but into these other lives that briefly crossed with mine.

> I was not a victim of these informers, as many East Germans really were of theirs. They did me no serious damage. Yet, knowing how the system worked, I may fairly guess that they did harm others. I cannot say how typical they are of Stasi informers in general, although I know enough of other cases to say that some elements are common. However, the fact that they happen to have informed on me gives me a special chance to test the accuracy of the files—and to enter into their own experience. Why did they do it? What it was like for them? How do they see it now?

After reading the file the Stasi kept on him during his time in East Germany, Ash decided to confront the people who had informed on him to the Stasi. He was able to gain access to the files of those individuals and also to the informants themselves: firstly, by stating that he has a professional interest in their activity as a historian and secondly, a personal interest because they participated in keeping records on him.

First on Ash's list of persons to be contacted and confronted is his former academic advisor at the Humboldt University, Laurenz Demps. "I telephone Professor Demps, one day in June 1995, to arrange my appointment. I have had no contact with him since 1981. He is clearly surprised by my call and the news that I have 'something I want to discuss' with him, but agrees to meet." (89) The two men set up a meeting in a café in Berlin. Ash recalls their rendezvous: "Eleven sharp, and there he sits outside the café....A slightly tense greeting. Tea and coffee ordered. Then I come to the point. I have read my Stasi file and it would appear that they had him down as an informer of the HVA." (89) [HVA = Hauptverwaltung Aufklärung / Main Directorate for Reconnaissance, Ministry of State Security] Ash explains what the file says and shows Demps copies of the relevant pages. Shaken, Demps says no, he was not an informer, he had nothing to do with the Stasi. (89-90) In the course of their conversation, the two historians discover that a misleading error—a case of mistaken identity—had been made in the IM report. Professor Demps is an innocent man after all, and Ash is very, very relieved after this unexpected turn of events. He says he has nothing but sympathy—and some admiration—for the way Demps copes with the shock he has just given him.

Before introducing Ash's most assiduous informer, IMV "Michaela," I would like to explain what it was that attracted him to communist-ruled Eastern Europe and East Germany in particular. Fortunately, Ash clarifies this for his readers:

> The ideological evaluation in my Stasi opening report—"bourgeois-liberal"—was just about right. I cared passionately for what I saw, with a rather simplistic romantic patriotism, as the British heritage of individual liberty. And I wanted this liberty for other people. . . . But liberal anti-communism was not the primary source of my fascination with the East. I was fascinated because here, in East Germany, people were actually *living* those endlessly difficult choices between collaboration with and resistance to a dictatorship. (51)

Ash says that his fascination with dictatorship and resistance, with the extremes of good and evil, civilization and barbarism, also led him to travel through Albania in the summer of 1978 and through all six countries of what was then called Eastern Europe the next summer. In Poland he would discover the "spirit of resistance" that he had long been seeking. (52)

According to Ash, British journalists, writers and scholars working abroad were very often thought to be engaged in spying for the British secret service, and some "journalists" and "students" were indeed more than they seemed.

> So I am not surprised or outraged that the Stasi decided to take a closer look at me. What is shocking is the way they were spying on their own people and getting them to spy on one another: that vast army of surveillance, intimidation and repression, in which my own "Schuldt," Smith" and "Michaela" were just a few foot soldiers. But the mere fact of this investigation of me is, in itself, just about within the range of a "normal" security service's work. (63)

> [...]

> To a communist state like East Germany, built on total control of the media, censorship and organized lying, any probing research or critical journalism was subversive. Western journalists were routinely covered by Stasi counterintelligence department II/13. Partly this was because they were looking for spies under journalistic cover, but it was also because, for the Stasi, the distinction between journalist and spy was not clear-cut. For them, a Western journalist and a Western spy were both agents of Western intelligence-gathering, and both alike threats to the security of the communist system. (64)

Let me now put the spotlight on IMV "Michaela." A four-page report by Stasi Lieutenant Küntzel focuses on Ash's June 30, 1979 meeting in Weimar with older Jewish communist, Dr. Georg, and his wife, who live in a castle. Ash had arranged the meeting so he could gather information from Georg for a piece in the English weekly "*The Spectator*" on the antifascist resistance struggle. At some point Georg's wife ("Michaela") unexpectedly entered the living room. The report states: "She was introduced by her husband with the words: 'My wife, director of the Weimar Art Galleries.'" (30) Ash explains that the V after the IM indicates that "Michaela" belonged to the Stasi's highest class of informer, those deployed in direct contact with the enemy. "Michaela" and her husband were both surprised that Ash immediately brought the subject around to the current exhibition on the Bauhaus organized by the Art Galleries. Angered by Ash's rudeness, Georg excused himself and left the room. Now Ash explained to the IMV that he was working on an article about the development of the artistic and cultural life of the GDR and was therefore interested in her comments. The conversation with the IMV lasted only twenty minutes, but served to establish their connection. After receiving a copy of an exhibition catalog from Ash on January 5, 1980, she writes: "In order to implement further measures to strengthen the contact as well as *Blickfeldmassnahmen* [a special Stasi term meaning keeping someone in view] I will send a letter of thanks to the address given below:

> Tim Gartow [sic] Ash
> Kunstgalerie
> Berlin-West."

In the summer of 1980, "Michaela" reports on another visit Ash paid to them and also gives Ash's telephone numbers in East and West Berlin to her Stasi handler.

Fifteen years later, Ash decides to visit Weimar again and ask "Michaela"—if she is still there—why she did it and what she has to say for herself. After he learns that "Michaela" has moved, he races up the autobahn to Berlin and checks into a hotel. In the phone book, he finds one entry with "Michaela"'s real name. He dials the number. "'Ah Herr Esch, you visited us in Weimar, didn't you, and I've since read your book. . . .'" Ash explains that he is very briefly in Berlin and has a particular reason for wanting to see her. They fix a time in the following afternoon for him to call. "You'll certainly have many questions," she says, adding, "really I'm looking forward to it."

Ash seeks a possible motive for her collaboration as an informer: "As a senior state employee, 'Michaela' was certainly obliged to cooperate with the Stasi, but she did not have to be an IM. Why did she do it? Probably for her career. She went on, after her husband's death, to work in the state art-dealing business in Berlin." (107) But in addition to her career, "Michaela" was clearly an opportunist, eager to take advantage of all the privileges and perks that would become available to her. Lodging in the state-owned castle was both an enviable privilege and a perk, as was having a cleaning lady, which in those days was very unusual in East Germany. And she hoped, somewhat naively, that she might be dispatched to America to collect two Dürer pictures U. S. Army soldiers had stolen from the Weimar collection at the end of the war.

Ash's dramatic meeting with "Michaela" the next day is without question the high point of his book. While she no longer lives in a castle, she continues to lead a life marked by privilege. Ash sets the stage for their encounter:

> A gray tower-block of characteristic socialist-modernist design, well located and smart by East German standards. Privileged. A tall rather loud woman greets me: "Hello, how are you?" Large features, bright lipstick, gray eyes behind metallic spectacles. Trousers and high heels. A hand-me-down Marlene. Tasteful interior decor, neo-Biedermeier furniture. (111)

When they are settled with coffee and cakes, Ash asks Frau [real name], "'do you have an inkling of why I have sought you out today?'" (112) After a pause, just slightly too long, she answers: "'No, not really.'" That "really" again. (112) Then he tells her.

"'Yes,'" she says immediately, "'one was obliged to [collaborate] in my position.'" About once a month they would come to see her. They said they were from the local council, but gave only their first names. "The conversation was purely in her official capacity, '*dienstlich, nur dienstlich* [only official business].'" . . . "How she clings to the sheet anchor of *dienstlich*." (112) Even when Ash asserts, "'But surely my visit was an entirely private one?'" she explains that her husband Georg was convinced he was working for British intelligence, "'so this was at least a semiofficial matter, *halbdienstlich*.'" (112)

Ash gives her photocopies of the reports and she starts reading. She is shaken by the detail and by the information on Georg. He asks how the interview normally proceeded. Did they have a notebook? "'Yes, yes, they had an open notebook and they carefully wrote everything down. And really one cooperated. One was obliged to. And one tried to tell as many harmless details as possible.'" (112)

She tells him Dr. Georg died in 1984. She herself moved to Berlin, took early retirement—with a good pension as the widow of a "fighter against fascism"—and, in 1987 resigned from the Party. (113)

"But then she goes back to reading the photocopies. . . . Suddenly she puts the papers down and says, 'I can't read any more. I feel sick. I want to puke.'" (113-114) Crying now, her voice is strangled as she says, "'This can't be excused.' Still, she tries to explain." (114)

In 1975 she got this good job in Weimar, but with it came the unofficial work as an informer. "As she talks, emotionally, disjointedly, she reveals rather vividly the mixture of motives that made her collaborate. Some residual belief in the system. The sense that it was an official duty. . . . Then there was the hope of using the Stasi as a player in the bureaucratic game. For her own purposes too: through Dürer to America!" (114-115) While that trip didn't materialize, she was able to obtain permission to take many official trips abroad, including to countries in the West, something of which most East Germans could only dream.

And fear?

"'Yes, of course, underneath one was shit-scared of them. So one tried to disarm any suspicion, to show how cooperative one was, by chatting away, giving all sorts of harmless detail. And this is what comes out. . . .'" (115)

"As she looks at the photocopied reports of IM 'Michaela' she nearly breaks down again, the eyes behind the metallic spectacles filling with tears." (115) She says, "And now you want to write something? And you wanted to see my reaction? And now I've reacted like this and that's good for you, isn't it?' She laughs bitterly, then asks, 'Will you name names?'" (115)

Ash explains that he does not want to hurt anyone and will not use her real name. But, it will be very difficult to tell the story without her being identifiable, to family and acquaintances at least. Ash observes that "Michaela" is "buffeted by conflicting thoughts and emotions." (115) As their conversation nears its end, she says: "We repressed so much. . . . *Why* didn't I apply to see my file? Because I didn't want to know what was in it . . . and about my husband. . . . Who knows what else there is. . . . I think this was the only time I reported so extensively on private matters. I thought it [reporting on Ash to the Stasi] was *dienstlich* but—Well, I hope if you do write you'll try to explain the subjective as well as the objective conditions. How it was then. But probably that's impossible. Even I can't really remember now." (116)

The conversation comes to an end. Now Ash has said everything that really needed to be said and he leaves the photocopies with her.

As they shake hands at the front door "Michaela" does not say, "'Sorry.'" She says, "'How did you get here, by car?'" (116)

"'No, by subway.'"

"'Oh, it's a very good connection isn't it?' Struggling for self-respect and normality, as if nothing had happened. Nothing really." (116)

When Ash sits down in his hotel room half an hour later and takes out a pen, he finds that his own hand is trembling.

Following this uncomfortable encounter with "Michaela," Ash addresses his readers who need to keep in mind that the passages below were written and published in the mid-1990s:

> You must imagine conversations like this taking place every evening, in kitchens and sitting rooms all over Germany. Painful encounters, truth-telling, friendship-demolishing, life-haunting. Hundreds, thousands of such encounters, as the awful power of knowledge is slowly passed down from the Stasi [. . .] to individuals like me, who then hold the lives of other people in our hands, in a way that most of us would never otherwise do.

> Might it not, after all, be wiser to allow them their own particular imaginative mixture of memory and forgetting, of self-respect built on self-deception? Or is it better to confront them? Better

not just for yourself, for your own need to know, but for them too? Even in her first confused reaction, "Michaela" herself said, "Really it's good that you've shown me this." (117)

IV
STATE SECURITY

UNDER SURVEILLANCE

Persons who have read the German or English version of my memoir, *Von Oberlin nach Ostberlin* (From Oberlin to East Berlin), or heard me speak about my secret police file, often ask questions like these: Were you aware that you were under surveillance during your stays in the GDR? How did the secret police go about keeping tabs on you? How did you manage to obtain your file? (The answer to the last question may be found in the snapshot entitled *In Search of My Stasi-File*.) And virtually everyone who has visited the GDR at some point, even for a short period of time, will inevitably volunteer something like this: "I attended a conference in Leipzig back in the summer of 1982, so I probably have a file too. I really have to look into that one of these days." In his compelling memoir, *The File*, Timothy Garton Ash has coined a term for this particular impulsive reaction; he calls it "file envy" (22), something I also have experienced on numerous occasions.

When it came to surveillance, the East German police were experts and used all sorts of methods and tools to gather information and spy on persons of interest. In this effort they were assisted by an army of civilian informants who were called unofficial collaborators. Each collaborator had a code name and a Stasi handler who would give that person assignments and conduct debriefing sessions. A collaborator's real name never appeared in reports, only the alias was used so the identity of that person would be known only to his/her handler. Stasi agents were assigned to work in hotels and restaurants that had guests from Western countries; they frequently used phone bugging devices and also bugged some hotel rooms and even the dwellings of GDR citizens whose activities they wanted to monitor. They conducted observations of suspicious individuals, some of which lasted for several days. The Stasi focused its attention chiefly—but not exclusively—on those individuals, groups of persons, and organizations known or thought to be hostile toward the GDR's ruling SED Party. It also monitored and gathered information on real and potential enemies of the state as well as on oppositional elements engaging in subversive activities.

The evidence in my file indicates that I became a person of interest to the Stasi in the fall of 1975, a few months after I began work in East Berlin on a book project that involved having meetings with a large number of GDR authors. Using a questionnaire and a tape recorder, I was conducting interviews with each of these writers and also gathering texts from them for publication in my book. The Stasi's initial interest in me probably resulted from an understandable uneasiness about my project, since it brought me into direct contact with writers of all political persuasions, including dissidents and regime critics, and it was difficult for anyone to monitor my activities closely. What were the writers telling me in the private interview sessions, what sort of literary texts were they giving me for publication in my book, and how was I going to package and present all of this material back in the US? Was I a friend or an enemy of the GDR? Their answer to the last question is, of course, to be found in my file.

My file contains reports from five types of secret informers; each has a code name preceded by one of the following acronyms: IM, IME, IMV, IMS, and IMB. IM stands for "Inoffizieller Mitarbeiter" (unofficial collaborator), the most common type of informant in the GDR. The file also reveals that there were at least nine unofficial collaborators of one sort or another who reported on my GDR-related activities and gathered information on me for the Stasi. For more information on the types of secret informers and the identities of those nine persons, see the snapshot entitled *My Stasi-File*.

When visiting the GDR for longer than one day, I would either stay in an apartment that had been assigned to me by the Humboldt University or in an Interhotel room that I had booked and paid for in advance. I always assumed that both the telephone and the room were bugged. I also assumed that my suitcase and other belongings would be searched when I was away from the apartment house or hotel. By using a clever trick I learned from a John le Carré spy novel, which involved the careful placement of a single hair in the lid of my suitcase, I was able to ascertain that such searches had indeed been conducted on several occasions. I also heard clicking sounds now and then while using the telephone in my hotel rooms or apartments; I used the phone frequently to set up meetings with writers in Berlin and elsewhere. Here and there in my Stasi-file, there are references in reports to phone calls I placed and things I said over the phone. The Stasi was most certainly listening in and keeping a sharp eye on me.

Surveillance operations involving several Stasi agents had to be justified in advance and authorized in writing by the Ministry for State Security. Observation reports in my file, which were prepared by Stasi personnel, reveal that I was the object of three such operations in East Berlin during the 1970s; one of these lasted for three days before it was terminated. From March 7 until March 17, 1985, I was again under "operative surveillance" while attending the Leipzig Book Fair and functioning as presider at the US Embassy fair booth. This observation yielded a comprehensive report on my "activities and operatively relevant behavioral patterns." As one reads this seven-page document, which is labelled "top secret," it becomes apparent that the Stasi and the GDR authorities were interested most of all in ascertaining the "real" purpose of my visit to Leipzig.

The most interesting surveillance report by far covers a farewell dinner party I had decided to have before returning to Oberlin in mid-December, 1977. The event was held in Berlin at the new Hotel Metropol, which had an excellent restaurant where I would be able to pay the bill with East German marks. This would be an opportunity to thank and say goodbye to my GDR writer friends and others who had helped me during my two-month visit as an IREX scholar. The writers in attendance were Christa and Gerhard Wolf, Ulrich Plenzdorf and his wife Helga, Klaus Schlesinger, and Martin Stade. Willy Moese, a well-known caricature artist was there, as was his wife Maria, a well-known GDR television personality. Also present were Dirk Strassenberger, a lawyer I had gotten to know while living in East Berlin; Helga Schrader, a friend from West Berlin; and Carlos, a Chilean doctoral candidate who was living across the hall from me in our apartment house.

As the file reveals, the Stasi had advance notice of my farewell party and decided to conduct a surveillance operation inside the hotel, beginning at 7:00 p.m. on December 13, and ending shortly after 3:00 a.m. on December 14. This report is supplemented by a long, detailed narrative one of my guests (IMV "Kurt") provided a few days later. When one reads and compares the two reports, it is obvious that the Stasi surveillance team did not know one of my guests was an informant. He has a different alias in their report ("Milan," not "Kurt"), and therefore his identity is protected. All but one of the other guests in the Stasi-report were given ornithological code names—"Blackbird," "Starling," "Titmouse," "Finch," "Raven," "Magpie," "Swallow," and "Siskin," probably so they would not seem out of place at "Eagle's" farewell party. One guest has the code name "Hook", which he had been given at an earlier point in time. The event itself (including conversations among groups of guests at the dinner table) is described in considerable detail—from start to finish—in the observation report, which is much too long to reproduce here.

The Stasi and the GDR authorities eventually concluded—largely on the basis of circumstantial evidence—that I was working for a branch of the US secret service, but that was simply not the case. Since they had come to view my activities within the GDR as "subversive" and begun to consider the possibility that I was an operative, the Stasi recommended measures to be taken in the future in an informational report dated January 7, 1978. Had I not been an IREX scholar, I clearly would not have been able to obtain a visa for my next stay in East Berlin (May 15 – June 15, 1978). When I read the final section of this report, I was frankly astonished.

- It is recommended, for the further monitoring of Zipser as well as the clarification of his contacts and intentions, especially in the light of possible espionage activity, that the following measures be taken under the auspices of Main Department XX/7:

- Zipser is to be put under investigation. When he enters the GDR on short notice, ways should be devised to allow Main Department VIII to keep tabs on him.

- His known contacts in the GDR up to now have to be examined thoroughly and screened with regard to their operative usefulness. With Main Department XX/5 as well as with Main Department VIII, one needs to consider possible ways to illuminate his contacts in Westberlin.

- It needs to be established whether Zipser can be so compromised by operative measures that he can be denied entry into the GDR in the future.

- One needs to ensure, through consultation with Main Department XX/2 and Department XV of the regional headquarters of the Ministry for State Security in Magdeburg, that the unofficial resources of this administrative unit will be utilized in a coordinated supervision of Zipser.

- By way of Main Department XX/3 one needs to ensure that Zipser, whenever he re-enters the GDR under the auspices of the UNESCO Organization IREX's scholar exchange through a predetermined program, will be so burdened by attending lectures at the Humboldt University, among other things, that it will no longer be possible for him to expand and maintain the connection to his GDR contacts, to a large extent unchecked until now. One needs to make certain that he is assigned a reliable minder, an unofficial collaborator with professional as well as political-operative qualifications.

- Through the assignment of appropriate living quarters it will be guaranteed that operative-technical measures can be carried out.

- One has to make certain that Zipser does not, by virtue of using his contacts, gain access to the Writers Congress that will take place in May 1978.

- It needs to be established whether Zipser's reputation can be so tarnished, by unofficial collaborators and within the Writers' Union through fitting well-directed remarks, that the negative forces [*i.e., voices of opposition*] will also avoid having further contact with him.

By way of conclusion, there is an interesting memory I want to share with my snapshot readers. On the afternoon of March 22, 1976, I visited prominent dissident GDR writer Reiner Kunze at his home in Greiz, a small city in Thuringia. My recollection of that visit is hazy after all these years, but I do remember Kunze's passion, intensity, frustration, and anger as we discussed the Prague Spring and the Soviet-led invasion of Czechoslovakia in 1968, human rights issues in the GDR and other Eastern Bloc countries, the ban on his publications and public readings in the GDR, also the suffering of his wife and the mistreatment of his daughter due to his persistent opposition to repressive state practices and policies. Kunze told me, as we conversed and while I tape recorded the interview, that he was certain the secret police had bugged his house. Every so often he would make a comment the GDR authorities and secret police would find offensive, if they heard it, then he would look at a place in the room where a bug might have been planted and say in a loud voice: "What do you think of that?!" Indeed.

LITERARY CENSORSHIP

Let me begin this piece by stating emphatically that the so-called German Democratic Republic was not democratic, nor was it a republic; it was a repressive dictatorship, whose behavior was similar in many ways to what the world has witnessed for years in China, North Korea, Russia, Cuba, Venezuela, Syria, Iran, and unfortunately the list goes on and on. Repression is the act of subduing someone or something by force or other means of restraint, in order to keep someone or something under control. Dictatorships use various means to maintain control, especially of those elements in society they view as hostile or oppositional. Surveillance is one of the means all dictatorships use to keep voices of dissent and opposition in check; censorship is another. Literary censorship is the topic of this snapshot, and I am going to explain just how it was carried out in the communistic GDR, what types of censorship were practiced there, and what the true purpose of censorship was. I also want to provide the rationale for censorship in East Germany and mention some of the things GDR authors were expected not to write about, the taboo topics.

A concise rationale for censorship can be found in the GDR *Wörterbuch der Literaturwissenschaft* (Dictionary of Literary Studies), ed. Claus Träger. Leipzig: Bibliographisches Institut, 1986, p. 582). It explains when literary censorship is appropriate: "In socialist societies the publication and dissemination of printed matter is governed by the principle of centralized democracy and is the full responsibility of everyone involved (authors, publishing houses, editorial boards, etc.). Publications that endanger peace, the harmonious relationship that exists among people everywhere, the dignity of human beings, and social progress are strictly forbidden." There was however another, much more important, unstated rationale: Through censorship and other measures, the state authorities tried to keep authors writing in a non-critical manner and thereby curb political dissent in the GDR. It is important to note that the constitution of the GDR did not provide any legal basis for cultural censorship. In fact, Article 27 of that document unequivocally guarantees freedom of speech, freedom of the press, radio and television: "1. Every citizen of the German Democratic Republic has a right, in accordance with the principles set forth in this constitution, to express his opinion freely and publicly. This right cannot be limited by the nature of one's work or service to the country, and there can be no prejudice against anyone who exercises this right. 2. Freedom of the press, of radio broadcasting and television, is guaranteed." (*Verfassung der Deutschen Demokratischen Republik vom 6. April 1968 in der Fassung des Gesetzes zur Ergänzung und Änderung der Verfassung der Deutschen Demokratischen Republik vom 7. Oktober 1974.* Berlin: Staatsverlag der DDR, 1989, p. 29.)

Since censorship did not officially exist in the former GDR, and since there was no official censorship policy in written form, how was it carried out? When the GDR was founded in 1949, the communist state authorities implemented an elaborate filtration system to ensure that all works of literature and other published materials would be ideologically acceptable, if not ideologically pure. The forms of state censorship, the filters that a written work had to pass through as it made its way from author to reader, were these:

Editorial censorship: An editor employed by the publishing house would read the book manuscript and recommend that the author make certain changes. This very informal procedure, which has frequently been called "pre-censorship" or "gentle censorship," depended on a good working relationship between the writer and his/her editor. Once the manuscript had been completed and revised, it would be scrutinized by a committee composed of knowledgeable persons (including some professors) who were known to be ideologically reliable. Their job was to uncover some heresy that at other stages of censorial review might pass unnoticed.

State ideological censorship: This form of censorship relied on two state agencies, the Publishing and Book Trade Administration (which regulated the activities of all GDR publishers) and the Copyright Office (which was empowered to authorize the publication of works by GDR authors in foreign countries, such as West Germany). Strictly speaking, this is the first level at which formal literary censorship began and the level at which most of it took place.

Party censorship: Censorship by the ruling communistic SED Party occurred at every level since party appointees occupied key positions in the main censoring agencies, such as the publishing houses, the GDR Writers' Union, the Cultural Ministry, and the all-powerful Politburo under the leadership of the SED Party First Secretary.

Readers might now be wondering, who were the censors? The Publishing and Book Trade Administration employed a small team of censors, highly-trained individuals whose love for literature was combined with a real commitment to communism. They believed that the GDR, in contrast to West Germany, was committed to certain values: socialism, humanism, anti-fascism, anti-racism. We know now from interviews with some of them that the GDR censors eliminated very little of the literature that reached them. Formally, they never censored anything at all; they simply refused to give undesirable books an official authorization to print (*Druckgenehmigung*). No printer in the GDR could accept a work that was not accompanied by the official authorization, and all printing houses were owned by the ruling SED Party. So, in practice, the process of securing an authorization to print and censorship amounted to the same thing. Therefore, it is fair to say that the GDR had actually developed an air-tight system of censorship, despite the provisions of its constitution. And throughout its short history the GDR state demonstrated that censorship, if exercised properly (that is, with predictable unpredictability), can help control people as efficiently as prison bars and walls.

What did the censors look for when going through a novel or a collection of essays? Above all, a censor had to be familiar with the sensitivities of SED Party leaders and have an eye for language that was likely to offend them. For example, the censors had to beware of all things American and West German. Also off limits were references to military defense, protest movements, and church dissidents. Any unflattering references to the Soviet

Union or provocative references to the Berlin Wall would be expunged from literary texts, as would references of any sort to the secret police and emigration to West Germany. Certain topics like alcoholism, unemployment, suicide, homosexuality, crime, pollution—things deemed to be nonexistent in the GDR—were taboo until the late 1980s. In making decisions about what to cut from a text, the censors did not work from a check-list; they were guided instead by experience, instinct, and a very human desire to protect their own skins.

The most important and insidious form of literary censorship in the GDR was self-censorship, what I like to call the scissors in heads. Simply put, the GDR authors themselves, using their knowledge of what was and was not acceptable for publication, would censor their own works. Although much has been said and written about the mechanisms of state censorship, almost all of the censorship in the GDR took place in the heads of writers. Many writers poured considerable creative energy into the game of outwitting the censors, and in the process they probably succeeded in outwitting only themselves. For it is clear, at least to me, that literary self-censorship was the ultimate goal of the censoring agencies. The system forced writers to censor their own works, consciously and subconsciously, and this is precisely what the state authorities wanted to achieve in the GDR—to make each author decide what was suitable for print and what was not.

Most GDR writers learned the rules of the censorship game by a process of trial and error, and many tried to bend the rules while appearing to observe them. Those writers who absolutely refused to play the game, or who insisted on playing by their own rules, faced a series of possible penalties and punishments. The most drastic of these included imprisonment, house arrest, expatriation, and exile—punishments reserved for the most troublesome and persistent dissenters. Serious offenders might also be denied the privilege of publishing or reading, lecturing, and performing in public. They and their families might even be threatened with bodily harm or openly harassed by the secret police, if they were too prominent to silence in other ways; this is precisely what Günter Kunert and Christa Wolf experienced for "misbehaving" in t he late 1970s. Lesser penalties included expulsion from the SED Party, expulsion from the local and/or national Writers' Union, the denial of visas for travel to the West, and the publication of one's books in ridiculously small editions. Some of these punishments had dire financial consequences for the affected writers, as one can easily imagine.

The Case of Prominent Poet Sarah Kirsch

Let me now present a first-hand account of the severest form of censorial repression in the GDR, one step short of incarceration. The victim in question was Sarah Kirsch, the GDR's most celebrated woman poet who was one of my favorite authors and my friend. She was born Ingrid Bernstein in 1935 in Limlingerode in the region of Thuringia, located in the part of Germany that after WW II became the GDR. I got to know her in the fall of 1975 when I was working in East Berlin on a major book project focusing on GDR literature in the 1970s. The cruelty of the GDR government authorities was on full display after they decided to prevent Sarah Kirsch from earning a living by publishing her writings or speaking in public, in order to discipline and silence her for behavior they viewed as hostile and oppositional to the SED regime.

Sarah Kirsch, who—unlike her famous colleagues Wolf Biermann, Reiner Kunze, Jurek Becker, Günter Kunert and Stefan Heym—was never considered a troublemaker, would eventually become a nonperson in the eyes of the GDR's cultural bureaucracy. Her sin was to protest, along with eleven other leading GDR writers, the government's expatriation in November 1976 of dissident songwriter and poet Wolf Biermann, while he was on a concert tour in West Germany. Her punishment for this transgression turned out to be worse than the ones other protesters received. She was informed that her writings would no longer be published in the GDR, that she would not receive any more free-lance translation work, the main source of her income at that time, nor would she be allowed to participate in public events of any sort. Since Sarah was divorced, and since she had a six-year-old son, her sudden inability to earn an income soon became a major existential problem. Her solution was to apply for a permanent exit visa that would enable her to move to the West. She did that, but the visa was not forthcoming. The government authorities had clearly decided to make an example of her, so other writers would know not to follow in her footsteps.

Sarah lived in a modern high-rise apartment house on Fisher Island in the River Spree, in central Berlin. At that time, she was romantically involved with a West German writer who resided in West Berlin; he would come to East Berlin periodically to visit her. This unusual across-the-Wall relationship contributed significantly to her desire to move to West Berlin, but for more than six months her visa application was ignored. Eventually, in the summer of 1977, Sarah was finally permitted to emigrate to the West and made the move to West Berlin. I visited with her that fall and asked how she had managed to get the visa. "I was so desperate," she said, "that I finally decided to appeal directly to [SED Party leader] Erich Honecker. I wrote him a letter and told him that I had applied for a permanent exit visa more than six months ago, but—despite my repeated inquiries—had not yet received a response. I said that I desperately needed his help and wanted him to intervene soon, very soon. I emphasized that this was an urgent life-and-death matter and concluded by asking him to keep in mind that my apartment was located on the seventeenth floor." Honecker then intervened, presumably because of her veiled threat of suicide, and her visa application was approved right away. In August 1977, Sarah Kirsch and her son Moritz relocated to West Berlin, without any fanfare.

Volker Braun, a prominent East German writer and close friend of Sarah Kirsch, memorialized her desperate flight to West Berlin in one stanza of his 1978 poem, "Der Müggelsee" (Lake Müggel): "and Sarah leaps over the Wall / From the seventeenth floor, her Love- / Song full of ravens! Ravens! / Black, under water." Black as midnight, raven symbolism and meaning is often associated with death and the underworld. But here it signals that something is about to transform Sarah Kirsch's life. Whether positive or negative, the impending transformation is certain to be dramatic. So the ravens, fierce protectors, are there to help guide her safely through the fray.

[Note: For detailed information on the forms and function of literary censorship in the GDR, see *Fragebogen: Zensur. Zur Literatur vor und nach dem Ende der DDR*, ed. Richard A. Zipser (Leipzig: Reclam, 1995. 341 pp.). This documentary work contains a critical introduction and interviews with 70 former GDR writers on the topic of literary censorship. All of the interviews were conducted in the early 1990s, after the fall of the Berlin Wall and the unification of the two Germanys. Also, see *Literary Censorship in the German-Speaking Countries*, a special issue of *THE GERMANIC REVIEW*, ed. Richard A. Zipser. Part Two: *Literary Censorship in the Federal Republic of Germany and the German Democratic Republic* (Summer 1990, Vol. 65, No. 3, 97-131). This volume contains my essay on "The Many Faces of Censorship in the German Democratic Republic, 1949-1989," also essays by and interviews with 11 GDR writers from the late 1980s and 1990, with observations from the period before the reunification of Germany. Most of these authors had already left the GDR and moved to the West, so they were not constrained in any way by the prevailing East German restrictions on open discourse.]

UNOFFICIAL AND ILLEGAL PUBLICATIONS

In my snapshot on *Literary Censorship*, I have illuminated and discussed the various forms and mechanisms of censorship that existed within East Germany as well as its ultimate goal in the cultural sphere—the stimulation of self-censorship. In their efforts to circumvent the near-perfect censorship process and to avoid prosecution or other suppression, GDR writers produced several types of unofficial and illegal literature, three examples of which will be discussed in this piece. These are 1) desk drawer literature; 2) *samizdat* (Russian: self-publishing), a form of clandestine or underground literature; 3) unauthorized and therefore illegal publication of books in other German-speaking countries such as West Germany, Austria and Switzerland.

Drawer Literature

Drawer literature as a concept originated in the People's Republic of China during the Maoist period (1949-1976). It referred to literature that had been written during this turbulent period but which for political reasons could not be published until years later, if at all. *Schubladenliteratur* is the German term for desk drawer literature, and it can be traced back to the end of World War II. After the war ended in 1945, some German writers who had been Nazi sympathizers during the Third Reich presented texts they claimed to have retrieved from their desk drawers as evidence that they were not collaborators but good democrats after all. [For further information on this distasteful subject, see Ernst Klee's reference work, *Das Kulturlexikon zum Dritten Reich. Wer war was vor und nach 1945?* (Cultural Encyclopedia of the Third Reich. Who was What before and after 1945?). Frankfurt am Main: S. Fischer, 2007. 720 pp.]

In the GDR the desk drawers contained a different sort of literature, texts by so-called dissident writers who were critical of their communistic society and authoritarian government. These texts had no chance of being published in their own country and, if they were made public, would probably have landed their authors in prison. That notwithstanding, the desk drawers of oppositional writers were not filled with literature written during decades of censorship in the GDR and just waiting to be published. One way or another, well-known East German authors who produced *Schubladenliteratur* always managed to publish what they had written, usually in West Germany. In the late 1970s and 1980s many dissident GDR writers moved voluntarily or were forced to emigrate to the West, where their previously unpublishable writings found their way into print. Hence, most literary critics with a serious interest in the GDR would be hard pressed today to name a single important work that emerged from storage in a desk drawer during the 1990s.

Samizdat

Samizdat was a form of dissident literary activity in the Soviet-ruled post-World War II communist countries in which individuals reproduced censored and makeshift underground publications, often by hand, and passed the documents from reader to reader. This illegal literature, secretly written then copied and circulated privately, was usually critical of the practices of the Soviet government; for this reason it was unpublishable and forbidden. My one and only encounter with Samizdat made in the GDR came at the Leipzig Book Fair in March 1985.

I turn to my Stasi-file to refresh my memory of what I have come to realize was a unique experience, something far more significant from a literary-historical perspective than I perceived at the time. A report in my file reminds me that I stayed in the drab, somewhat run-down Interhotel am Ring which was a short distance away from the Trade Fair House, the multi-storied home of the Book Fair. The file also reminds me that I had met (for the first time) with outspoken dissident writer and poet Lutz Rathenow, who was not permitted to publish his works in the GDR. He had published his first book illegally in West Germany, a collection of short texts critical of the GDR, *Mit dem Schlimmsten wurde schon gerechnet* (Already Prepared for the Worst, 1980). For this transgression Rathenow was arrested and imprisoned for three months. From then on he was under close surveillance by the Stasi, but he and his friends continued to smuggle their manuscripts into West Berlin and West Germany, to be published there. We had a dinner meeting that lasted several hours and were joined by Hans-Jürgen Schmitt, an editor with the West German Fischer Taschenbuch Verlag who had published several paperback anthologies of GDR literature.

Before we parted company, Rathenow gave me an unusual present, a handmade booklet containing typewritten texts by eight younger oppositional writers who were unable to find a GDR publisher for all or some of their works. In the GDR and elsewhere in the Soviet bloc, banned authors such as Rathenow would reproduce censored and underground publications by hand, and then these documents were circulated among readers. The purpose of this clandestine self-publishing practice, a key form of dissident activity, was to circumvent official state censorship. It was not without danger, however, as harsh punishments were imposed on persons caught possessing or copying censored materials. I thought it was quite an honor to be given an authentic *samizdat* literary anthology by Lutz Rathenow.

The booklet has a large wraparound cover made of heavier weight paper. The cover has a black ink woodblock image of two human faces, a woman and a man, and the artist's seal. Inside the cover, stapled together, one finds a table of contents followed by nine texts, the first of which is "A Letter from Prague" ("Ein Brief aus Prag") dated January 1984. Although the author of the letter is not identified, it is likely it was written by Rathenow who is listed as the author of the final literary text. The writers who contributed the other literary texts are Lothar Trolle, Stephan Ernst, Elke Erb, Raja Lubinetzki, Johannes Jansen, Eberhard Häfner, and Katja Lange. Rathenow was hounded by the East German secret police in the years leading up to reunification, but since 1990 he has garnered considerable acclaim as a writer. Erb and Lange (now Lange-Müller) have also established themselves as mainstream writers in today's unified Germany.

Illegal Book Publications

It was illegal for GDR authors to publish their works in countries other than the GDR—in German or in translation—without first securing official approval from the government authorities. But from time to time frustrated and defiant writers, such as Lutz Rathenow, would proceed to do just that. Their willingness to break the law usually had evasion of censorship as its purpose, but it could also be for ideological or financial reasons. West German publishing houses were eager to publish books by high-profile GDR writers, especially those who were considered controversial. However, before a work could be considered for publication in the West, it would have to be submitted to an East German publisher and from there undergo the censorial review process. If a work was cleared for publication in the GDR, the East German

Copyright Office would then assist its author with the legal and bureaucratic work associated with a book being licensed for publication in the West.

Consider the case of German-Jewish writer Stefan Heym, the GDR's most famous and widely read author, who had emigrated from Germany to the US in 1935 and later become a US citizen. Heym was able to establish himself as a freelance author, writing in English. His first novel, *Hostages* (1942), was a bestseller, and his novel *The Crusaders* climbed to sixth place on *The New York Times* list of best sellers. In 1952, he wrote a letter to President Eisenhower protesting the Korean War and the fascistic policies of the American government. He then decided to move back to Europe with his American wife and requested asylum in communist East Germany. In 1953, the GDR government restored his former German citizenship, enabling him and his wife to move to East Berlin.

Heym's political activism intensified in the GDR and before long SED Party officials came to regret their decision to repatriate him. His first major conflict with the GDR authorities occurred in 1956 when his novel about the June 17, 1953 mass uprising of workers in East Berlin, *5 Days in June* (5 Tage im Juni*)*, was published in West Germany and in English translation but rejected for publication in the GDR. The fact that Heym's novel was banned in East Germany underscored how dangerous his fictional recounting of history was in the minds of the GDR's leaders.

Heym continued publishing his books in Western countries, both in German and in English translation, and these publications earned him large sums of hard currency that GDR authorities were eager to share in accordance with a formula the state had established. Heym resisted, and in 1969 he was convicted of violating the GDR's currency exchange regulations after publishing his novel *Lassalle* in West Germany. In 1979 he was again convicted of breaching the GDR's currency exchange regulations, this time in connection with the publication of his novel *Collin* in West Germany. This violation resulted in his expulsion from the GDR Writers' Union and a major confrontation with government officials that would eventually involve eight prominent writers who supported Heym and, for so doing, would also be expelled from the Writers' Union. Facing prosecution for alleged currency offences, Heym wrote to me (in English) in late April of 1979: "If you've been following the news, you may have noticed that there's trouble brewing in this place—I am going to be prosecuted on a trumped-up charge of violation of foreign currency rules, in reality, because I refused to ask the GDR authorities for permission to have my books printed abroad if they're forbidden here." A few months later, Heym was tried and fined 9,000 West German marks for having published his novel in the West without securing authorization from GDR officials and for neglecting to report the income he had received in foreign currency.

East German writers like Stefan Heym who published books illegally in Western countries, and in the process violated the GDR's foreign currency regulations, faced a series of possible penalties and punishments. The most drastic of these included imprisonment, house arrest, expatriation, and exile—punishments reserved for the most troublesome and persistent dissenters. Serious offenders might also be denied the privilege of publishing or reading, lecturing, and performing in public. They and their families might even be threatened with bodily harm or openly harassed by the secret police, if they were too prominent to silence in other ways. As I mentioned earlier, this is precisely what Günter Kunert and Christa Wolf experienced for "misbehaving" in the late 1970s. Lesser penalties included expulsion from the SED Party, expulsion from the local and/or national Writers' Union, the denial of visas for travel to the West, and the publication of one's books in ridiculously small editions. In Heym's case the punishment amounted to little more than a cautionary slap on the wrist, since GDR authorities did not want to stem the flow of hard Western currency into their coffers. However, in many instances the punishments for illegal publication had dire personal and professional consequences for the affected writers. For some examples, see my snapshots on Bernd Jentzsch, Sarah Kirsch, and Reiner Kunze in sections VI and VII.

SUPPRESSED LITERATURE

In 2001, more than a decade after the reunification of the two Germanys, two former GDR writers—Joachim Walther and Ines Geipel—began working on a government-financed project that involved collecting unpublished literary texts that had been suppressed in the dictatorial East German state that was created after World War II. Between 2001 and 2005, they were able to uncover texts that 100 or so GDR writers had been unable to publish in communistic East Germany. Using both conventional and unconventional research methods, combined with sophisticated detective work, they located unpublished literature written by some writers who had disappeared and by some who had previously not been known to exist. In many instances, the Stasi had arrested dissident authors, confiscated their writings and kept that material on file to use as evidence against them in trials. Writers who were deemed to be hostile to the ruling SED Party and its actions were often made to disappear, along with the unpublished texts they had written which were retained in their or in another individual's Stasi-file. In connection with this mammoth undertaking, Geipel and Walther established an Archive of Suppressed Literature in the GDR (Archiv unterdrückter Literatur in der DDR). The archive houses the collection of unpublished works of literature by GDR authors, many of whom are no longer living, a total of 70,000 manuscript pages.

Walther and Geipel's work on suppressed GDR literature, which some scholars have called "the third German literature," was far from finished in 2005. They began publishing some of the texts from the archive in a book series entitled *Die Verschwiegene Bibliothek* (The Concealed Library); ten volumes, each one devoted to a single author, appeared in the Edition Book Guild between 2005 and 2009. The material in the archive led them to undertake yet another project, the publication of a co-edited book entitled *Die Gesperrte Ablage: Unterdrückte Literaturgeschichte in Ostdeutschland 1945-1989* (The Locked Repository: History of Suppressed Literature in East Germany 1945-1989). Düsseldorf: Lilienfeld Press, 2015. The last section of this book is an appendix (311-408); it contains valuable information on 85 of the authors whose writings are housed in the archive. For each of these writers, who are presented in alphabetical order, there is a short biography, a listing of works available in the archive's holdings, and a list of selected publications; for some there is also an interview, which the editors conducted while collecting materials for the archive. In a brief introduction to the appendix, Walther explains that the founders of the archive were not merely interested in gathering the unpublished evidence of a counterworld and storing it in the archive. For them it was more about giving a voice to these authors who had been pushed aside and the literature that had been suppressed, in addition to making both known to the public as authentic evidence of the SED's cruel dictatorship (310).

As I write this piece in the COVID-19 summer of 2020, a time when all lives matter and no lives matter, I remind myself that almost thirty years have passed since the world witnessed the reunification of Germany. During that time span, several of the authors represented in the Archive of Suppressed Literature in the GDR were able to establish themselves as mainstream writers in unified Germany. Among the best known within this group are: Siegmar Faust, Jürgen Fuchs, Uwe Grüning, Wolfgang Hinkeldey, Jürgen Hultenreich, Freya Klier, Lutz Rathenow, Andreas Reimann, Gabriele Stötzer-Kachold, Lothar Trolle, Gerhard Zschorsch.

In conclusion, let me mention that Joachim Walther died on May 19th of 2020. The next day Ines Geipel published an article in the online Berlin Newspaper (*Berliner-Zeitung*) announcing his death and paying tribute to him. Her article is entitled "The Person in Charge—upon the Death of Joachim Walther" ("Der Zuständige—zum Tod von Joachim Walther"). Geipel spent the first thirty years of her life in the GDR, where as a young woman she suffered brutal physical abuse at the hands of the Stasi. Her collaboration with Walther on a number of projects spanned a fifteen-year period (2001-2015). For discovering, uncovering, and preserving "the third German literature" and illuminating a dark chapter in German history, we who believe in freedom for all people and free speech owe Joachim Walther and Ines Geipel a debt of gratitude.

BERLIN STORIES: AN ILLEGAL ANTHOLOGY PROECT

In November 1975, during my first lengthy stay in East Berlin, I became involved unwittingly in an illegal anthology self-publishing undertaking called *Berliner Geschichten* (Berlin Stories). As I have mentioned elsewhere, officials at the GDR Writers' Union were very suspicious of me and wary about the project I had proposed and begun carrying out on GDR literature in the 1970s. Therefore, the East German secret police (Stasi) were keeping an eye on me, monitoring and writing file reports on my activities, and also keeping track of the persons with whom I conferred and had contact. As I would learn many years later, my 400-page Stasi-file was a work in progress from 1973 to 1988.

A 15-page informational report in my Stasi-file, compiled from a number of unidentified sources and dated January 7, 1978, discloses that I first attracted attention operatively in 1975. It then goes on to explain why the secret police became interested in me: "ZIPSER's 1975 stay in the GDR coincided time-wise with the activities of SCHLESINGER, PLENZDORF and STADE related to the realization of their 'Berlin Stories' anthology project, which was hostile to the SED Party." I discover that on November 10, 1975, the Stasi had sent a report to SED Party officials at the highest level on a subversive initiative spearheaded by three oppositional writers: Ulrich Plenzdorf and his good friends, Klaus Schlesinger and Martin Stade. These writers were quietly and without authorization assembling an anthology of short stories to be published under the title "Berliner Geschichten." Each of the stories was to focus on a societal, political, or other problem that its author was concerned with as a writer. The plan was to offer the anthology to an East German publishing house and to insist that it be published without editorial revisions—i.e., in its original, uncensored form. Furthermore, as I learned from informal conversations with and among the three editors, if the anthology were rejected for publication in the GDR they were prepared to offer it directly to a West German publisher, without the approval of the GDR Copyright Office. Many GDR writers had been asked to participate in this unauthorized and therefore illegal project, so before long the Stasi and the GDR Writers' Union officials heard about it from some of their informants. Working together and using various kinds of threats, they were able to block this 'dangerous and subversive' self-publishing initiative in January 1976. Ironically, I was a beneficiary of their action, since several writers gave me the short stories they had written for the "Berlin Stories" anthology to publish in my book, *DDR-Literatur im Tauwetter* (GDR Literature During the Thaw, 1985). The section of the informational secret police report on "Berliner Geschichten" concludes with the following observation: "Due primarily to his connection to PLENZDORF and SCHLESINGER, one can assume that ZIPSER has received detailed information on this undertaking. After it was certain that the anthology was not going to come into being, SCHLESINGER demonstratively handed over his contribution to ZIPSER." As I can recall, that is precisely what happened, but how did the Stasi learn about it?

My anecdotal Berlin story has a happy ending: Twenty years later, in 1995, Suhrkamp Verlag in Frankfurt am Main published a paperback edition of *Berliner Geschichten*. The anthology had three editors: Ulrich Plenzdorf, Klaus Schlesinger, and Martin Stade. The book also relates what had happened back in 1975-76 when three enterprising authors launched a bold self-publishing experiment that had to be stopped by the Stasi—yet another Berlin story!

THE STASI'S LONG ARM

As I explained in my snapshot on *The Stasi*, the Ministry for State Security (MfS) was responsible for both domestic surveillance and foreign espionage in the Soviet-occupied German Democratic Republic. At its peak, it employed 90,000 secret police officers (commonly called "Stasi") whom East Germans hated and feared. It has been described as one of the most effective, repressive, and despised intelligence and secret police agencies that ever existed, comparable to the Soviet Union's ruthless KGB. With the help of almost 200,000 informants, the Stasi monitored and gathered intelligence on GDR citizens it considered to be possible enemies of the state. It also conducted covert operations in West Berlin, West Germany, and elsewhere in the West, including the United States. The Stasi was proud of its "long arm," which it used on many occasions to incapacitate enemies of the GDR's communist government living in the West, persons who presumed they were safe and beyond the Stasi's reach. Unfortunately for them, they were very wrong.

It appears that the Stasi acted with impunity not only within the borders of the GDR, but also in West Berlin and West Germany where it time and again perpetrated various types of crimes in violation of international human rights law. Ralph Pickard, in his article on "The Awarding of the East German Patriotic Order of Merit in Bronze to a Ministry for State Security Officer for Kidnapping a West German Citizen During the Cold War," reports on the kidnapping operations of the MfS in the West and the fate of those persons affected.

> It is estimated during the early period of the Cold War that between 400 and as many as 600 German citizens were abducted in West Germany and taken to East Germany (GDR) after the creation of the GDR in 1949, through the mid-1960s. Those involved in the abductions were members of the East German Border Police/Guards, DDR Ministry for State Security (MfS – STASI) and, to a lesser extent, the USSR Committee for State Security (KGB). Based on historical research of the STASI Archives, some of the persons who were abducted by the East German state were found guilty under East German law and, in some instances, were sentenced to death. However, in other instances, some abductees were given prison sentences that were as long as 15 years. Abductions in West Germany and West Berlin involved multiple MfS departments, which in itself provides some insight on the coordination that was necessary to bring the abductees back into East Germany. (*Regimes Museum Journal*, Vol. 6, No. 1, Feb. 2019, p. 14)

Following this introduction to the topic of abductions orchestrated by the GDR's MfS, Pickard focuses attention on two of the many individuals who were kidnapped from West Berlin, Gerd Sommerlatte and Karl Wilhelm Fricke. Gerd Sommerlatte was a GDR citizen who had managed to become an East German border guard. On September 10, 1961, he was assigned to the Brandenburg Gate dividing East and West Berlin and on that day, he decided to defect to the West. A short time after his defection to the West, West German criminals hired by the MfS leadership abducted Sommerlatte in West Berlin. They drove him to the East Berlin border, where they handed him over to the GDR authorities. He was charged with espionage and sentenced to ten years in prison in 1962. He was released in 1965 and handed over to West German authorities.

Pickard proceeds to tell his readers about Karl Wilhelm Fricke, a West German journalist who was abducted on April 1, 1955. Before his abduction, Fricke was a GDR citizen who had fled the East German People's Police after they arrested him in 1949. He settled in West Germany, became a political journalist and wrote several articles that were critical of East Germany's ruling SED Party. In the middle of 1954, the MfS leadership planned an operation designed to lure Fricke back to East Berlin. Two Secret Employees (Geheime Mitarbeiter – GM) of the MfS, Kurt Maurer and his wife were assigned to carry out the kidnapping of Fricke.

According to Pickard, the Maurers established a friendship with Fricke in West Berlin. On April 1, 1955, they invited Fricke to their apartment for drinks and drugged him so that he lost consciousness. They then quickly transported him to East Berlin, where they handed Fricke over to other MfS employees. On June 11, 1956, following several months of interrogation by the Stasi, Fricke was found guilty of crimes against the GDR State and sentenced to four years of solitary confinement. He was released on March 31, 1959, and handed over to West German authorities. He continued to work as a political journalist and author until the end of the Cold War and well into this century. He has produced several of the standard works on resistance and state repression in the GDR (1949-1990).

Pickard's primary focus in his article is on Stasi officer and Secret Employee Kurt Maurer, whose real name was actually Kurt Rittwagen. He returned to East Germany as a hero and was awarded the East German Patriotic Order of Merit in Bronze medal with award document on May 8, 1955. The award document, presented to Rittwagen for his role in kidnapping West German journalist Karl Wilhelm Fricke, was hand signed by GDR President Wilhelm Pieck. This document is the earliest of three that were produced during the Cold War. Pickard reports that Rittwagen continued to work actively in the MfS in East Germany until his retirement in 1974. During his active duty career in the MfS, he earned several additional East German awards and advanced from the rank of second lieutenant to major.

A Case in Point: Karl-Heinz Jakobs

In the final section of this snapshot, I want to give my readers an example of how the Stasi sought to intimidate and influence the behavior of oppositional writers who were living in the West with its "long arm." I have elected to put the spotlight on prominent East German prose writer Karl-Heinz Jakobs, who spent most of the spring 1986 semester at Oberlin College as Max Kade German Writer-in-Residence. I should mention that I had been a faculty member in Oberlin's German Department since 1969. Our choice of Jakobs, who was living in West Germany when we issued the invitation, angered officials in both the GDR Writers' Union and the Ministry of Culture. For Jakobs, much like the two GDR writers in exile who preceded him as our visiting authors—Bernd Jentzsch in 1982 and Jurek Becker in 1979—had evolved into an outspoken critic of the Honecker regime, the GDR state, and its communistic brand of socialism.

A down-to-earth writer who had never been viewed as a troublemaker, Jakobs surprised many of his East German colleagues and functionaries at the GDR Writers' Union when he turned into one of the more vociferous of the intellectuals who protested the expatriation of the famous dissident chansonnier Wolf Biermann in November 1976. His harsh criticism of the ruling SED Party led to his dismissal from the Berlin Writers' Union as well as from the executive committee of the GDR Writers' Union, and finally to expulsion from the SED Party in 1977. Because of his deteriorating relations with the GDR authorities, he was given a three-year "visa" and asked to leave the country for that period of time. When it expired in April 1980, the visa was extended for four more years, but Jakobs decided not to return and stayed in West Germany.

After being forcibly exiled to West Germany in 1977, Jakobs increased his commitment as freelance author and journalist to confront the problems of the GDR's government directly, focusing on the dictatorial SED regime. In the spring of 1986, when he was visiting writer at Oberlin College, we frequently discussed his experiences as a writer in the GDR. These leisurely conversations often took place at my house, where he would join my wife Ulrike and me for dinner two or three times each week. One evening, Karl-Heinz told us about his departure from the GDR. Shortly before he was "shoved" into the West ("abgeschoben" is the word he used), he had a meeting with a high-ranking and very powerful official from the GDR's Ministry for Culture. This individual told him to be careful in West Germany, to behave himself and refrain from attacking SED Party leaders or their policies and actions. He was warned to beware of "the long arm of the Stasi" which would be able to reach him anywhere.

Jakobs' defiant response to the Deputy Minister's threat came in the form of the first major work he wrote while living in West Germany, *Wilhelmsburg* (1979), a novel that examined the dynamics of a provincial city in a nameless, German-speaking socialist state. The hero brings to mind the typical GDR citizen: he is a man who keeps his opinions to himself for fear of the consequences, a man who says "yes" even when he thinks "no," something Jakobs himself had done on many occasions. Shortly before the novel's publication, Jakobs remarked that an East German writer conscious of history must tell what happened, and what happened unjustly. He declared that—for him—the moment of hesitating to do this was gone forever.

Jakobs would continue to be a vocal critic of the SED regime in the GDR, but his voice would grow weaker with each passing year. It became apparent in the late 1970s and 1980s, as the number of East German writers living in Western exile increased steadily, that it was nearly impossible to live in West Germany and effectively protest or criticize what was happening unjustly in East Germany. Only Wolf Biermann was able to do that successfully and over an extended period of time. The East German authorities became aware that the exiled GDR writers did not pose much of a threat to them, so deportation became their solution to a problem. As for Jakobs, he was very fortunate. The MfS leadership did not hire thugs to abduct him, nor did they go out of their way to make life difficult for him. He was able to continue working as a journalist and as a writer for radio and television broadcasts, all the while in opposition to the SED regime. Luckily, the Stasi's long arm did not reach for him.

V PEOPLE

THE INVENTOR

When we think of famous inventors, names like Johannes Gutenberg, Leonardo da Vinci, Benjamin Franklin, Thomas Edison, Alexander Graham Bell, Marie Curie, Orville and Wilbur Wright, and Steve Jobs quickly come to mind. I have always thought that it must be incredibly interesting and satisfying to be an inventor, but I learned that this was not the case in East Germany. Inventors in that country could not pursue their interests in an unrestricted and creative way; rather, they were government employees and as such assigned to invent specific things that were needed in the GDR. I learned about this in the strangest way.

In 1976, I spent the first two weeks of June in East Berlin, in order to continue interviewing East German writers and gathering various materials from them for a book project on GDR literature. I stayed in the Interhotel Stadt-Berlin, a four-star hotel that was supposed to offer its guests a taste of the West in the East. This forty-story hotel on the Alexanderplatz, a huge public square located in the most central district of Berlin (Mitte), boasted the best of the GDR in an attempt to compete with Western standards. It had a panorama restaurant on the 37th floor, a favorite place to dine for diplomats and tourists with hard currency, and unusually fast elevators for that time in the GDR. It also had a restaurant on the ground floor where one could pay the bill with East German marks. The food and service were exceptionally good there, and—as a hotel guest—I never had difficulty being seated at a table or at the long bar that stretched along one side of the dining room.

On the evening I am recalling, I returned to the hotel after a particularly exhausting day that had involved long meetings with three GDR writers who lived in different districts of Berlin. Usually, I scheduled such meetings in the morning and the afternoon, but on this day I had been invited to dinner at one writer's house, a very special occasion. Our 'business meeting' took place after dinner, then I drove back to the hotel and went to the ground-floor restaurant for a nightcap. I took a seat at the bar and observed that someone was sitting to the left of me, with one barstool between us. I would soon learn that this person, a man who looked to be about forty years old, was an East German inventor.

I was tired and not at all eager to have a conversation with a stranger, so it was he who spoke first. He looked in my direction and asked me what he surely knew from the Western-style clothes I was wearing: "Are you from here?" I replied: "No, I'm not from here." Whereupon he said, "Then you must be from over there (*drüben*)," the reference being to West Berlin or West Germany. I responded: "No, I'm not from over there, I come from outside Germany (*draussen*). I'm from the United States." Being curious, he didn't hesitate to ask me what I thought of the GDR, a question that took me by surprise. When I told him I thought it was OK, he gave me a weird look that signaled disbelief and said, "You can tell me the truth. Tell me what you really think." This prompted me to tell him about my project on East German literature that brought me together with very interesting people, such as the GDR writers I'd met with that day.

At some point, I asked this man about his line of work. "I'm an inventor," he said. When I commented that being an inventor must be an extremely interesting and satisfying occupation, he replied: "On the contrary, here in the GDR it is a frustrating and unrewarding job." He went on to explain, so I would understand the GDR inventor's unhappy fate. "I'm a creative person with many original ideas for new things I'd like to invent. But, I can't do that. I'm employed by the state and work together with other inventors at a facility in Potsdam. We're all assigned to invent things that the GDR desperately needs. These things have already been invented and are readily available in Western countries, but we don't have the hard currency to buy them. So, our task is to come up with ways to produce something comparable here, using materials that are available in the GDR. This is not always possible, of course, and when we 'invent' a product it is always inferior to what already exists. For forward-looking persons like myself, this is frustrating beyond belief."

I must have asked him for examples of things he had reinvented, but in truth I cannot recall any. However, he did indicate that his team of inventors worked on producing equipment for use in hospitals, doctors' and dentists' offices, electronic data processing, banking, and manufacturing, also household appliances of every type, and more. An exemplar of the item to be copied or imitated would be purchased in a Western country, disassembled, and studied by the inventors who had been assigned to work on the project, and then they would proceed to reinvent something that had already been invented.

Our conversation went on for quite some time and gave me several new insights into life in the GDR under communism. Shortly before the restaurant and bar closed I finished my beer, said good night to the inventor, and went to my room, still thinking about this strange but revealing encounter.

THE MARLBORO MAN

The Marlboro Man is a figure that was used in tobacco advertising campaigns for Marlboro cigarettes. It is considered the most powerful mascot in American tobacco marketing in history. In the US, where the advertising campaign originated, it was used from 1954 to 1999. The images initially featured rugged men portrayed in a variety of roles but later primarily featured a rugged cowboy, in nature with a cigarette. Over the years, dozens of men (some of them "real" cowboys) have modeled for television commercials, magazine and newspaper advertisements, billboards, and other advertising materials promoting the Marlboro brand of cigarettes. The iconic Marlboro Man was synonymous with America's image of itself—tough, self-sufficient, hard-working. The Marlboro Man had no home and no family tied him down; he was at home alone on the range. He epitomized resilience, independence, and free enterprise. Some of us still remember the TV commercial with a moving image of a rugged mustachioed man on horseback, cloaked in a shearling range coat and wearing a cowboy hat, charging across the prairie in the American West while smoking a Marlboro. Or, the one with a man wearing cowboy chaps, leading his horse out of a corral, a cigarette between his lips. "Come to Marlboro Country," the caption urged.

In the summer of 1977, while vacationing on the island of Martha's Vineyard, I bought a custom-fit "Country Marlboro Shearling Sheepskin Coat." I did not smoke Marlboro cigarettes (or any other brand), nor was I eager to capture the spirit of the American West. I simply wanted to own a coat that would keep me warm in the frigid winter weather we typically had in northern Ohio, where the bone-chilling wind from Lake Erie would blow across the flat, prairie-like countryside. I was teaching at Oberlin College at that time and needed a coat I could wear every day during the winter. The handsome cognac-colored shearling sheepskin coat I found in a leatherworks store was just perfect for me. It had a substantial wind-cutting shearling collar and shearling lining that would hold out the weather and keep in the heat. Even in Oberlin, where the wind could drive snowflakes with the force of shotgun pellets, I would never be cold again!

On October 15, 1977, with the support of an IREX (International Research and Exchanges Board) grant I had been awarded in the spring of that year, I returned to East Berlin for a two-month period in order to continue work on a major book project. The project involved interviewing writers and gathering literary texts and other materials from them; hence, this stage of it had to be carried out in the GDR. Since my stay in East Berlin and work as an IREX scholar had the approval of the GDR Ministry of Higher Education and the sponsorship of the Humboldt University, I had a more elevated status than before. I was really excited about returning to East Germany and resuming work on the project that later became a three-volume book on GDR literature in the 1970s.

Packing clothes for this stay was somewhat problematic. I was limited to 44 pounds of luggage for the international flight, as I recall; for additional pounds I would have to pay a hefty penalty. I selected clothing items for my trip carefully, with a preference for casual wear. I knew that Berlin often has very cold weather in the late fall and winter, so I decided to take along my new shearling sheepskin coat. This I would carry onto the plane, along with my tote bag, and store it in an overhead bin. For rainy days, I decided to take along my London Fog raincoat, which I would wear onto the plane. Two overcoats for two months in East Berlin, that was all I needed. I could not have imagined the awkward wardrobe situation I would have to deal with when I reached my destination.

The Humboldt University provided me free of charge with a very modest studio apartment in a high-rise building in a neighborhood known then as the "Hans-Loch-Viertel." It was situated in the locality of Friedrichsfelde and not very close to the center of East Berlin, "Berlin Mitte." But the Friedrichsfelde subway station was nearby, and I had wisely purchased an older Volkswagen in West Berlin, so I would not be wholly dependent on public transportation.

After I had gotten settled in the studio apartment, I began contacting writers in East Berlin and made appointments to visit them. I drove all over Berlin in my VW and also used the city railway. I did a lot of walking as well, especially when I was in Berlin Mitte and in the vicinity of the Alexanderplatz. In October I usually wore my lined London Fog trench coat while outdoors, but as the days became chillier I began wearing my beloved shearling sheepskin coat. I also wore blue jeans most of the time and brown leather boots. At this point I should mention that I had a full head of long brown hair, long sideburns, and a manly mustache (of the Burt Reynolds variety) on my upper lip. I had what one might call "the 1970s look."

One day as I was strolling along Unter den Linden boulevard, heading toward the Alexanderplatz clad in the outfit described above, I noticed that passersby were staring at me. I thought to myself, what is going on? When a woman with her young son came walking toward me, I found out. As they were both looking at me, the young boy suddenly pointed his finger at me and said excitedly: "Look, it's the Marlboro Man!" The Marlboro Man, indeed, even without the ubiquitous cigarette and cowboy hat. This was the beginning of something that caused me much embarrassment until I eventually got used to it. People everywhere would stare at the Marlboro Man from the US, even in the elevator in my apartment house; the adults would stare in silence, but young children would often point and exclaim: "The Marlboro Man!" There was no easy solution to this problem. In frigid East Berlin I had to keep wearing the warm cowboy coat, and I had to keep enduring the stares and exclamations whenever I was in public places. In retrospect, I am amused by this memory and pleased to have been an object of mistaken identity—not once, but time and again!

While writing this piece, I began to wonder how the East Berliners had become familiar with the Marlboro Man. Marlboro cigarettes were not sold in East German stores or vending machines, and naturally there were no ads for them on East German TV stations. But Marlboros were a popular brand in West Germany and commercials for them appeared frequently on West German TV stations. Most East Germans had access to a TV, but they were not permitted to watch West German stations. However, broadcasts from West Germany were of great interest to GDR citizens. There they could view the news of the day in an uncensored form and also watch other programs that interested them more than many of those GDR stations had to offer. They were especially interested in the West German commercials, according to a friend of mine who grew up in the GDR, and could all recite the lines and sing the melodies that went along with them. Hence, many East Germans pointed their TV antennas toward the West so they could receive the West

German broadcasts, even though they were officially forbidden to do so. And that's how they got to know the Marlboro Man who conjured up magical images of the Wild West of the US, the fascinating land of cowboys and Indians they had so eagerly read about in adventure novels by the renowned German author Karl May! Interestingly enough, Karl May had not visited the American West before or while he was writing books about it, so he and the East Germans had something in common.

PHOTOGRAPHER ROGER MELIS

May 18, 2019, 12:34 p.m. My East German friend and colleague, Heinz-Uwe Haus, sends me the link to an online announcement of an exhibition in Berlin of Roger Melis's photographs from the GDR era. Melis (born October 20, 1940; died September 11, 2009) was an East German photographer specializing in portraiture, photo-journalism, and fashion photography. He was one of the first to present a wide-ranging portrait of the GDR and the people who inhabited it. Above all, he was known for his powerful portrait photographs of the GDR's leading literary and artistic figures including Anna Seghers, Christa Wolf, Thomas Brasch, Wolf Biermann, Franz Fühmann, Heiner Müller, and Sarah Kirsch. According to the announcement, "Hardly any other photographer documented the East Germans and their everyday experience for so long, so intensely, and in so many respects as Roger Melis. For three decades the co-founder and 'Master of East German Photorealism' (*Die Zeit*, June 21, 2007) travelled far and wide across the GDR, a country that he often found 'silent' and 'ossified' under the rule of the SED. As a critical observer and chronicler, Melis captured the urban and rural lives of people in atmospherically dense, often symbolic photographs. His empathetic portraits and careful reportages create a complex picture of East Germans in the years between the construction and fall of the Berlin Wall."

In the introduction to his book *In a Silent Country, Photographs 1969-1989*, Melis writes: "My most important task has always been to create powerful portraits of people, whenever possible in their natural living and working environments, and to avoid stealing their souls and instead to approach them sensitively, remaining—and I use this antiquated expression deliberately—in awe of the individual, a respect which the police and Party secretaries also deserve. You cannot choose the yardstick by which you are measured, but if I could, it would be this one above all." (Leipzig: Lehmstedt, 2007, 12-13)

In the summer of 1975, while on my first sabbatical leave from Oberlin College, I travelled to East Berlin to begin work on a project that would become the three-volume book *DDR-Literatur im Tauwetter* (GDR Literature During the Thaw). The objective of this book was to introduce readers to the leading East German writers of the day, especially to those who were shaping the new sociocritical direction of writing during the 1970s. Each author would be introduced by a bio-bibliographical sketch, portrait photograph, and a personal statement about his or her goal as a writer; this would be followed by a recent representative text—a short story, poems, essay, or chapter from a novel—a text focusing on some problem in GDR society that was of concern to the writer as a writer; and finally, there would be an interview based on a questionnaire I had designed to elicit each writer's responses to issues in contemporary GDR society.

Klaus Schlesinger, the first GDR writer I interviewed, contacted Roger Melis and arranged for me to meet with him. In mid-November 1975, I stopped by Melis's apartment in the central district of Berlin and had tea with him while we discussed my project. He was extremely accommodating and offered to give me (free of charge!) portrait photos of any writers I wanted, as long as I had their permission and would give him credit in my book. I would meet with Melis again in the summer of 1976, as well as in late fall of 1977, and once more in the spring of 1978. In his apartment Melis had a separate file for each of the writers he had photographed and in advance of our meetings would select some photos for my consideration. In all instances, I followed his recommendations—with one exception. The exception was Jurek Becker, with whom I got together frequently and who over time had become a friend. Jurek had a splendid sense of humor and was a remarkable storyteller. For the most part, the stories and anecdotes he told would make people laugh—and

Jurek would often laugh as well. But there also was a quiescent sadness that Melis had managed to capture in his black and white photos of Jurek, as if he had looked through the lens of his camera and been able to see beneath the surface. One photo in particular captured my attention: It showed Jurek sitting on a swing in his yard, relaxed and smiling broadly. That was the photo I wanted, the happy Jurek, not the sad and pensive one depicted in the other photos. That photo was not one of Melis's favorites, nor was Jurek fond of it. Still, that photo found its way into my book and to this day Jurek's comment reverberates in my mind: "You Americans always want to have smiling people in your photos. That is not natural!"

There are black and white portrait photos, taken by Roger Melis, of twenty of the forty-five GDR writers represented in *DDR-Literatur im Tauwetter*. Those authors are: Erich Arendt, Jurek Becker, Volker Braun, Günter de Bruyn, Fritz Rudolf Fries, Franz Fühmann, Peter Hacks, Stephan Hermlin, Bernd Jentzsch, Rainer Kirsch, Sarah Kirsch, Karl Mickel, Irmtraud Morgner, Heiner Müller, Erik Neutsch, Siegfried Pitschmann, Hans Joachim Schädlich, Klaus Schlesinger, Anna Seghers, and Martin Stade. If you want to view these marvelous photos, go to my website (https://richard-zipser.com) and click on the tab labelled "Photos of GDR Writers."

In retrospect, I realize how very fortunate I was to have met the master of East German photorealism and received from him, as a gift, those twenty portrait photographs. Roger Melis's stature as an artist has grown considerably during the years that have gone by since we met back in 1975, and his contributions to my book have enriched it and enhanced its value as a literary-historical document. Moreover, Melis and I have something very important in common: he was the chronicler of a world that ceased to exist—and so am I.

THE SORBS

Four officially recognized national minorities live in today's Germany: the Danes, the Frisians, the German Sinti and Roma, and the Sorbs. They receive special protection and specific funding from the federal and state governments. According to information provided by the German Federal Ministry of the Interior, the federal government regards as national minorities those population groups who meet the following five criteria: they are German nationals; they differ from the majority population in having their own language, culture, and history and thus their own distinct identity; they wish to maintain this identity; they have traditionally resided in Germany (usually for centuries); they live in Germany within traditional settlement areas. While the Danes, Frisians and Sorbs are typically settled in certain geographically defined regions, German Sinti and Roma have customarily lived in almost all parts of Germany, generally in small groups. The fact that they have traditionally resided in Germany distinguishes the national minorities from immigrants, who have not customarily resided in Germany. Unlike Jewish groups in some other countries, Germany's Jewish community does not consider itself a national minority, but a religious community.

Germany's indigenous Slavic community, the Sorbs, have lived for centuries in Lusatia (the *Lausitz*), a region that is located between the German federal states of Saxony and Brandenburg. The region is the home of the ethnic population of Lusatian Sorbs, which was an officially recognized and protected minority group in the GDR. This community of some 60,000 people is comprised of descendants of the Slavic tribes who settled the Central German Uplands more than 1,400 years ago. However, fewer than half of these people are bilingual speakers of German and Sorbian. Their unique language can be observed on the bilingual road signs, and signs of their unique culture can be observed throughout the Spreewald forest area, a UNESCO protected biosphere. In the stunning Spreewald thousands of manmade waterways cross picturesque meadows with houses that have stood untouched since before Germany became one nation in the nineteenth century. Just an hour southeast from Berlin, accessible by car or train, the Spreewald offers an ideal escape from city life. The two major Sorbian writers of the twentieth century, prose writer Jurij Brězan (b. 1916) and poet Kito Lorenc (b. 1938) are among the 45 authors presented in my book, *GDR Literature During the Thaw* (*DDR-Literatur im Tauwetter*). They both wrote and published their works in Sorbian and in German. In the remainder of this snapshot I will discuss some of the things I experienced and learned while visiting and interviewing them at their homes in Lusatia.

Jurij Brězan (b. 1916)

Jurij Brězan's career as a freelance writer began in 1949, spanned the entire existence of the GDR (1949 to 1990), and continued beyond German reunification until his death in 2006. As I was beginning work on the above-mentioned book in the fall of 1975, functionaries at the GDR Writers' Union in Berlin proposed that I add Brězan's name to the list of authors I was planning to include in my study of East German literature in the 1970s. They asserted, and they were right, that Brězan would add an important dimension to my work since he published his works bilingually, usually writing the Sorbian version first and soon thereafter a German version. But they were primarily interested in promoting the Sorbian author because he was a staunch communist and SED Party loyalist as well as a vice president of the Writers' Union, a position he held from 1969 to 1989.

The Germanist, Dr. Peter Barker, in his article on Brězan's autobiographical writings, observes that he "was known above all for his novels, a genre which before 1945 hardly existed in Sorbian literature. Despite his view that his most important task was the protection of the Sorbian language and identity, he was a significant literary figure at national level in the GDR. His two major autobiographical works, *Mein Stück Zeit* [My Piece of Time] (1989) and *Ohne Pass und Zoll* [Without Passport and Customs] (1999), illustrate the dilemmas of a socialist writer caught between politics and writing in the GDR who in the end gave up his belief in the power of literature to have a direct influence on politics." ("Rewriting My Life and Work: Jurij

Brĕzan's Autobiographical Writings." In "The Self in Transition." *German Monitor* 1, 2012: 199.) Note that both of his autobiographical works have only appeared in German.

In post-WW II Germany Brĕzan lived in Bautzen, a hill-top town in eastern Saxony with a rich history. Bautzen is the most important cultural center of the Sorbian minority, which constitutes about ten percent of that city's population. It has a very compact, well-preserved medieval town center with numerous churches and towers and a city wall on the steep embankment to the river Spree. Bautzen was infamous throughout East Germany for its two penitentiaries. "Bautzen I" was used as an official prison; it was nicknamed "Gelbes Elend" (Yellow Misery) due to the color of its exterior, whereas the more secretive "Bautzen II" was used as a facility to hold political prisoners, dissidents, and prisoners of conscience. Bautzen II, which like Bautzen I was operated by the GDR's Ministry for State Security, has served as an open memorial since 1993 and is accessible to the public. A permanent exhibition depicts the misery suffered by its occupants; visitors may tour detention cells, the isolation area and the yards where prisoners were allowed to exercise.

On March 28, 1976, I drove from Berlin to Bautzen and from there proceeded on to Brĕzan's house in Dreihäuser, a tiny hamlet in the municipality of Räckelwitz, which is located about 15 kilometers northwest of Bautzen. The Sorbian-German author was waiting for me, appearing eager to hear more about my project and contribute to it. After we exchanged greetings, he guided me into his comfortable study, which was decorated with Sorbian folk art and cultural artifacts of various sorts that had been produced by Sorbs. There we spent the next few hours chatting and taking care of business. With most of the East German writers I interviewed, I was able to establish good rapport as we discussed the nature and purpose of my undertaking. However, this was decidedly not the case with Brĕzan. His bearing was guarded, distant and somewhat aloof, so I was unable to "connect" with him in the way I had with most of his colleagues. Through his involvement with the Writers' Union, he probably had learned much more about my activities than most GDR authors, and he may have disapproved of some things I was doing. The questions he asked me reflected his wariness and revealed that he had certain reservations about my project, first and foremost regarding the writers I had selected and invited to participate. That being said, I should also report that he was not unfriendly in any way; our conversation was cordial and our meeting was enjoyable. The taped interview went smoothly from beginning to end. The transcribed version of it is in volume 3 of my book, *DDR-Literatur im Tauwetter*.

An unofficial collaborator's report in my Stasi-file provides additional insight into my admittedly negative perception of Brězan. The collaborator, whose alias is IMV "Julia," had been assigned to gather my views on certain GDR writers. In her tape-recorded report dated June 6, 1978, which focuses on our dinner meeting the previous day in the restaurant of Hotel Berolina, she states: "We talked about the quality of the GDR writers' works, also about how he had been received by these persons here in the GDR. Zipser asserted upfront that all writers are very egotistical and to some extent egocentric, but said he had grown accustomed to that. He made very derogatory remarks about Jurij Brězan. His writings are, in Zipser's opinion, mundane. He says that Brězan regularly makes use of our national minority issues in a distasteful way to promote himself. From a telephone conversation I had with Zipser on 6/5/1978, it was apparent that he must have spent this day with Brězan, since he mentioned that he had just returned from Lusatia." I had indeed visited with Brězan for a few hours that afternoon, in order to finalize the interview we had done in 1976 and get his authorization to publish it and various other materials.

Jurij Brězan is without question the most prolific, most prominent, and most praised Sorbian writer of the twentieth century. Dedicated throughout his literary career to the survival of the Sorbian language and culture, he is recognized as the most influential and outspoken advocate for the Sorbian people, their culture and literature. Not all of his works deal with Sorbian matters, but the most prominent theme in his writings is Sorbian identity, how the identity of a small ethnic group of people indigenous to Germany has been preserved, cultivated, and threatened throughout their history. Perhaps because of this narrow focus, he was unable during his lifetime to develop a significant readership outside the borders of the GDR, where his books were published in large editions and marketed aggressively. Brězan is a Sorbian storyteller first and foremost, even though he also wrote and published in German, and that is his singular legacy.

Kito Lorenc (b. 1938)

Kito Lorenc belongs to the "middle generation" of East German writers, those born between the mid-1920s and late 1930s, who started writing after WW II. It is with this group of writers that one generally dates the beginning of East German literature *per se*, for this literary generation was the first to be shaped, wholly or at least decisively, by the conditions of a socialist society within a divided Germany. Lorenc, the son of a Sorbian lumber merchant, was born in Schleife, Lusatia. In his youth and as a young man he was engaged in learning about various aspects of his Sorbian heritage, including their culture, history, customs, and language. From 1952-1956 he attended a Sorbian boarding school in Cottbus, and after graduation he majored in Slavistics at the university in Leipzig. From 1961-1972 he worked at the Institute for Sorbian Ethnic Studies in Bautzen, then as a dramaturge with the State Ensemble for Sorbian Folk Culture. In the early 1970s, Kito moved with his family to the tiny Lusatian village of Wuischke am Czorneboh, located in eastern Saxony, and became a freelance writer.

Lorenc, his wife Elke and their children lived on what once had been a farm located in an idyllic rural setting in the Lusatian countryside. The main farmhouse and other buildings had been purchased by a group of poets who were friends—Adolf Endler and Elke Erb from Berlin, who were married at the time; they occupied a historic mill which they used for summer vacations and weekend retreats. Lorenc and his family lived in their farmhouse throughout the year. Heinz Czechowski, the Halle poet, had acquired an adjacent dwelling, a traditional Lusatian country house (*Umgebindehaus*) that he and his then partner were in the process of restoring. In this close-knit community located in the middle of nowhere, these writers were able to take refuge and shield themselves from the stifling socialist cultural industry that thrived in larger East German cities.

Peter Barker, in a short piece he wrote about Kito Lorenc after the writer's death in 2017, recalls first meeting Kito in Leipzig in 1990, also getting together with him in Wales during the 1990s when the Lorenc family came to the Welsh coast in the summertime. Kito would rent a cottage in a bilingual area and also visit with the Barkers in their Welsh cottage. As Barker recalls, "He was fascinated to experience directly an area, where the minority language had been able to grow significantly, over the whole of Wales to over half a million mother-tongue speakers in the census of 2001, about 20% of the population, with only the border area with England, the Welsh Marches, and parts of South Wales remaining for the large part monolingual." ("Memories of Kito Lorenc," *The Wendish Research Exchange* 3, 2018: 1.)

From that time on, Barker "visited Kito and his family in his rural paradise of Wuischke and watched with great interest his advocacy on minority cultures and writers exploiting the productive possibilities of bilingualism in its relationship with the majority language. His play *Die wendische Schiffahrt* [The Wendish Cruise], which was premiered in Bautzen in 1994, is suffused with water images, which emphasize the possibilities of fluidity, whereby both cultures can reach the 'Neuwasser' [hybrid water] of mutual cross-enrichment. Implicit here is a critique of forms of nationalism, which seek to create barriers between cultures, a view, which was not uncontroversial in the Sorbian context. But he argued that linguistic exclusiveness was no longer possible, and the bilingual writer has here a great advantage, able to exploit the frontiers between the two languages." (Ibid., 1)

In the conclusion to this splendid tribute to his friend, Barker tells us he will "miss Kito's somewhat wicked humour and his intense interest in language and the relationship between different cultures and languages." He mentions that Lorenc received an Honorary PhD degree at the University of Dresden in 2008, "which represented well-deserved recognition of his great achievements as a bilingual poet and his immense contribution to the study of language, in particular in relation to Sorbian." (Ibid., 2)

While on a research visit to the Humboldt University Berlin, I arranged to meet with Kito Lorenc on June 3, 1978, at his home in Wuischke am Czorneboh. I drove to Wuischke from Berlin and without difficulty found the remote farmhouse that was the Lorenc family's permanent residence. The purpose of my visit was to gather materials from him for my book on GDR writing and writers in the 1970s, *DDR-Literatur im Tauwetter*, as well as texts for another book project, a bilingual anthology of contemporary East German poetry. Lorenc greeted me warmly when I arrived and immediately invited me to stay overnight in his house, which I was delighted to do. This gave me an opportunity to have lengthy discussions with him and the poet Adolf Endler, his neighbor, about problems associated with the 8th GDR Writers Congress that had just concluded in Berlin and the recent developments in the GDR literary scene. Before continuing, let me say for the record that Kito was a marvelous host, who did everything possible to make my visit a memorable one.

In my Stasi-file there is a one-page report on my visit with Kito Lorenc, his wife Elke, and Adolf Endler on June 3 and 4, 1978. The report was prepared in the nearby city of Bautzen and then sent to secret police headquarters in Dresden, and forwarded from there to the Ministry for State Security (MfS) in Berlin. It is based on information provided by an anonymous unofficial source—i.e., an unidentified informant. The date, June 27, 1978, is stamped onto the report, along with the following information: MfS/ DR 32, 3422, Main Department XX. It is particularly interesting to see that there is no reference to Lorenc's wife Elke in the report, which appears in its entirety below.

Regional Headquarters for

State Security Dresden

County Authority Bautzen

Ministry for State Security

Main Department XX

Comrade Generalmajor Kienberg

<u>B e r l i n</u>

via Regional Headquarters Dresden – Division XX

Bautzen, 06/26/1978

Reh/Thr

Binder-No.: 2332/78

Visitation of the American Germanist <u>Z i p s e r</u> with the <u>Sorbian lyric poet L o r e n c, Kito und the translator E n d l e r, Adolf</u>

Unofficially, it became known that the American Germanist Zipser spent time visiting the Sorbian lyric poet Lorenc, Kito in 8601 Wuischke, Bautzen County. Zipser was seeking contributions from Lorenc for a GDR poetry anthology as well as for another book on the topic of GDR literature, which is supposed to be about 1,000 pages in length. For this purpose he plans to interview 40 prose writers and poets from the GDR; he will present these interviews together with a short biography and a picture of each writer as well as some poems or short prose works by each.

Zipser stayed overnight at Lorenc's place and engaged in a longer conversation with the translator Endler, Adolf in his dwelling, also located in Wuischke. It was not possible to gather any information regarding the content of their conversation.

The discussions between Lorenc and Zipser focused on, among other things, problems associated with the Writers Congress as well as with the development of GDR literature. Zipser was very cautious during this process and noncommittal in his comments. His conduct was characterized by constant self-control and impartiality. Zipser confirmed that he would get back in touch with Lorenc and also with Endler in due course. A fixed date was not set. Nothing was learned about Zipser's further travel destinations.

Director of the County Authority

[*signature*]

On behalf of Kubel

- Major –

I made two more trips to Wuischke in the month of June, and each time the poet Elke Erb and her young son Konrad accompanied me. The purpose of these trips was to gather materials for the two book projects I mentioned earlier from Heinz Czechowski, Kito Lorenc, Adolf Endler and Elke Erb. I enjoyed being in the company of such a talented group of writers and learned a great deal from them about East German poetry and how poets managed to survive financially in the GDR, where their works were usually published in small editions. We had fascinating conversations on these and other topics, including politics and aspects of life in America.

I would like to conclude my piece on the Sorbs by focusing briefly on the relative importance of Jurij Brězan and Kito Lorenc as bilingual Sorbian/German writers, and again I am relying on Peter Barker to provide us with his knowledgeable perspective on this matter. In a letter to me dated March 15, 2021, Barker writes: "As far as his [Brězan's] literary standing is concerned, I found a lot of his writing fairly uninteresting, especially the early 'socialist realism' novels, but he was an important figure in the development of bilingual writing. But, Kito Lorenc is a much more interesting and substantial literary figure, who had a more nuanced idea of the relationship between majority and minority cultures."

GDR WRITERS AT OBERLIN COLLEGE

During my seventeen years as an Oberlin College faculty member (1969 to 1986), I had the pleasure of co-hosting and interacting with twelve Max Kade German writers-in-residence, always during the spring semester. Five of these writers were East Germans: Christa Wolf (1974), Ulrich Plenzdorf (1975), Jurek Becker (1978), Bernd Jentzsch (1982), and Karl-Heinz Jakobs (1986). Typically, the visiting writer would arrive in mid-February and depart in mid-May. During their residency, the writers would live in an apartment located in a dormitory on campus or in a house owned by a professor away on sabbatical leave. Their official duties were minimal, since we wanted them to have plenty of time to write and participate in the life of the college community. All the writers had some formal responsibilities during their stay in Oberlin, but these were not very time-consuming and meant to bring them together with students, members of the German-speaking community, and some colleagues from other colleges and universities in Ohio. Each writer was asked to do the following: 1) conduct an informal two-hour colloquium once a week on a topic of their choice; 2) have a few office hours each week so that interested students could stop by and chat informally with him/her. Each author was also asked to prepare and deliver a public lecture (in English, if possible) at a special event to which we would invite guests from a number of German departments in Ohio. In addition to the lecture, there was another session that featured the writer reading from his/her works. This half-day special event provided an opportunity for our department to showcase the visiting writer and share him/her with interested individuals in our community and colleagues from other institutions in Ohio and neighboring states, some of whom were understandably envious.

The first East German writer to visit the US was Günter Kunert, who was writer-in-residence at the University of Texas from September 1972 until January 1973. He was forty-four years old at the time and one of a handful of GDR authors who had achieved an international reputation that stretched beyond the Eastern European Bloc into the West. Hence, his residency at the

University of Texas was viewed by many as quite a coup, which it indeed was. The person who engineered this initiative was A. Leslie Willson, who at the time was chairman of the Germanic Languages & Literatures Department at UT. Willson's reputation as an innovator and entrepreneurial spirit was enhanced by Kunert's visiting professorship, as was the already fine reputation of his department.

In the spring of 1973, Oberlin College awarded me an internal H. H. Powers Travel Grant for a 30-day study trip through the GDR that was to take place in the summer of that year. This was an exciting and important professional opportunity for me, as I was going to spend an extended period of time in 'the other Germany,' so as to learn more about its culture, people and their way of life under socialism. The thirty days I spent touring East Germany that summer provided a fascinating introduction to that country, as I absorbed as much as I could while sightseeing at an exhausting pace and engaging in cultural activities of every imaginable sort.

Early in the fall 1973 semester, I learned at a meeting of the German faculty that the prominent West German author we had invited months earlier to be our writer-in-residence in spring 1974 had declined our invitation. This was a regular occurrence, since we always aimed very high with the initial invitation and then, if necessary, lowered our sights and invited a second- or third-tier writer who would be likely to accept. Mindful that Günter Kunert had just been visiting writer at the University of Texas, and eager for more rewarding East German experiences, I proposed that we invite GDR writer Christa Wolf. With the 1968 publication of her novel *The Quest for Christa T.*, the work that firmly established her reputation as a prose writer, Wolf had gained international recognition. Soon after it appeared in print in East Germany, *Christa T.* was translated into multiple languages and became the object of critical acclaim everywhere. As a result, Christa Wolf acquired celebrity status almost overnight. Such was her fame in 1973 that my colleagues doubted that she would be willing or able to visit Oberlin. Furthermore, there was the obstacle the East German authorities posed—i.e., even if she wanted to come to our college for a residency, would they permit her to leave the GDR? I shared my colleagues' misgivings and understood their hesitancy, but persuaded them that we should give it a try. If we got lucky and Christa Wolf did come to Oberlin, it would be a major coup. The fact that Kunert had been able to spend four months in Texas proved to be a persuasive argument and, in the end, decisive. We proceeded to issue the invitation, agreed to shorten the length of the stay to suit Christa Wolf's spring schedule, and she accepted! I was delighted, of course, as were all of my colleagues!

CORRUPT GDR WRITERS

During the Cold War period (1947-1991), the Ministry for State Security (Ministerium für Staatssicherheit or MfS) was responsible for both domestic surveillance and espionage in the Soviet-occupied German Democratic Republic. The Cold War was the geopolitical, ideological and economic struggle between two world superpowers, the US and the USSR and their respective allies. It started after World War II and lasted until the dissolution of the Soviet Union on December 26, 1991. Today, some thirty years after the Cold War ended, we are unfortunately witnessing the onset of another Cold War as the US, Russia, and China struggle for economic and military dominance on a global scale.

The MfS, headquartered in East Berlin, was widely regarded as one of the most effective and repressive intelligence and secret police agencies in the world. At its peak, the MfS employed 90,000 officers full-time. Stasi, an abbreviation for Staatssicherheit (literally: State Security), is what the secret police of East Germany were commonly called. With the assistance of approximately 190,000 informants, it monitored East German citizens; kept track of those persons who were considered enemies or potential enemies of the communistic GDR state and its ruling SED Party; and conducted covert operations in West Germany, West Berlin, and elsewhere in the West, including the faraway US. The Stasi was formed in 1950 and dissolved after German reunification in 1990.

The army of secret informants that helped the Stasi carry out its surveillance and espionage activities included persons from all segments of GDR society. They were called unofficial collaborators (*unoffizielle Mitarbeiter*) and the identity of each was known only to that individual's secret police handler. Each collaborator had an alias or code name that was used in the written reports they or their handlers made; their actual identities were not recorded anywhere and were therefore at the highest level of top-secret information. These unidentifiable informants were often in direct contact with persons considered to be enemies of the state, not only in the GDR but occasionally in foreign countries as well. The information they collected and reports they made to their secret police handlers on individuals under surveillance were kept in so-called Stasi-files. In the early 1990s, not long after German reunification, I learned that such a file had been compiled on me and was able to obtain a copy of it in 1999. My file is almost 400 pages long. It is filled with information Stasi officers and their collaborators had assembled on me in the 1970s and 1980s when I was thought to be engaging in activities that were hostile to the GDR state. Reading and digesting the file's contents was a fascinating but unsettling exercise that spanned several years. For the first time in my life, I was able to view myself—for better or for worse—through the eyes of others. Rarely does one have such an opportunity.

The file reveals that there were nine and possibly ten unofficial collaborators of one type or another who reported on my GDR-related activities and passed along information on me to the Stasi. Not surprisingly, most of these were in the literary field. Three were writers: Paul Wiens (code name "Poet"), a well-known, well-connected author and communist party loyalist; the prominent prose writer and opportunist Fritz Rudolf Fries (code name "Pedro Hagen"); and the poet Uwe Berger (code name "Uwe"), a cunning opportunist motivated more by careerism than ideology. Three other unofficial collaborators were connected in various ways to the GDR's literary world: Konrad Reich, the unscrupulous head of the Hinstorff Verlag, a prestigious publishing house in Rostock; Anneliese Löffler (code name "Dölbl"), a professor of German literature at the Humboldt University who was assigned to keep tabs on me while I was carrying out a major project in Berlin as an IREX (International Research and Exchanges Board) scholar; and Eberhard Scheibner, a functionary in charge of the international department of the GDR Writers' Union. At some point, as I continue to transform my memories into snapshots, I intend to devote a piece to each one of these corrupt individuals who eagerly betrayed East German writers and intellectuals for personal gain. In addition, I am going to put a bright spotlight on prominent prose writer Hermann Kant, who in my view was the most despicable scoundrel of all.

VI

GDR WRITERS IN OHIO

CHRISTA WOLF, 1974

My interest in GDR literature was awakened in the spring of 1974, when prominent East German prose writer Christa Wolf spent six weeks in Oberlin as German Writer-in-Residence. She was accompanied by her husband Gerhard, a well-known literary scholar and editor with connections to many contemporary GDR authors and publishers. I spent a lot of time with the Wolfs while they were in Oberlin, and they introduced me to the GDR literary scene through carefully selected readings and instructive conversations that were truly fascinating. When I told the Wolfs that I would be taking a one-year sabbatical leave in 1975-1976, they encouraged me to think about doing a project on GDR writing in the 1970s and promised to assist me. During the course of our discussions, the outline of a possible project gradually emerged. The focus would be on new directions and trends in East German literature during the period of "thaw" that occurred shortly after Erich Honecker replaced Walter Ulbricht as leader of the Socialist Unity Party in 1971. Another prominent East German author—Ulrich Plenzdorf—came to Oberlin as writer-in-residence in the spring of 1975. Plenzdorf and I became good friends that semester, and he too helped me shape and finalize plans for my first sabbatical leave, a good portion of which I intended to spend in the GDR.

Christa Wolf, the seventh Max Kade German Writer-in-Residence at Oberlin College differed in several ways from her predecessors. She was the first novelist, while those who came before her were lyric poets, playwrights, and short-story writers. Also, as the first East German writer to visit Oberlin, she was able to give our community valuable insight into that other, very different, German culture. Finally, she was not only one of the first two women writers in residence (the first being Helga Novak in 1973), but also the first to integrate the sexes by bringing her spouse with her.

Born in 1929 in Landsberg an der Warthe (former German territory, located in western Poland today), about one hundred miles east of Berlin, she spent her childhood years under Hitler and in time of war. After WW II ended in 1945, she worked for a few years as the secretary to the mayor of a village in Mecklenburg. In 1949 she began studying literature, first at the University of Jena, then at the University of Leipzig, receiving her diploma in 1953. She then became an editor for the magazine *Neue Deutsche Literatur* (New German Literature) and for *Neues Leben* (New Life), a publisher of books for children and young adults. Later she worked as an editor for the *Mitteldeutscher Verlag* (Mid-German Publishing House) in Halle, which published her *Moskauer Novelle* (Moscow Story) in 1961. For this first work she received the prize of the city of Halle, and for her next prose work, *Der geteilte Himmel* (Divided Heaven, 1963), both the Heinrich Mann Prize and the national prize of the GDR. Her third book, *Nachdenken über Christa T.* (The Quest for Christa T., 1968), became a bestseller in its West German original and paperback editions. When this novel was first published in East Germany, it immediately created a storm. GDR authorities instructed book dealers in East Berlin to sell it only to well-known customers who were engaged professionally in literary matters. Also, the novel was severely attacked at the 1968 meeting of the East German Writers Congress, and it was condemned by government officials who eventually banned it, even though it has nothing explicit to say about politics in the GDR. But those of us who are able to read between the lines will easily see why Christa Wolf's *Christa T.*, the novel, its main character, and its author stirred up SED Party leaders and made them apprehensive. On the surface it is a straightforward story of the unremarkable life of an introspective young woman growing up in Nazi Germany, then dying at age thirty-one in Communist East Germany. Beneath the surface it is a first-hand, subjective account of everyday life in a repressive society that does not tolerate persons who question socialist beliefs and the way of living in a socialist state that expects all of its citizens to conform. Christa T. is shown to be a victim of this restrictive, inflexible society.

All three of Christa Wolf's major early works are concerned with the inner development of their central character. In all three, a heroine searches with increasing awareness to find herself. The search, not so much for self as for the right way in life, is at the same time a search for truth. In each instance the reconstruction of the past, even one's own past, gives rise to the question that concerns so many novelists: What really happened? Thus William Faulkner shows the hero in *Absalom, Absalom!* setting out to learn from the protagonists about what had happened in their lives and what to them was the meaning of the past. Similarly, the heroine of *Moscow Story*, a young doctor on a trip with a professional group to Russia, again meets the Russian whom she knew eight years earlier as an enemy officer in her German village after the war. Only after making clear to themselves and each other the love and hostility each felt back then for the other are they able to resume with new strength the useful lives they have made for themselves in their own countries.

The decision about which life (communism vs. capitalism) and which country (East vs. West Germany) is more difficult for the heroine of *Divided Heaven*, Rita. This is a very romantic and sad story, which takes place at the time the Wall was built. Here, too, the past—the Nazi years as well as the early years of the GDR—is reconstructed through conversations with many of the novel's characters. The gradual recreation of Rita's past reveals to the reader that it is because of her love for a young chemist, Manfred, that she has left her village and secretarial job to join him in Berlin where she will study to become a teacher. Rita is required to work in a factory during her student years and becomes increasingly involved in the affairs of her workplace. In the process, she comes to identify with the socialist aims of her country and the factory workers. This leads to conflict with her lover Manfred, whose dishonest father is guilty of wrongdoing while managing the factory. Despite his hostility toward his father and mother, who had both collaborated with the Nazis, Manfred asserts his bourgeois heritage and leaves for the West where he believes he can better fulfill his goals as a scientist. Rita remains behind to lead the more difficult but useful life in the East, thereby choosing to sacrifice her personal love and asserting her commitment to a new, progressive society.

Christa Wolf's third novel, *The Quest for Christa T.*, is the most controversial of all with its insistence on finding oneself while at the same time serving society. The coincidence of both author's and heroine's first names underscores the autobiographical component in the novel. Christa Wolf's teacher of German literature at the University of Leipzig, Professor Hans Mayer, attests to the existence of a student there whose life closely paralleled the heroine's; he also recalls Christa Wolf's own examination essay on the same topic as the heroine's. Clearly then, though Wolf's heroine is a composite of fact and fiction, much in her crises of conscience is real and part of Wolf's own experience. The author's insistence on the search for truth and the discovery of it in this novel goes hand in hand with her ongoing search for new ways of writing. Here she makes use of entirely new narrative techniques, which represent a radical departure from the prescribed principles of socialist realism, the officially sanctioned style of writing in the GDR during the 1950s and 1960s. The narrative structure of *The Quest for Christa T.*, described by some critics as an interweaving or merging of narrative voices, provides a marvelous example of the "subjective authenticity" that is a distinctive characteristic of Wolf's style. For further information on her literary style and her observations on the function of literature in East and West German societies, see *Lesen und Schreiben* (Reading and Writing), a collection of essays she published shortly before coming to Oberlin, Ohio (Darmstadt: Luchterhand, 1972. 220 pp.).

The time has come to report on Christa Wolf's activities while she was in Oberlin, from April 3 until May 12, 1974. I have elected to let Christa tell the story in her own words, which she fortunately did in an essay she wrote in July 2003. The essay represents her contribution to a volume chronicling Oberlin College's German writers-in-residence program from 1968 to 2003 (*Willkommen und Abschied* [Welcome and Departure]. *Thirty-Five Years of German Writers-in- Residence at Oberlin College*, ed. Dorothea Kaufmann and Heidi Thomann Tewarson. Rochester: Camden House, 2005. 398 pp.). My translation of her essay, which is located on pp. 55-58 of the book cited above, appears below.

Writer-in-Residence in Oberlin, 1974

When we, my husband Gerhard Wolf and I, arrived in Oberlin, Ohio on April 3, 1974, we had never before set foot on American soil; we didn't know the meaning of the term "Midwestern," nor did we know what a "dry town" was, nor how to behave if there is a tornado. So the next day, blissfully trusting Richard Zipser from the German Department, we drove out into the countryside in order to buy beverages outside the city limits that were not available in the puritanical "dry" town, this even though a banner with a tornado warning was showing continually on our television set and outside the wind was blowing pretty hard. Back in those days, there were wines available in the USA with bright labels that stated "like Liebfraumilch," which were—and I am expressing myself politely—disappointing. (Not only that— the entire gastronomic culture has in the meantime improved immensely!) But the gusts of wind quickly developed into a storm and, as we once again sat happily watching television in the evening, we were shown that a small nearby settlement made up of wooden houses similar to those in Oberlin had for the most part been blown away.

The same thing—almost the same thing—was bestowed upon us as we were about to depart. On May 11, as we were gathered at our farewell party and waiting for the steaks to finish grilling, the radio again broadcasted a tornado warning for Oberlin. This time we went into the so-called "tornado cellar" in the neighbors' house—nothing more than a corner of the cellar that was reinforced with crossbeams and sturdier materials, which measured by our European standards would be blown away by any gust of air. There we stood, along with well-dressed members of another party, holding cocktail glasses as we heard on the radio that the tornado had caused serious damage on Cedar Street. But that's where we are living!, we cried out. Our friends calmed us down though, saying: Cedar Street is long. After midnight, however, as we approached our house—which actually belonged to Professor Kurtz who had rented it to us while he was on vacation—the area right in front of this house was bathed in bright light; a huge municipal repair vehicle was blocking the street, and workers in orange-colored overalls were busy cutting up the large tree that at this very spot, together with its entire root system, had been twisted out of the earth and tossed onto the street. There was an electrical power outage; our neighbors were worried about the turkeys in their deep freezers and offered us emergency aid—just as a couple of students had stopped by our place at the beginning of our stay with homebaked bread: We Europeans would surely have our issues with the American white bread . . .

Indeed, and these issues persisted; all the same I gradually learned to find those grocery items at Fisher's that appealed more to our taste, yet there was one more crisis when Gerhard came down with a serious stomach ailment and was supposed to eat oatmeal, which was only available in various "flavors," the scent of which had caused him to develop an allergic reaction, until I discovered—after numerous failed experiments—"Quaker's unflavored oatmeal."

So much for "culture shock." Or, perhaps a couple more additions after all. Whenever we ventured to take a walk, after just a few hundred meters a car would inevitably pull up beside us and a friendly driver would ask if our car had broken down and if he could take us somewhere. In the supermarket a black employee would pack my purchases in the famous paper bags, and then his jaw would drop with regularity when outside he had to place the bag in the basket of a rusted bicycle I had borrowed and which responded to the name "Horatio," rather than in the trunk of a fancy automobile. In the school bus driving by the white children were sitting up front, the black ones together in the back in a tightly knit group; in the school I visited one time they were seated the same way in separate groups in the classroom. And when the teacher asked a sixteen-year-old girl after class: What do you know about the GDR?, a one-word response came after a long pause for thought: The Wall.

Now this was the other side of the culture shock that we may have inflicted on our American partners: We came from a country, the existence of which was unknown to the female and male students from the farms in the Midwest, and the literature of which they had heard nothing about previously. We were prepared for that and had sent diverse packages with books in advance, the foundation of a small GDR library. Hence we offered colloquia in which names like Anna Seghers cropped up, but we focused chiefly on the "middle" and younger generations of authors: Erwin Strittmatter, Hermann Kant, Volker Braun, Johannes Bobrowski, Karl Mickel, Ulrich Plenzdorf, Günter de Bruyn, Irmtraud Morgner, Brigitte Reimann, Sarah Kirsch, Rainer Kirsch, Reiner Kunze, Uwe Gressmann. I took on the prose writers, Gerhard the lyric poets. Once a week we hosted a wine and snacks gathering at home for persons interested in readings and discussions that frequently proceeded along these lines: It's like this where we live, how is it where you live?

On our free evenings we sat in front of the television and watched, somewhat stunned, as the stack of tape cassettes beside President Richard Nixon's chair—the "tapes" he had to hand over—grew higher and higher and convicted him of having illegally wiretapped his opponents during the election battle. Then I would sit at Professor Kurtz's desk, work for a while on *Kindheitsmuster* (Patterns of Childhood, published in 1976) or read *Doctor Faustus* by Thomas Mann from the professor's library. Breathing all around me was that perfect American house, with its umpteen bedrooms and just as many bathrooms, that got warm and cold automatically (we were experiencing cold weather, even snow) and that devoured kitchen garbage amidst irritating gargling sounds in the drain. Was that the future? Or was the future the doctor who refused to have Gerd admitted to the hospital, in order to diagnose the cause of his medical condition: "It's very expensive, madam!" Or the family of the truck driver with whom he eventually shared a room, who—as soon as they had greeted the husband and father— would gather around his bed and stare intently at one of the two televisions that were hanging from the ceiling? We could not get this man to turn off the television, not even once: "After all, he has paid for it!"

Max Frisch [Swiss playwright and novelist] called one evening from his hotel room in New York, 5th Avenue, and berated me because the GDR had planted a spy on Willy Brandt's staff, which brought about his resignation. He had been drinking a lot of whiskey, and so had I. In the end, we became reconciled by way of shared outrage.

We acquired friends. We marveled at the College's music hall and its well-endowed art museum. When we went for a walk on the campus, we could tell if older married couples were European immigrants by the way they walked. I had to deliver a lecture in English: "Prose Writing Today," which I wrote in German, had Dick Zipser translate, and then rehearsed for days. In the early morning I went swimming in the indoor pool; at midday or in the evening we frequently would go to the German House and dine there. I attended a lecture on the Shakers and responded to questions by a women's group about the emancipation of women in the GDR. I was not certain that we had the same understanding of emancipation, but it was clear that we were interested in one another. I knew that this interest would stay with me.

On May 12, we flew from Cleveland to New York, on May 13 from New York to Prague; there we were already as good as home.

July 2003

I could write much more about Christa Wolf, who was a central figure in East German literature and politics during the 1970s and 1980s. However, my focus here is on the time she spent at Oberlin College, where I first met and got to know her and her husband Gerhard in 1974. During the later 1970s, I visited her a few times at her home in Kleinmachnow and, after she and Gerhard moved to Berlin's central district (Mitte), in her Friedrichstrasse apartment on numerous occasions. In those and later years, she wrote many more important prose works that enhanced her reputation significantly and perhaps should have paved the way to a Nobel Prize. But that did not happen, unfortunately in my view, possibly because of her brief collaboration with the Stasi as an informant in the early stages of her career as a writer. After the collapse of the Berlin Wall and the GDR state, Christa Wolf continued to write and publish in post-unification Germany until her death in December 2011, and would eventually become one of the most celebrated German authors of the twentieth century. In 2002, she was awarded the first German Book Prize for her lifetime achievement. The jury lauded her for "courageously confronting the great debates of the GDR and reunified Germany." In closing, let me say how pleased I am to have known Christa Wolf personally and how immensely grateful I am for the assistance and guidance she and her husband Gerhard gave me in the 1970s. Without their help I never would have been able to carry out my first major book project on GDR literature and most of the GDR-related book projects in the years that followed.

ULRICH PLENZDORF, 1975

What really knocks me out is a book that, when you're all done reading it, you wish the author that wrote it was a terrific friend of yours and you could call him up on the phone whenever you felt like it.

Holden Caulfield, *The Catcher in the Rye*

Ulrich Plenzdorf, Berlin prose writer, playwright, film director and scenarist, was the second author from the GDR (the first being Christa Wolf in 1974) to visit Oberlin College as Max Kade German Writer-in-Residence. In April and May of 1975, he and his wife (Helga Plenzdorf) lived and took their meals in a dormitory, along with undergraduate students. Nearly everyone who met him found it difficult to believe that Uli (as he came to be called) was already in his early forties, so easily did he relate to young people and their problems. How else can one describe him? Soft-spoken, extremely modest and approachable, fond of sports cars, detective stories, jazz, and drinking beer out of a can, yet more opposed to smoking than the Surgeon General, casually clad in a leather jacket and blue jeans (for further information, see the snapshot entitled *Blue Jeans* in section IX)—this is the Ulrich Plenzdorf who made a lasting impression on many of us.

Plenzdorf, the son of working-class parents who were active members of the Communist Party of Germany (KPD), was born in Berlin in 1934. After completing his *Abitur* in 1954, he studied philosophy in Leipzig, and served as a stagehand for the state-owned DEFA film studio from 1955-1958. Following a year of military service, he completed a four-year training program at the Babelsberg Academy for Film and Television in 1963. He then worked as a screenplay writer for the DEFA studio in Babelsberg. Plenzdorf had not published extensively prior to his arrival in Oberlin; he had written seven screenplays, five of which had been produced. Nevertheless, he had achieved widespread international acclaim for his controversial yet highly regarded short novel, *Die neuen Leiden des jungen W.* (The New Sufferings of Young W.), which in 1972 propelled him to the pinnacle among young writers of the GDR. Hence, Ulrich Plenzdorf's residency at Oberlin College—like that of Christa Wolf the previous spring—was generally viewed as a prestigious coup.

Plenzdorf's innovative novel parallels and parodies Goethe's epistolary masterpiece, *Die Leiden des jungen Werthers* (The Sufferings of Young Werther, 1774), one of the most important works of the Storm and Stress period in German literature. It presents the story of a young revolutionary in a socialist society, Edgar Wibeau, who breaks off his apprenticeship in the small town of Mittenberg, flees the restraints of a broken home and escapes to the "freedom" of the metropolis (Berlin), where he lives alone in a dilapidated garden house, makes music, "not just any old Händelsohn Bacholdy," but "genuine music," plays and sings a "Bluejeans Song," paints in the abstract, dances by himself, admires J. D. Salinger's *Catcher in the Rye*, has an affair of the heart with a young kindergarten teacher, Charlie, who later marries her stodgy twenty-five-year-old fiancé. At her suggestion, Edgar briefly joins a work-brigade as a housepainter, but he finds it difficult to conform to their rules. In the end, he "crosses the Jordan" as he tries to invent a new electric paint gun: "It was probably better that way," Edgar asserts from the other side of the Jordan. "I wouldn't have lived through this failure anyway. . . . But I never would've *really* gone back to Mittenberg. I don't know if you understand me. That was maybe my biggest mistake. My whole life I'd been a bad loser. I just couldn't swallow anything. Idiot that I am, I always wanted to be the winner."

Edgar Wibeau, one of the most intriguing characters in all of East German literature, is a frustrated teenager who rebels against the **conformity** that was so prevalent in every segment of GDR society. While he is not against socialism per se, he is in favor of almost everything the SED Party officials and others in positions of power were against, preferring to live a life without rigid constraints and picky regulations, opting instead for individualism and creative self-expression, while rejecting phoniness and stodginess in favor of that which is genuine and natural. Edgar bears a resemblance in some ways both to Salinger's Holden Caulfield and Goethe's Werther. And in many respects, he is also very much like the free-spirited Ulrich Plenzdorf I met in Oberlin back in 1975, a true GDR "original."

Die neuen Leiden des jungen W. was first published as a screenplay in *Sinn und Form* (March 1972), the leading literary journal in the GDR. Plenzdorf wrote a prose version as well, which was published in East Germany by the Hinstorff Publishing House (1973) and in West Germany by the Suhrkamp Publishing House (1976). The book became a phenomenal success, selling over 4 million copies in 30 languages. In West Germany it was adopted as required reading for high school students, and it was also made into a film for West German television. The stage version of *Die neuen Leiden des jungen W.* was performed extensively to full houses in Eastern and Western Europe; it saw 60 stage productions in German theaters alone. By the mid-1970s, mainly as a result of this work's extraordinary popularity, Plenzdorf had become the most discussed, reviewed, and performed GDR writer since the death of Bertolt Brecht in 1956. A leading and influential contemporary critic, Marcel Reich-Reinicki, rated Plenzdorf's short novel among the significant literary documents of the post-WW II era.

During his stay in Oberlin, Ulrich Plenzdorf visited German language and literature classes on all levels and participated actively in my Intermediate German course, where he discovered how passionately involved American students had become in *Die neuen Leiden des jungen W.* Upon his return to the GDR, he helped me secure permission from Hinstorff for a textbook edition of his famous novel. I began preparing the textbook edition in the fall of

1976 and completed work on it during the summer and early fall of 1977. It was published by John Wiley & Sons in 1978 and remained in print for about fifteen years. It was the only work by an East German author to be published in its entirety, in a special textbook edition, in the English-speaking world.

While in Oberlin and with my assistance, Ulrich Plenzdorf purchased a car, a bright red Chevrolet two-door coupe. From the sale of his books in West Germany and West Berlin, he had been able to accrue a significant amount of hard currency in the form of West German marks, a sizeable portion of which was siphoned off by the GDR Copyright Agency. He had a bank account in the West, where his share of the book royalties was deposited, and he used this money mainly to purchase durable goods that were unavailable in the GDR and to fund his travel in Western countries. In Berlin he had a spiffy Renault sports car, the only such vehicle I ever saw in East Germany, which he liked to drive in a "sporty" manner. The Chevy looked rather sporty, but it definitely was not a sports car. However, Plenzdorf enjoyed driving it like a sports car, pushing the vehicle to its limits and beyond. After a short while, less than two weeks as I recollect, all the double clutching and downshifting he did led to a dropped transmission. Although the car was brand new, the transmission, clutch, and some other parts had to be replaced. The Chevrolet dealership honored the warranty, but they told Plenzdorf to be more careful and indicated that they would not do this a second time.

In May of that year, after their Oberlin residency had ended, Helga and Uli embarked on a grand auto tour of the United States. From Ohio they drove in a northwesterly direction toward the West Coast, along the way visiting some of our breathtakingly beautiful national parks and the Rocky Mountains before reaching the Pacific Ocean. After sightseeing in California, they drove through the southwest and the Gulf Coast states to the East Coast. When I saw them in Berlin that summer, they told me this had been the trip of a lifetime for both of them, as they literally "saw the USA in their Chevrolet."

As I conclude this snapshot on Ulrich Plenzdorf's stay at Oberlin College, I want to express my gratitude for the advice, assistance, and encouragement he gave me as I was preparing to take my first sabbatical leave in 1975-1976. Like Christa and Gerhard Wolf the year before, Uli helped me develop and shape the project I proposed to undertake involving GDR writing and writers who were active in the 1970s. Moreover, when I was working on the project in East Germany, he continued to assist me in meaningful ways. Helga Plenzdorf always treated me like a member of their family, as did Uli, and the friendship that began in Oberlin grew stronger over the years. In retrospect, I realize that I could not have produced an 840-page book like *DDR-Literatur im Tauwetter* (GDR Literature During the Thaw), nor most of my other major publications on GDR literature, without the strong and unwavering support of the Plenzdorfs and Wolfs. I remain very indebted to them.

JUREK BECKER, 1978

I first met Jurek Becker in November 1975, when I visited his home in Berlin-Köpenick for the purpose of doing a tape recorded interview for *DDR-Literatur im Tauwetter*. In addition to being an exceptionally talented prose writer, Becker was a very likeable man; he had a marvelous sense of humor, a great deal of personal warmth and charm, and was one of the best storytellers I ever met. He was also candid, outspoken, and not afraid to express his views on controversial topics, such as problems within GDR society and his country's oppressive system of government. His criticism of the SED leadership and their violation of human rights brought him into conflict with the GDR authorities on numerous occasions.

International recognition came to Becker following the publication of his first and, in my view, most powerful novel, *Jakob der Lügner* (Jacob the Liar, 1969), which was translated into many languages and made into a motion picture of the same title. His books are serious in theme and, at the same time, highly entertaining reading. The Swiss writer, Max Frisch, said of himself: "I try on stories like clothes," an assertion that Becker could have made with equal force. Indeed, when it came to the not-so-simple art of telling a story, Becker was a master craftsman able to employ all the tools of his trade with uncommon skill.

During my visits to East Berlin in 1976 and 1977, I met with Becker on numerous occasions and over time we became friends. As I got to know him better, I became convinced that he was a perfect candidate for the German Writer-in-Residence program at Oberlin College. His outgoing personality, friendly and unassuming demeanor, and ability to relate to people—in addition to his talent and international reputation as a novelist—made him an ideal choice. And when he came to Oberlin for most of the spring 1978 semester, he dedicated himself to making his residency as successful as possible—and in every regard it was a memorable visit.

In December of 1977, Becker quietly moved from East to West Berlin. He was in possession of a unique two-year exit visa that enabled him to go back and forth from the West to the East, where his two teen-age sons were living. At that time, he was the only East German writer to be permitted such freedom of movement. In November 1976, Becker had become embroiled in a human rights conflict with the government when he—along with eleven other GDR writers—publicly protested the forced exiling of dissident poet-singer, Wolf Biermann. In the ensuing months, he resigned from the GDR Writers' Union, was thrown out of the SED Party, and then barred from making public appearances and publishing his writing in the GDR.

Becker's decision to spend a semester as writer-in-residence at Oberlin College coincided with his decision to leave East Germany for a year or two. In June 1977, when Becker and many other writers were still preoccupied with the Biermann affair, I first discussed with him the possibility of coming to Oberlin. Following the expulsion of his good friend Biermann, a move Becker had protested more vociferously than most, his life had been a series of upheavals. "I've gotten out of everything," he jokingly told me, "out of the Writers' Union, out of the Party, and out of my marriage." Upon separating from his wife, Becker exchanged a comfortable home on the outskirts of Köpenick for a modest, rear-building apartment (with no bathroom or telephone) in the working-class neighborhood of Friedrichshain [*Köpenick and Friedrichshain are districts of Berlin*]. This not only provided an interim solution to the problem of where to live, it also enabled him to withdraw and devote himself full time to writing the novel *Schlaflose Tage* (Sleepless Days). Barred from reading in public, uncertain about his future, and in the midst of a midlife crisis of sorts, Becker sought and found refuge in his work.

Before the end of June 1977, *Schlaflose Tage* had been completed and submitted to the Hinstorff Verlag in the GDR and the Suhrkamp Verlag in the FRG. Initially, Becker was assured by the editors at Hinstorff that they would be able to publish the novel. But later on, when he steadfastly refused to make certain recommended changes, it became clear that his novel would not appear in his own country. Becker, who maintained that he—unlike some of his colleagues— could not live and write in one Germany, only to be published and read in the other, was forced to begin contemplating possible solutions to his dilemma. In an interview printed the following month in the West German news magazine, *Der Spiegel* [*The Mirror*], he expressed a desire to remain in East Germany and the hope that his books would continue to be published there. "If it's a question of keeping my mouth shut," he remarked, "then I'd rather keep it shut in the Bahamas." However, the airplane carrying Becker to the New World landed not in the Bahamas but near Oberlin, Ohio.

Becker, our third writer-in-residence from the GDR, arrived in Oberlin on February 20, 1978, just a few weeks before *Schlaflose Tage* was published in the West by the Suhrkamp Verlag. For the next three months he lived in a dormitory on campus, where the Plenzdorfs had lived before him, and dined with students at the Max Kade German House most of the time. Jurek spent almost every morning in his apartment, writing short prose texts, then made himself available in his office every afternoon to those who wanted to stop by and talk with him. His office in Rice Hall was across the corridor from mine, so we saw each other and conversed almost every day, often about GDR-related topics. When he had finished a draft of a *Splittertext* (splinter text), as he called these experimental short prose works, he would come to my office and read it to me, eager to hear my reaction. In Oberlin I was his one and only link, and he was also my only link, to the GDR.

Despite the publicity that had accompanied Jurek's departure from East Germany and his trip to the US, few people at Oberlin College were aware of the tremendous upheaval that had occurred in his life during the previous fifteen months, and very few—if any—were in a position to appreciate the impact that these violent changes had had upon him. From the outset, Jurek found himself both isolated and insulated by his new, unfamiliar environment. He had been a celebrity in West Berlin, but in Oberlin he was for most people a nobody, and at first he had difficulty adjusting to his new status. He had been removed, suddenly and physically, from the problems that had consumed so much of his time and emotional energy in Berlin, from the problems that had led him to write a book like *Schlaflose Tage*, and now he was in Oberlin, a tranquil college town in northern Ohio with a year-round population of 8,600.

Jurek, a gregarious man who liked and related well to young people, welcomed the daily contact with Oberlin students. He took an interest in their lives and concerns, suppressing for a time all thought of those difficulties and decisions awaiting him in Berlin. On Tuesday evenings he held a two-hour colloquium in the German House lounge. Sometimes, eager to get a response, he would read the latest of his prose texts, or he would simply talk about whatever happened to be on his mind (e.g., Jurek Becker, New York City, the so-called American way of life, similarities between the US and the GDR), or he would ask questions so that he could listen and learn. On Thursday evenings he always held an open house for anyone who cared to come, an opportunity to get to know the writer Jurek Becker as a flesh-and-blood human being and a chance for him to become better acquainted with persons who were interested in him.

While in Oberlin, Jurek learned to love Baskin-Robbins ice cream and, to my amazement, the game of baseball which he said was "not at all boring, you just have to know the rules." He was amused by his own appearance in an

OBERLIN sweatshirt, unafraid of his second-hand Ford Pinto—despite our unsafe-at-any-speed warnings—and fascinated by the AAA and all its services. He came to like the "apolitical" climate in Oberlin, and joined the rest of us in complaining about the nasty weather. Oberlin was good for Jurek, and he was good for us. He had time to write, to think, to take stock of the past, and to prepare for what the future had in store for him. After leaving Oberlin in late May of 1978, Jurek spent seven weeks touring the US—Miami Beach, New Orleans, Taos, and San Francisco—and visiting some of his new friends.

One of Jurek's friends at Oberlin was 18-year-old Hannah Zinn from Hayward, California, who was a first-year student when he met and began dating her. Hannah, a beautiful and highly intelligent young woman, was a student in my Elementary German class that spring. She lived in the Russian House and dined at the Russian Table in the dining room of the German House, where Jurek usually ate lunch and dinner. I introduced him to Hannah, and soon thereafter they began dating. It was the beginning of a romance that lasted for more than five years. In the summer of 1978, Jurek visited Hannah in California and met her parents. Infatuated with Hannah, he contemplated staying in the US, but eventually decided to return to Germany and invited her to join him. He flew back to West Berlin in July of that year, but without Hannah who wanted to complete her college education. However, at the end of the fall 1978 semester, she dropped out of Oberlin College, flew to West Berlin, and moved into Jurek's apartment. They lived together until the fall of 1983, when Jurek broke off the relationship.

After spring break, two journalists from Germany—Eva Windmöller and Dirk Sager—descended on Oberlin to do articles on Jurek. Windmöller's article, "Jurek Beckers Urlaub von der DDR" (Jurek Becker's Vacation from the GDR), appeared in the July 1978 issue of Stern [Star] magazine (No. 29, 116-120). It is illustrated with photos of Jurek interacting with students in the German House lounge and dining room, talking on the phone in his dormitory apartment, and chatting with a sheriff at the Midway Mall. Nice memories! Dirk Sager, whom I had met on several occasions in East Berlin, was a correspondent for the German TV channel ZDF. He interviewed Jurek for his weekly news program *Kennzeichen D* [literally: License Plate G (G for Germany)], and he kindly included a short conversation with me in the segment—my first and only appearance on television.

For me, Jurek Becker's visit as German writer-in-residence was the most enjoyable of any I experienced during my seventeen years at Oberlin College, probably because I knew him well and regarded him as a friend before he arrived. I know he regarded me as a friend as well, not only because he gave me a pre-publication copy of *Schlaflose Tage* with the following inscription: "Für Dick in Dicker Freundschaft" [For Dick in close friendship] "Jurek Becker, Oberlin, Feb. 24, 1978." After leaving Oberlin and touring the US, he returned to West Berlin in late July, and when his special visa expired he decided to remain in the West. He remarried and lived in West Berlin until a short time before he died of cancer at age 59, much too young to depart this world, on March 14, 1997. [In preparing the section above on Jurek Becker in Oberlin, I relied heavily on my essay, "Jurek Becker: A Writer with a Cause," *DIMENSION*, Vol. 11, No. 3 (1978), 402-406.]

STEFAN HEYM, 1978

In June 1976, I met with prominent German-Jewish writer Stefan Heym at his villa in Berlin-Grünau. The purpose of my visit was to conduct a tape recorded interview and gather some materials for a book on East German literature in the 1970s, *DDR-Literatur im Tauwetter*. Heym, an internationally acclaimed novelist and essayist, was not only East Germany's most famous writer but its most controversial one as well. In response to a letter I had sent him in February 1976, Heym had graciously invited me to meet with him at his home. Of course, I was very eager to do so.

At the time of my visit in June 1976, Heym was living under open Stasi surveillance. A secret police vehicle occupied by at least two officers was always parked on the street right in front of his residence, so he would know they were monitoring the coming and going of all persons to his house, and to discourage people from visiting him. Inside the house, his informant housekeeper (code name "Frieda") was able to overhear and report on his conversations with visitors, photograph documents that might be of interest to the Stasi, and keep a watchful eye on her employer whose telephone was most certainly bugged. The fact that he was constantly being observed must have bothered Heym, but he was not easily intimidated and seemed to consider it a badge of honor, a tangible sign of his success as a SED regime critic and human rights advocate.

After we and his wife Inge had coffee and cake in their elegantly appointed living room on the first floor, Heym guided me to his study on the second floor where we proceeded to do the interview. In retrospect, I can say that Heym was one of the very best interview subjects I encountered in the GDR. At that point in his life, he probably had more experience with interviews than any of his writer colleagues and nothing fazed him. He was extremely cooperative and answered my questions in a straightforward manner, with no hesitation. He came across as self-assured and confident, but without any hint of arrogance. I felt comfortable in his study; we were surrounded by books which reminded me of my office at home. When we finished the interview, Heym handed me a typewritten copy of a prose text he had written earlier that year and a portrait photo, along with his written permission to publish both in my book. I had the sense that he really liked my project and also was pleased to have an American Germanist with an interest in GDR literature visit with him.

"Mein Richard" (My Richard) is the title of the short story Heym gave me that day. The story takes place at a time when the GDR, after a few years of relaxed domestic politics in the earlier 1970s, was once again utilizing harsh methods of repression. The text deals directly with two topics that were taboos in the GDR: flight from the Republic and the Berlin Wall. For that reason, this piece of fiction could not have been published in East Germany, as Heym and I both knew. In the story fifteen-year-old Richard and his friend have crossed over the Wall into West Berlin fourteen times through a window in Richard's house, which is located right next to the wall. But they were not planning to remain in the other Germany, they only wanted to go to the movies there. After doing just that, the boys always returned home promptly from their illicit excursion. Eventually, the East German secret police found out about these illegal acts; the boys were arrested, put on trial, and sent to prison. At the very end of the story, the boys' lawyer comments on the bizarre irony of the situation, addressing the prosecuting attorney: "If I were you, comrade, I would have awarded the two boys a gold medal. . . . Because they have, as is now known to the court, demonstrated their absolute loyalty to our Republic fourteen times in a row." Heym's fictional commentary is all the more effective because he utilizes the literary conventions of socialist realism, the officially sanctioned style of writing in the GDR during the 1950s and 1960s.

The name of the protagonist in "My Richard" is Richard Zunk; the name of his seventeen-year-old friend is Richard Edelweiss. So Heym has given us two Richards, which in Germany is an uncommon first name, one whose last name begins with the letter Z. Is this a strange coincidence, or is it possibly related to the fact that my name is Richard Zipser? I think the latter is likely, and this might have been the author's humorous way of personalizing his Wall story and indirectly dedicating it to me. Thank you very much, Stefan Heym!

Heym had led a most unusual and eventful life. Born in Chemnitz in 1913, he fled the Nazis in 1933, moving first to Prague, and from there emigrating to the US in 1935. He completed his education at the University of Chicago, where he received a master's degree, and then for two years was editor-in-chief of the German-language weekly, *Deutsches Volksecho* (German People's Echo). From 1939 to 1942, Heym worked as a printing salesman in New York City while trying to establish himself as a freelance author, writing in English. His first novel, *Hostages* (1942), was a bestseller, and his novel *The Crusaders* (1948) climbed to sixth place on *The New York Times* list of bestsellers. He became a US citizen and served in the US Army during World War II. For his meritorious service as Technical Sergeant in 1944 and 1945, he was awarded the Bronze Star Medal. In 1952, he wrote a letter to President Eisenhower, protesting the Korean War and the fascistic policies of the American government. Heym claimed to have sent his Bronze Star and his US Army commission to Eisenhower, but he remained a US citizen. He moved back to Prague with his American wife and requested political asylum in communist East Germany, where he hoped to find the personal rights that he said were lacking in the US. In 1953, the GDR government restored his former German citizenship, enabling him and his wife to move to Berlin, where he had been a student in the early 1930s.

SED Party officials would soon come to regret their decision to repatriate Heym, as he would demonstrate time and again to their chagrin that he was a rebellious, fearless dissident, a thorn in the side of the authoritarian government. His first major conflict with the GDR authorities occurred in 1956 when his novel about the June 17, 1953 mass uprising of workers in East Berlin, *5 Tage im Juni* (5 Days in June), was rejected for publication in the GDR. The novel was published in West Germany and in English translation, but the fact that it was banned in East Germany underscored how dangerous Heym's fictional recounting of history was in the minds of the GDR's leaders.

Heym began publishing his books in the West, both in German and in English, and these publications earned him large sums of hard currency that GDR authorities were eager to share in accordance with a formula the state had established. Heym resisted, and in 1969 he was convicted of violating the GDR's currency exchange regulations after publishing his novel *Lassalle* in West Germany. In 1979 he was again convicted of breaching the GDR's currency exchange regulations, this time in connection with the publication of his novel *Collin* in West Germany, which loyalist GDR writers described as "anti-communist rubbish." This violation resulted in his expulsion from the GDR Writers' Union and a major confrontation with government officials that would eventually involve eight prominent writers who supported Heym and, for so doing, would also be expelled from the Writers' Union. Facing prosecution for alleged currency offences, Heym wrote to me (in English) in late April of 1979: "If you've been following the news, you may have noticed that there's trouble brewing in this place—I am going to be prosecuted on a trumped-up charge of violation of foreign currency rules, in reality, because I refused to ask the GDR authorities for permission to have my books printed abroad if they're forbidden here." A few months later, Heym was tried and fined 9,000 West German marks for having published his novel in the West without securing authorization from GDR officials and for neglecting to report the income he had received in foreign currency.

Heym had written many of his works in English and welcomed the opportunity to converse with me in that language when we met. He told me proudly that he subscribed to *The New York Times* and read it every day. Unlike other East German writers, Heym as a US citizen was able to leave the GDR and take trips abroad, such as his two-month visit to the US in the fall of 1978. He was extremely pleased when I invited him to visit and give a talk at Oberlin College as part of his lecture tour. He came to Oberlin for two days and on November 17, 1978, he gave a memorable hour-long lecture to a huge audience on the inherent conflict between writers (he called them "practitioners of literature") and cultural policymakers in the GDR. I am pleased to report that the tape recording of this special event is still in my possession today.

Many GDR writers were eager to visit Oberlin College and give a lecture or public reading from their works. They were not only interested in travelling to and around the US, but also in becoming closely identified with their internationally famous colleagues who—as all of them knew—had been guest authors in residence at Oberlin College: Christa Wolf (1974), Ulrich Plenzdorf (1975), and Jurek Becker (1978). Some of the GDR writers who unabashedly asked me to invite them were outed as Stasi informants in the 1990s—e.g., Hermann Kant, Fritz Rudolf Fries, and Uwe Berger. I was also pressured by the GDR Writers' Union and the GDR Embassy in Washington, DC to invite certain writers of their choosing, whose honorarium, travel, and other expenses would be fully covered by the GDR. But during my seventeen years as a faculty member at Oberlin College (from 1969 to 1986), Stefan Heym was the only GDR writer to receive an invitation to come and speak on our campus. The five other GDR authors who visited Oberlin prior to my move to Delaware in 1986 were Max Kade German Writers-in-Residence.

BERND JENTZSCH, 1982

In the fall of 1981, following my return from a one-year research leave at Stanford University's Hoover Institution, I resumed my teaching and other duties at Oberlin College. My most important service assignment was to function as chair of the German faculty in the Department of German and Russian, albeit without that official title. At our first department meeting of the fall semester, the German faculty members approved my recommendation that we invite former GDR writer Bernd Jentzsch to be the 15th Max Kade German Writer-in-Residence during the spring semester of 1982. Jentzsch, a well-known poet, prose writer, editor and translator, who also worked as a publisher's reader, was delighted to receive our invitation and accepted immediately.

When I met Jentzsch in November 1975, he and his family—which included his mother—were living in Wilhelmshagen, a town situated on the outskirts of East Berlin. Jentzsch led a quiet life until the fall of 1976, when his fortunes took a dramatic and unexpected turn. That fall, when he was in Switzerland doing spadework for an anthology of Swiss poetry, he learned about the expatriation of prominent poet-singer Wolf Biermann and the expulsion of fellow writer Reiner Kunze from the GDR Writers' Union on the order of GDR government authorities. Stunned and angered by the harshness of these actions, he spontaneously demanded that the regime reverse its decision; he wrote a scathing and detailed open letter to head-of-state Erich Honecker, submitting it for publication to several newspapers in the GDR, in West Germany, and in Switzerland, without considering possible negative consequences. The reprisals against Jentzsch, his family, his long-since widowed mother, and his friends were not long in coming. His open letter was not published by any GDR newspapers but turned over to the Stasi, which promptly indicted him for "hostile agitation against the State." Faced with the prospect of a mock trial and two to ten years of imprisonment, he decided to stay in Switzerland. His wife, her brother, his son, and even his pensioned active socialist mother were harassed, humiliated, and ostracized by the GDR authorities.

In the spring of 1977 Jentzsch's wife, Birgit, and their son, Stefan, were finally permitted to leave the country with a passport for stateless persons and joined him in Switzerland. His elderly mother, however, was repeatedly denied permission to visit him and his family; their correspondence was scrutinized, their occasional telephone conversations were monitored and disrupted; she was driven to despair and, ultimately, to suicide in the fall of 1979. Jentzsch himself was officially branded as a criminal fugitive from the GDR; his publications were banned, his name was removed from reference books, and his contributions were deleted from subsequent editions of anthologies. From 1977 on, the Jentzsch family lived in Küsnacht near Zurich; Jentzsch was able to find work as a publisher's reader, and his wife became director of a home for deaf-blind children.

It is worth noting that both of Jentzsch's parents were social democrats in post-World War I Germany. During the Third Reich they lived and suffered under the constant surveillance and harassment of the Gestapo. After WW II, in 1946, they were automatically integrated into what would become the GDR's Socialist Unity Party (SED). Bernd Jentzsch, born in 1940, was raised and educated in the eastern portion of Germany and embraced the GDR's communistic brand of socialism while he lived there. However, he understandably became disillusioned and very embittered while living in Switzerland, as a man without a country, and eventually had this to say about socialism in the GDR: "Everything that made socialism great has been liquidated. This is the terrible truth."

Our decision to invite Jentzsch to spend three months at Oberlin College as German writer-in-residence infuriated government and Writers' Union officials in the GDR, especially since the previous GDR writer to visit Oberlin had been outspoken regime critic Jurek Becker in 1978. Functionaries in the GDR Writers' Union would soon formulate and seek to implement the "delegation principle" (*Delegierungsprinzip*), a procedure that would enable them to pre-select authors from the GDR for Oberlin College and other institutions with guest writer programs in the US, such as the University of Texas and the University of Iowa.

Bernd Jentzsch's main literary activities have been those of writing poetry and short narrative prose fiction, including stories for children; translating poetry by outstanding poets of various nationalities; also, editing anthologies, with texts from different periods of German literature and works by individual authors. His anthologies are distillations of profound knowledge, sharp judgment, and refined taste. One of his most important achievements in the GDR was his editorship of a poetry series, *Poesiealbum* (Poetry Album), a monthly periodical which presented the public with new (and old) poets, both native and foreign, many of whose works had for political reasons not previously been accessible in East Germany; one hundred and twenty-two booklets appeared in large editions between 1967 and 1976, when the period of self-imposed exile began.

During my seventeen years as an Oberlin College faculty member, I had the pleasure of co-hosting and interacting with twelve Max Kade German writers-in-residence, always during the spring semester. Typically, the visiting writer would arrive in mid-February and depart in mid-May, which is precisely what Bernd Jentzsch did. Of all the writers I experienced in Oberlin, Bernd was probably the most even-keeled and modest, also one of the least self-absorbed. He was an unusually good listener, genuinely interested in what others had to say and eager to hear their comments on his literary texts and various issues. His responses to these comments were always measured and thoughtful. He was less emotional and more cerebral than most of the writers we hosted, an intellectual in every respect, and both the small college setting and academic environment seemed to suit him well. My wife Ulrike and I spent many hours in his company each week. We enjoyed his presence at our dinner table on numerous occasions as well as the friendly conversations we frequently had on a wide range of topics.

In March, I scheduled a short trip to New York City to meet with Dr. Erich Markel, President of the Max Kade Foundation which supported our German writer-in-residence program, the on-campus Max Kade German House and its library, and the Max Kade Lecture Series that brought an eminent German scholar to our campus annually. I needed to secure Dr. Markel's funding approval before inviting the next writer to visit our campus, and I also wanted him to meet Bernd Jentzsch. The three of us stayed at the Barbizon Hotel, right across the street from Central Park South. The highlight of our trip was without question our visit to the World Trade Center NY, a large complex of seven buildings located in the Financial District of Lower Manhattan. At the time of their completion in April 1973, the twin towers—the original One World Trade Center and Two World Trade Center—were the tallest buildings in the world. While most of the World Trade Center complex was closed off from the public, the Top of the World Observatory located on the 107th and 110th floors of tower two was open for all spectators. The Top of the World was an indoor and outdoor observation deck that delivered a spectacular 360-degree view of New York City, allowing visitors to see up to 50 miles away with clear skies. A photo Ulrike took of Bernd while we three were "on top of the world" provides a lasting memory of our visit and the twin towers that were destroyed in the terrorist attacks of September 11, 2001.

Another vivid recollection: That spring, as newlyweds, Ulrike and I were in the process of completing the construction of a new house on a quiet cul-de-sac close to the college campus. On a daily basis, we would check on the progress of work being done inside the house. Bernd would often join us and help us make decisions regarding aspects of the interior design. He also visited home furnishing stores with Ulrike and helped her select such items as floor tiles, wallpaper, lighting fixtures, etc. He marveled at the number of options available to us in every category, as he recalled how few choices he'd had in the GDR when renovating his family's dwelling in the mid-1970s. We recognized that his artistic creativity extended to the areas of design and decor, so we welcomed his input. Bernd, who had not had an easy life since resettling in Switzerland, benefited greatly from his stay in Oberlin which

I think was in many ways therapeutic, just as it had been for Jurek Becker in 1978.

HELGA SCHÜTZ, 1985

Acting on my recommendation in the fall of 1984, the German faculty at Oberlin College decided to invite GDR prose writer Helga Schütz to be the 18th Max Kade German Writer-in-Residence during the spring semester of 1985. I had visited her a few times at her beautiful villa overlooking Gross Glienicke Lake, and had also toured the nearby DEFA (Deutsche Film-Aktiengesellschaft, the first film production company in post-WW II Germany) studios in Potsdam-Babelsberg with her. Helga's personality and warm smile were very engaging, so I was confident that she would interact well with our undergraduate students and Oberlin's German-speaking community. Since I was on sabbatical leave that fall, the acting chair of the department—Dr. Peter Spycher—issued the official invitation to her. Helga Schütz was not a controversial or oppositional writer, so I did not expect her to have any difficulty securing permission and a visa for the trip to the US, but as luck would have it the unexpected happened. In mid-January 1985, just a few weeks before the beginning of the spring semester, Peter Spycher received the following heart-wrenching letter from her, which he later passed along to me. The letter, which bears testimony to the cruel and inhumane nature of the GDR Writers' Union functionaries and higher authorities, is cited below. (I translated it from German into English.)

Berlin, 12/31/84

Dear Peter Spycher,

Today this year is coming to its end, a year rich with experiences, a year full of hope and plans, so that I have lived and worked during this time contentedly and happily—almost offensively so. I had plans for Oberlin, first and foremost, for the months with you at the College. It seemed to me that everything was moving forward and going well—until the day before Christmas. I found a telegram in my mailbox, telling me to visit the Writers' Union. There, too, I still did not sense that anything was wrong. I thought that perhaps a signature was missing or a precise travel date. I had always presented your invitations right after their arrival and expressed my strong interest. Things turned out differently—I was informed that there was no interest in my residency in Oberlin and that the exit visa would not be issued. The justification got lost in a nebulous exchange of words from which it was just possible to glean that you were always selecting the wrong writers for Oberlin (Wolfs, Plenzdorf and Jurek Becker, Bernd Jentzsch) and that the Writers' Union does not expect sending me to Oberlin would benefit the GDR in any way. I was stunned, regretted right away that I had let myself engage in a verbal exchange, wanted to leave just then, as the man from the Union advised me to use illness as the reason for cancelling my residency with you. I cannot tell you how I felt at that moment. Afterwards I crept through the streets like a lowly insect and, with what remained of the positive mood I had stored up over the last months, I prepared the Christmas celebration for our family. I then sat down over the holidays and wrote a letter to the Minister of Culture, wherein I tried to explain to him that I was being deprived of many important experiences and that I had for months been preparing myself mentally for Oberlin. In addition, I wanted to work on the manuscript of my novel in a foreign setting, with a foreign language all around and new images and, of course, solitude as well. I wanted to think about some chapters, fresh and from afar, while reminiscing about home. I planned to let the students participate in that. It would have been an attempt, a venture, but perhaps possible after all in a way not to be described in advance. I was very curious about this situation.

Under the new, shabby circumstances I now do not know how I ought to approach the manuscript. There is actually no substitute for the plan I devised and was longing to carry out.

While writing the letter to the Minister I realized that in the best case scenario I might be able to encounter understanding, but through that nothing more would be salvageable. Should the gray powers revise their decision, it would surely again take weeks, even months, and the semester in Oberlin would have begun; the departure here would be nervous, without the necessary calmness and creative anticipation. I do not even know now what I want to achieve with my complaining. I would almost not want to waste my strength on a commiserative handshake.

In my situation I would now like to ask you point-blank whether there is the possibility—in the event of a revision and an understanding—that I can come to you later on, in the fall semester or in the following year. For only then would my revolting make practical sense.

Dear Peter Spycher, I think I could detect your sympathy for my situation on the telephone; nevertheless I would like to tell you once again that I am ashamed of the behavior of the Writers' Union. It is outrageous to say "no" in this cold and unreasonable manner, and just before the start of a wonderful undertaking prepared on your part with so much time and effort and with so much love.

Please accept my best wishes for the New Year.

Yours,

Helga Schütz

Eventually, the Helga Schütz story had a happy ending. The German faculty at Oberlin, appalled by the way she had been mistreated by the GDR authorities, resolved to keep inviting her and not to invite any other writers from the GDR until she had visited Oberlin. In the fall of 1985, we invited her to be writer-in-residence for the spring 1986 semester, but her visa application was again denied and she was unable to accept the invitation. We then invited Karl-Heinz Jakobs, a GDR writer who—following his vigorous public protest of Wolf Biermann's expatriation—had been forced to move to West Germany in 1977. Two years later the GDR authorities finally relented, and in the spring of 1988 Helga Schütz became the 21st Max Kade German Writer-in-Residence at Oberlin College.

Why did the GDR Writers' Union and, presumably, higher authorities treat Helga Schütz so harshly? In retrospect, I think they were very angry about our earlier selection of two outspoken dissident writers, Jurek Becker in 1978 and Bernd Jentzsch in 1982, who in their view did not in any way represent the GDR. They clearly decided to use Helga Schütz to punish us for selecting oppositional writers as representatives of the GDR, and that also would explain why they waited so long to deny her visa application. They knew we would have difficulty finding a replacement for her on such short notice, but fortunately we were able to do so. As I would learn in March 1985 while attending the Leipzig Book Fair, the Writers' Union was determined not only to participate in the selection process but to select appropriate writers for residency in Oberlin. In accordance with a newly established "delegation principle" (*Delegierungsprinzip*), they wanted us to contact them when we were ready to have a writer from the GDR; they would then either make the selection for us or propose two or three writers for our consideration. This would enable them to reward loyalist writers and at the same time ensure that the GDR would be represented by authors who were supportive of the SED Party's decisions and actions in the cultural domain. Needless to say, my colleagues and I at Oberlin College rejected the delegation principle, but some other US institutions of higher education with visiting writer programs of various types welcomed this "input" from the Writers' Union.

KARL-HEINZ JAKOBS, 1986

In the fall of 1985, the German faculty at Oberlin College again invited Helga Schütz to be German Writer-in-Residence, just as I had said we would do in my March 1985 conversations with GDR Writers' Union function-ary Eberhard Scheibner. We proposed that she spend approximately three months in Oberlin during the spring 1986 semester, from mid-February to mid-May, and asked her to let us know by no later than the end of October if she would be able to accept the invitation. Predictably, her application for a visa to travel to the US was again denied, so I proceeded to contact Karl-Heinz Jakobs, a prominent GDR prose writer who had been living in West Germany since 1977. (For more information on Helga Schütz, see the previous snapshot in this series.)

Jakobs was born in 1929 in the East Prussian village of Kiauken. After WW II he pursued several trades other than writing before finding work as an editorial assistant and journalist. These early jobs included construction work, mining, and masonry—employment that entailed international travel. In 1967-68, he worked for ten months building walls as part of a construc-tion crew that hoped to aid economic development in Mali. Manual labor, especially masonry, had a great attraction for him; Jakobs said he "couldn't live on poetry alone."

In 1956, Jakobs began two years of study at the Johannes R. Becher Literary Institute in Leipzig, after which he devoted himself full time to free-lance writing. As for his studies at the Becher Institute, he became convinced while there that "all good East German writers come from Leipzig." His first novel, *Beschreibung eines Sommers* (Description of a Summer, 1961), met with unprecedented success in East Germany, selling a half-million copies. Among his later works from the pre-Oberlin period are six additional novels (two of them based on travel experiences in the Soviet Union and Africa), three collections of stories, and a volume of essays. In 1983, he published a largely autobiographical book about the events that followed the revocation of Wolf Biermann's East German citizenship—*Das endlose Jahr: Begegnungen mit Mäd* (The Endless Year: Encounters with Mäd), another work critical of the GDR's government.

Jakobs was one of the more vociferous of the writers and intellectuals who protested the expatriation of dissident GDR writer/singer Wolf Biermann in November 1976. His harsh criticism of the ruling SED Party led to his dismissal from the Berlin Writers' Union as well as from the executive committee of the GDR Writers' Union, and finally to expulsion from the SED Party in 1977. Because of his deteriorating relations with the GDR authorities, he was given a three-year "visa" and asked to leave the country for that period of time. When it expired in April 1984, the visa was extended for four more years; however, Jakobs decided not to return and stayed in West Germany.

Although restricted in some ways by this special arrangement, just as Jurek Becker had been after moving to West Berlin, Jakobs increased his commitment to confront the problems of the communistic GDR directly. He maintained that the typical path of an East German writer led to schizophrenia, because one always had to paint the details but leave the whole out of sight. Early during his years in West German limbo, Jakobs broke with this schizophrenic tendency and wrote *Wilhelmsburg* (1979), a novel that examined the dynamics of a provincial city in a nameless, German-speaking socialist state. The hero brings to mind the typical GDR citizen: he is a man who keeps his opinions to himself for fear of the consequences, a man who says "yes" even when he thinks "no." Jakobs espoused the view that an East German writer who is conscious of history must tell what really happened, and what happened unjustly; for him, the moment of hesitating at this was a thing of the past.

Our choice of Jakobs as a substitute for Helga Schütz most assuredly angered officials in both the GDR Writers' Union and the Ministry of Culture. For Jakobs, much like the two GDR writers in exile who preceded him—Bernd Jentzsch in 1982 and Jurek Becker in 1979—had evolved into an outspoken critic of the Honecker regime, the GDR state and its brand of socialism. I like to think that the GDR authorities, when they realized that we had chosen Jakobs to be our German Writer-in-Residence in spring 1986, regretted their decision to deny Helga Schütz this opportunity. From their perspective, she certainly would have been a far better representative of the GDR than dissident writer Jakobs.

My memory of Karl-Heinz Jakobs's Oberlin residency is a bit sketchy, but I can recall some things very well. He occupied the office adjacent to mine in Rice Hall and spent a lot of time there, so we had plenty of contact; now and then I was able to observe him at work. He was an exceptionally disciplined worker, spending many hours writing every day. I was surprised to see that he wrote the first draft of his prose texts with the electric typewriter, not by hand as most writers did before the advent of personal computers. He would draft a short story, essay, or chapter of a novel from beginning to end, then would proceed to revise the pages in a really unique way. He would begin this process by making handwritten changes within the text and scribbling notes in the margins. Using scissors, he would then cut the pages into sections, each one a full paragraph or more. These he would reassemble on his desk and then Scotch tape them to the wall. While the strips of paper were hanging on the wall, Jakobs would review and rearrange some of them, thus creating a new whole. This "collage" technique of writing and editing is very common today, now that we work on computers with cut-and-paste features.

The picture of Jakobs in the photo galleries I posted online (www. richard-zipser.com) reminds me that he was a good-natured and sociable person, quite laid back, someone with whom you would enjoy having a beer and casual conversation. He came to our house and joined us for dinner frequently, and my wife Ulrike and I always enjoyed his company and our conversations. I recall that he was somewhat lonely that semester, and there were understandable reasons for that. His English was very poor, something that limited his ability to engage socially with persons outside the minuscule German-speaking community in Oberlin. Also, apart from mealtimes in the German House, he did not socialize with students. The downsized German faculty was not large enough to offer him adequate companionship, but Ulrike and I did our best to provide him with some semblance of a social life. We also introduced him to what by the end of his stay would become his favorite sipping whisky: Kentucky bourbon!

THE DELEGATION PRINCIPLE

The German Democratic Republic and the United States initiated full diplomatic relations on September 4, 1974. In the mid-1970s, after establishing an embassy in Washington, DC and joining the United Nations, the GDR was finally able to gain the international recognition it had long sought. From the platform of its embassy, the GDR began to systematically develop a network of sympathizers comprised chiefly of academicians from universities. The object was to identify persons, professors, and doctoral candidates working in the general area of German studies, who were interested in the GDR and sympathetic to its socialist form of government. In the effort to create a fifth column, two groups were targeted: first, intellectuals from the far left—i.e., would-be progressives who viewed the GDR with its brand of communistic socialism as a model society; and second, professors who could be cultivated in various ways and transformed into advocates for all that the GDR represented and cherished.

The GDR Embassy played an important role in this nationwide propaganda effort, by organizing lecture/reading tours for East German authors loyal to the SED Party and by disseminating pro-GDR materials in a remarkably effective way. The GDR needed to ensure that US universities and colleges would not just have oppositional East German writers visiting their campuses, but also a significant number of writers who had a positive view of the GDR state, political system, and society. These writers would be rewarded for their loyal support and, while visiting the US, they would be expected to help expand the network of GDR sympathizers that had already been established at some institutions of higher learning. This eventually led GDR authorities who were overseeing activity in the cultural sphere to formulate and implement a practice based on the so-called delegation principle (*Delegierungsprinzip*).

What was the delegation principle and how did it impact the process of selecting and inviting GDR writers to visit Oberlin College as Max Kade German Writers-in-Residence? In brief, the delegation principle was a procedure that would enable GDR Writers' Union officials to pre-select authors from the GDR for Oberlin College and other institutions with guest writer programs. Here is how it was intended to function in practice. When our German faculty was prepared to invite an East German writer for a residency at Oberlin College, I was supposed to inform the Writers' Union of our intention with adequate advance notice. The Writers' Union would then send us the names of two or three suitable authors, from their point of view, and we would be able to pick the one we liked best. Of course, this procedure was unacceptable to our faculty. We were not prepared to allow GDR functionaries to participate directly or indirectly in the selection process.

What prompted the GDR Writers' Union to create the delegation principle? The short answer to this question is: Oberlin College's visiting German writer program. From the ideological perspective of the SED authorities who were responsible for the GDR's cultural policies and activities, the first four GDR writers we invited and hosted—Christa Wolf, Ulrich Plenzdorf, Jurek Becker, and Bernd Jentzsch—were not good representatives of the GDR. Let me explain why.

Christa Wolf (1974) was undoubtedly viewed as an unfortunate choice, since her controversial novel *The Quest for Christa T.* (1968) had been condemned by government officials and was eventually banned in the GDR. Her novel is a subjective account of everyday life in a repressive society that does not tolerate persons who question socialist beliefs and the way of living in a socialist state that expects all its citizens to conform. Christa T., an introspective young woman, is shown to be a victim of this restrictive society. (A more detailed discussion of this novel is presented in the snapshot on Christa Wolf in section VI.)

Ulrich Plenzdorf (1975) was also someone the GDR Writers' Union would not have selected to send to Oberlin if we had invited them to recommend a few writers for our consideration. His most famous work, *The New Sufferings of Young W.* tells the story of a young revolutionary in a socialist society, Edgar Wibeau, who rebels against the conformity that was so prevalent everywhere in the GDR. While he is not against socialism per se, Edgar is in favor of almost everything the SED Party officials and others in positions of power were against. (A more detailed discussion of this work is presented in the piece on Ulrich Plenzdorf in section VI).

While Plenzdorf—like Christa Wolf—is critical of various aspects of GDR society, he—like Wolf, once again—has nothing explicit to say about politics in the GDR or the SED Party. This, along with their international prominence and popularity throughout East Germany, probably explains why they were allowed to come to Oberlin. In both instances, we issued the invitation directly to the author, and they then sought and secured permission to visit Oberlin with their spouses.

Jurek Becker (1978), the third author from the GDR to visit Oberlin, was as famous but more controversial than his two predecessors. He was very outspoken and not afraid to express his views on such topics as problems in GDR society and his country's oppressive system of government. His criticism of the SED leadership and their violation of human rights brought him into open conflict with the GDR authorities on numerous occasions. In November 1976, Becker became embroiled in a major conflict with the government when he—along with eleven other GDR writers—publicly protested the forced exiling of dissident poet-singer Wolf Biermann. In the ensuing months, he resigned from the GDR Writers' Union, was thrown out of the SED Party, and also barred from making public appearances and publishing his writing in the GDR.

Before the end of June 1977, Becker's novel *Sleepless Days* had been completed and submitted to the Hinstorff Verlag in the GDR and a West German publishing house. Initially, Becker was assured by the editors at Hinstorff that they would be able to publish the novel. But later on, when he steadfastly refused to make their recommended changes, it became clear that his novel would not appear in his own country. In December 1977, Becker decided to leave and quietly moved from East to West Berlin, and from there he came to Oberlin in February 1978.

At this time, Becker was in possession of a unique two-year exit visa that enabled him to go back and forth from the West to the East where his two teen-age sons were living. Since he already had this visa, GDR officials were not involved in any way in his decision to accept our invitation to become the eleventh Max Kade German Writer-in-Residence, which I delivered by hand in the fall of 1977. Years later I would learn that the GDR authorities were angered by our selection of Becker for a residency at Oberlin College, considering it an affront.

Bernd Jentzsch (1982), our fifteenth German author in residence, was far and away the most controversial GDR writer to visit Oberlin. Jentzsch had led a quiet life in a town on the outskirts of East Berlin until the fall of 1976, when he was in Switzerland preparing an anthology of Swiss poetry. There he learned about the expatriation of prominent chansonnier Wolf Biermann and the expulsion of fellow writer Reiner Kunze from the GDR Writers' Union on the order of GDR government authorities. To protest these actions, he submitted to East and West German newspapers a sharply critical and detailed open letter to head-of-state Erich Honecker, demanding that the regime reverse its decision. His open letter was not published in the GDR but turned over to the Stasi, which promptly indicted him for "hostile agitation against the State." Faced with the prospect of a mock trial and up to ten years in prison, he elected to stay in Switzerland. In retaliation, the GDR authorities harassed, humiliated, and ostracized his wife, her brother, his son, and even his pensioned active socialist mother who eventually committed suicide.

Our decision to invite Jentzsch to spend three months at Oberlin College as German writer-in-residence infuriated government and Writers' Union officials in the GDR, especially since the previous GDR writer to visit Oberlin had been outspoken regime critic Jurek Becker in 1978. It was after this that the GDR Writers' Union formulated and sought to implement the delegation principle. They hoped that this procedure would enable them to pre-select authors from the GDR for Oberlin College and other US institutions with guest writer programs, such as the University of Texas and the University of Iowa.

Helga Schütz (1985), a prose and screenplay writer who was definitely not a troublemaker and not in any way controversial, ironically became the first to fall victim to the delegation principle. Acting on my recommendation in the fall of 1984, the German faculty at Oberlin College decided to invite her to be the 18th Max Kade German Writer-in-Residence during the spring semester of 1985. I did not expect her to have any difficulty securing permission and a visa for the trip to the US, but—as luck would have it—the unexpected happened. In mid-January 1985, just a few weeks before the beginning of the spring semester, we received a heart-wrenching letter from Schütz. This letter, dated December 31, 1984, bears testimony to the cruel and inhumane nature of the Writers' Union functionaries and higher authorities in the Ministry of Culture. Cited below is a portion of the letter's first paragraph, which I translated from German into English.

> Today this year is coming to its end, a year rich with experiences, a year full of hope and plans, so that I have lived and worked during this time contentedly and happily—almost offensively so. I had plans for Oberlin, first and foremost, for the months with you at the College. It seemed to me that everything was moving forward and going well—until the day before Christmas. I found a telegram in my mailbox, telling me to visit the Writers' Union. There, too, I still did not sense that anything was wrong. I thought that perhaps a signature was missing or a precise travel date. I had always presented your invitations right after their arrival and expressed my strong interest. Things turned out differently—I was informed that there was no interest in my residency in Oberlin and that the exit visa would not be issued. The justification got lost in a nebulous exchange of words from which it was just possible to glean that you were always selecting the wrong writers for Oberlin (Wolfs, Plenzdorf, Jurek Becker,

and Bernd Jentzsch) and that the Writers' Union does not expect sending me to Oberlin would benefit the GDR in any way. I was stunned, regretted right away that I had let myself engage in a verbal exchange, wanted to leave just then, as the man from the Union advised me to use illness as the reason for cancelling my residency with you. I cannot tell you how I felt at that moment. Afterwards I crept through the streets like a lowly insect and, with what remained of the positive mood I had stored up over the last months, I prepared the Christmas celebration for our family. I then sat down over the holidays and wrote a letter to the Minister of Culture, wherein I tried to explain to him that I was being deprived of many important experiences and that I had for months been preparing myself mentally for Oberlin. . . .

Why did the GDR Writers' Union and, presumably, higher authorities treat Helga Schütz so harshly? In retrospect, I think they were very angry about our earlier selection of two outspoken dissident writers, Jurek Becker in 1978 and Bernd Jentzsch in 1982, who in their view did not appropriately represent the GDR. They apparently decided to use Helga Schütz to punish us for selecting oppositional writers as representatives of the GDR, and that also would explain why they waited so long to deny her visa application. They knew we would have difficulty finding a replacement for her on such short notice, but fortunately we were able to do so.

As I would learn in March 1985 while attending the Leipzig Book Fair, the Writers' Union was determined to enforce the delegation principle so as to participate in our selection process by pre-selecting some writers they viewed as suitable for a residency in Oberlin. This would enable them to reward loyalist writers and at the same time ensure that the GDR would be represented by authors who were supportive of the SED Party's decisions and actions in the cultural domain. Needless to say, my colleagues and I at Oberlin College rejected the delegation principle, but some other US institutions of higher education with visiting writer programs of various types welcomed this "input" from the Writers' Union.

In the fall of 1985, the German faculty at Oberlin College again invited Helga Schütz to be German Writer-in-Residence, just as I had said we would do in my March 1985 conversations with GDR Writers' Union functionary Eberhard Scheibner at the Leipzig Book Fair. We proposed that she spend approximately three months in Oberlin during the spring 1986 semester, from mid-February to mid-May, and asked her to let us know by no later than the end of October if she would be able to accept the invitation. Predictably, her application for a visa to travel to the US was again denied, so I proceeded to contact Karl-Heinz Jakobs, a prominent GDR prose writer who had been living in West Germany since 1977. If the GDR authorities were hoping that the denial of Helga Schütz's visa would make Oberlin more amenable to their delegation principle, they were mistaken.

Karl-Heinz Jakobs (1986) was one of the most outspoken of the writers who had protested the expatriation of dissident GDR writer/singer Wolf Biermann in November 1976. His harsh criticism of the ruling SED Party had led to his dismissal from the Berlin Writers' Union as well as from the executive committee of the GDR Writers' Union, and finally to expulsion from the SED Party in 1977. Because of his deteriorating relations with the GDR authorities, he was given a three-year "visa" and forced to leave the country for that period of time. When it expired in April 1984, the visa was extended for four more years; however, Jakobs decided not to return and stayed in West Germany.

Although restricted in some ways by this arrangement, as Jurek Becker had been after moving to West Berlin, Jakobs nevertheless increased his commitment to confronting the problems of the communistic GDR society directly. Our choice of him as a substitute for Helga Schütz was probably viewed as a provocation by officials in both the GDR Writers' Union and the Ministry of Culture. For Jakobs, much like the two GDR writers in exile who preceded him—Bernd Jentzsch and Jurek Becker—had evolved into an outspoken critic of the Honecker regime, the GDR state, and its brand of socialism. I like to think that the GDR authorities, when they realized that we had chosen Jakobs to be our spring 1986 German writer-in-residence, regretted their decision to again deny Helga Schütz this opportunity. From their perspective, she surely would have been a far better representative of the GDR than dissident writer Jakobs.

Eventually, the Helga Schütz story had a happy ending. The German faculty at Oberlin, appalled by the way she had been mistreated by the GDR authorities, resolved to keep inviting her and not to invite any other writers from the GDR until she had visited Oberlin. Two years later the GDR authorities finally relented and approved her visa application, so in the spring of 1988 Helga Schütz became Oberlin College's 21st Max Kade German Writer-in-Residence. With the unwitting assistance of oppositional writer and SED regime critic Karl-Heinz Jakobs, we had managed to thwart the delegation principle!

VII
FAVORITE GDR WRITERS AND WORKS

SARAH KIRSCH

In retrospect, I realize what I liked most about my seventeen years on the Oberlin College faculty (1969 to 1986) was the opportunity I had to interact each spring term with a prominent writer from a German-speaking country. The Max Kade German Writer-in-Residence program brought West German, East German, Austrian, and Swiss authors to our campus every year for a residency of about three months duration. In my first year at Oberlin, my department chairman gave me the assignment of looking after celebrated playwright Tankred Dorst, with whom I had lots of contact and many rewarding conversations. I was intimidated at first, since he was the first live writer I had ever met, but I soon got over that and came to enjoy interacting and socializing with him and the authors who followed in his footsteps. Without question, our visiting writer program prepared me well for the scholarly projects I would undertake during my first sabbatical leave and later in my career, since those initiatives brought me into direct contact with a large number of East German authors. While at Oberlin College, I had the pleasure of co-hosting twelve Max Kade German writers-in-residence, and I was instrumental in bringing five East German writers to our campus: Christa Wolf (1974), Ulrich Plenzdorf (1975), Jurek Becker (1978), Bernd Jentzsch (1982), and Karl-Heinz Jakobs (1986). But I also had two very disappointing experiences, both of which involved women writers from the GDR—Sarah Kirsch and Helga Schütz—persons I was eager but unable to bring to Oberlin. I have written elsewhere about Helga Schütz (see VI GDR WRITERS IN OHIO, "Helga Schütz"), explaining why the GDR Writers' Union initially would not allow her to visit Oberlin and why she eventually was permitted to do so after I had moved to Delaware. Sarah Kirsch was another matter altogether.

The first East German writer-in-residence at Oberlin College was Christa Wolf, who spent six weeks with us in the spring of 1974. She was accompanied by her husband Gerhard, a well-known literary scholar and editor who had connections to many contemporary GDR authors and publishers. The Wolfs were prominent figures in the East German literary scene; both were highly influential, albeit in different ways. Yet they were modest individuals; their comportment was unpretentious and down to earth, not self-absorbed or self-assertive. It was obvious that they viewed themselves as their country's goodwill ambassadors. I spent a lot of time with the Wolfs while they were in Oberlin, and they introduced me to the GDR literary scene through readings and conversations that were truly fascinating. Christa and Gerhard unveiled and led me into another, discrete world of German literature, one I had for some odd reason not been introduced to in graduate school. When I told the Wolfs that I would be taking a one-year sabbatical leave in 1975-76, they encouraged me to think about doing a project on GDR writing in the 1970s and promised to assist me. During the course of our discussions, the outline of a possible project gradually emerged. The focus would be on the more subjective and sociocritical literature that came into being in East Germany after Erich Honecker became leader of the SED Party in 1971. In a famous speech he proclaimed that there were to be "no taboos" in the arts, thereby relaxing the strict cultural policies of his predecessor, Walter Ulbricht. To my delight, another prominent East German author—Ulrich Plenzdorf—came to Oberlin as visiting writer in the spring of 1975. He helped me shape and finalize plans for my first sabbatical leave, a good portion of which I was hoping to spend in the GDR.

According to the plan I had developed with the Wolfs' and Plenzdorf's help, I was to prepare a book that would explore and document East German writing within a short-lived period of liberalization for literature and the arts in the GDR. The so-called "no taboos" period lasted for approximately five years; it ended abruptly in November 1976 when dissident writer Wolf Biermann was expatriated by the GDR authorities. The objective of my book project was to introduce readers to the leading East German writers of the day, especially to those who were shaping the new sociocritical direction of writing during the 1970s.

The Wolfs made good on their promise to assist me, long before I actually began working on my project. Christa sent a letter to the GDR Writers' Union in early 1975, endorsing my undertaking and asking them to let me proceed and also provide assistance. This set the stage for the initial meeting I had in September with several Writers' Union functionaries at their East Berlin headquarters. Without the Wolfs' involvement and intervention on my behalf, especially at the outset, I doubt that the GDR authorities would have permitted me to conduct interviews with writers and gather other materials for my book.

While I was in East Berlin that September, the Wolfs introduced me to two well-known writers in their circle of friends, Volker Braun and Sarah Kirsch, and also paved the way for meetings in November with three members of the GDR's literary aristocracy, Stephan Hermlin, Günter Kunert, and Franz Fühmann. Ulrich Plenzdorf introduced me to two of his close friends, prose writers Klaus Schlesinger and Martin Stade, persons I would see frequently during the next few years. When I returned to East Berlin in November, Plenzdorf lent me a portable tape recorder to use for the interviews with authors I was scheduled to visit.

Another writer I got to know well was Sarah Kirsch, who at that time was one of Christa Wolf's closest friends. I met her in the fall of 1975 and visited her on numerous occasions that year as well as in 1976 while I was working on various book projects in the GDR. She and her young son Moritz lived in a modern high-rise apartment house on Fisher Island in the River Spree, in central Berlin. During my visits to East Berlin, Sarah and I got together from time to time for dinner at a restaurant or a glass of French red wine and cheese (also French) at her place, and by degrees we became good friends. She was a reserved, unassuming person who kept her own counsel and preferred to avoid the spotlight. We got along well, she took a genuine interest in my work, and I enjoyed her company immensely. She was always eager to hear reports on my visits with these authors, also to hear how I as an outsider from the US viewed each of them and their works. One evening, after I had finished recounting what I had experienced that afternoon during my hours-long visit with prominent GDR playwright Peter Hacks, Sarah said: "Dick, your eyes are tiny, but those eyes see everything." What a compliment that was!

Sarah gained initial prominence in the 1960s as one of a group of GDR poets who challenged the official cultural-political dictate that literature should primarily reinforce the values and reflect the achievements of socialist society. In 1960, she married the controversial lyric poet Rainer Kirsch and then both were mentored by Gerhard Wolf. Sarah and Rainer Kirsch joined a group of other aspiring poets—Wolf Biermann, Heinz Czechowski, Elke Erb, Volker Braun, and Karl Mickel, among others—who collectively charted a new direction in GDR poetry. Their poems emphasized subjective approaches to reality as opposed to ideological affirmations of socialist society. In 1967, Sarah published her first solo collection of poems, *Landaufenthalt* (A Stay in the Country), in which she asserted formally and thematically a new poetic identity. Heinz Czechowski, the influential poet from Halle, commented: "With Sarah's poems a new, previously unheard tone could be heard in German lyric poetry." Some insiders referred to that tone as the "Sarah-Sound." Her poems were grounded primarily in personal experience and emphasized subjective feeling, and they were often subtly critical of GDR conditions. The independent-minded poet Sarah Kirsch was recognized as an important talent, but also eyed with suspicion by the cultural authorities of the SED.

However, unlike a number of her colleagues—e.g., Stefan Heym, Günter Kunert, Reiner Kunze, Jurek Becker, and Wolf Biermann—Sarah Kirsch was not openly hostile to the SED regime and was never considered to be a troublemaker. Nevertheless, for stepping out of line on just one occasion she would become a nonperson in the eyes of the GDR's cultural bureaucracy. Her sin was to protest, along with Christa Wolf and ten other leading GDR writers, the government's expatriation in November 1976 of dissident poet Wolf Biermann, while he was on a concert tour in West Germany. Her punishment for this transgression was extremely cruel and had dire financial consequences for Sarah. She was informed that her writings would no longer be published in the GDR, that she would not receive any more freelance translation work, the main source of her income at that time, nor would she be allowed to participate in public events of any sort. Since Sarah was divorced, and since she had a six-year-old son, her sudden inability to earn an income soon became a major existential problem. Her solution was to apply for a permanent exit visa that would enable her to move to the West. She did that, but the visa was not forthcoming. The government authorities had clearly decided to make an example of her, so other recalcitrant writers would not be tempted to follow in her footsteps.

As previously mentioned, Sarah was romantically involved with a German writer who lived in West Berlin, a lover who would come to East Berlin from time to time to visit with her. This relationship contributed significantly to her desire to move to West Berlin. But for more than six months, GDR authorities ignored her visa application. Eventually, in the summer of 1977, they finally permitted Sarah to emigrate to the West and move to West Berlin. I visited with her that fall and asked how she had managed to get the visa. She told me that she was so desperate that she ultimately decided to appeal directly to SED Party leader Erich Honecker.

I wrote him a letter and told him that I had applied for a permanent exit visa more than six months ago, but—despite my repeated inquiries—had not yet received a response. I said that I desperately needed his help and wanted him to intervene soon, very soon. I emphasized that this was an urgent life-and-death matter and concluded by asking him to keep in mind that my apartment was located on the seventeenth floor.

Honecker then intervened, presumably because of her veiled threat of suicide, and her visa application was approved right away. In August 1977, Sarah Kirsch and her son Moritz quietly relocated to West Berlin.

In the fall of 1977, I spent two months in East Berlin with the financial support of an IREX (International Research and Exchanges Board) grant. During this time I made several trips to West Berlin in order to visit with Sarah, who was having some difficulty getting resettled and acclimated to life in the West. One day she told me about something that had happened to her shortly before she left the GDR, in all likelihood due to her participation in the protest of the GDR's expulsion of Wolf Biermann, an incident that both repulsed and frightened her. She said she had returned to her apartment on the seventeenth floor one afternoon to find this painted boldly on the outside of the entrance door:

Saujüdin (Jewish Pig)

The irony here is that Sarah was not Jewish. In 1935 she was born Ingrid Bernstein in Limlingerode in the region of Thuringia, the part of Germany that following World War II became the GDR. She changed her first name to Sarah in order to protest against her father's anti-Semitism and to show solidarity with Holocaust victims. From 1960 to 1968 she was married to East German lyricist Rainer Kirsch, which explains the change in surname.

I returned to East Berlin in the middle of May, 1978, to complete the work that could only be done in the GDR on two projects that would culminate in book publications: *Contemporary East German Poetry* (a bilingual anthology) and *GDR Literature During the Thaw* (a three-volume documentary). With Sarah's permission, I published a selection of her poems in both of these books, as well as her written response to my interview questions in the book focusing on the period of thaw. We got together a few times in May/June of 1978, but little did I imagine that I would never see Sarah again—yet, that is what happened! In the summer she departed for Italy, where—thanks to a grant from the government—she was able to spend the next half year as artist in residence at the German Academy in Rome at Villa Massimo. The stay at Villa Massimo enabled Sarah to devote herself to writing again, after several years of emotional and mental turmoil, and it marked the beginning of a new chapter in her personal and professional life.

In 1979, after Sarah Kirsch had returned to West Berlin, I proposed to my Oberlin colleagues that we invite her to be our German writer-in-residence for the spring 1980 semester, and members of the German faculty were eager to do so. But, as I would learn, Sarah's life had gone in a new direction. She had met a young German composer at the Villa Massimo, Wolfgang von Schweinitz, and become romantically involved with him. She and Wolfgang had decided to move away from Berlin and its many distractions that made it very difficult for Sarah to write. When I contacted Sarah and issued the invitation, she told me they were preparing to relocate and embrace a different style of life in the rural township of Bothel in Lower Saxony. There, while living in the peaceful countryside with Wolfgang, son Moritz, and her mother, Sarah wrote the powerful collection of poems that were published under the title *Katzenleben* (Cat Lives, 1984).

Sarah's closest neighbor, Johanna Amthor, has written and posted online her "Memories of Sarah Kirsch in Bothel from 1980 to 1983" (Erinnerungen an Sarah Kirsch in Bothel von 1980 bis 1983). She recalls how much Sarah loved the flat, marshy landscape and country life. She also provides a description of Sarah which coincides with my recollection of Sarah, so I have translated it and am including it here. "Sarah was petite and slender back then. She had straight hair, tinted red, and wore eyeglasses with thick frames. She liked to wear flared pants and Norwegian sweaters. She also did knitting and later on knotted lovely carpets. But not before [moving to] Tielenhemme. Sarah seemed very modest in her demeanor, almost shy, one could say. She had a pleasant alto voice, smoked a lot, was a good cook, had a nice and also sometimes earthy sense of humor."

In the fall of 1982, during my first semester as chairman of the German and Russian Department at Oberlin College, I contacted Sarah and invited her formally to spend the spring 1983 semester in Oberlin, as German Writer-in-Residence. Below is my translation of the letter she wrote in response to my second invitation to visit Oberlin. It reflects her determination not to spend time travelling and reading from her works, but rather to do what she wanted and needed to do most—watch the flowers bloom, be there for her son, and write!

Bothel, 16 October 82

Dear Dick,

Many thanks for the long telegraphic invitation, but I can't and don't want to leave this place; everything that is here needs me, and I also wouldn't get to see my flowers bloom. Seriously, I'm able to work really well here and have granted myself a two-year break from public readings, otherwise one gradually comes to dread this activity. It was very nice that you thought of me several times, that you still think I have to visit Oberlin. Coming from the GDR that would have been something really different; there one seized every opportunity to be able to travel.

I hope that you are doing well along with those close to you, that your work is still a source of pleasure. Moritz, meanwhile, is almost as tall as I am, 13 years old, he is thriving here. Recently, he travelled by himself for the first time to visit a friend in Berlin-W.

Many good wishes from both of us!

Yours, Sarah

Most of all, Sarah craved the solitude of nature which stimulated her creativity more than anything else. In 1983 she moved with partner Wolfgang and son Moritz to Schleswig-Holstein. They moved into a former school-house in Tielenhemme (district of Dithmarschen), a rural municipality with a population of about 170 persons, located near the Danish border. Sarah was fascinated by the barrenness and expanse of the unspoiled landscape surrounding them. Joey Horsley, in her biographical essay on Sarah Kirsch, tells us: "Here she kept sheep, cats and a donkey, observed and absorbed nature and the world, and wrote daily for the next 20 years. She also took up painting; her watercolors appear in some of her publications." (*FemBio* "Sarah Kirsch," p. 6) Sarah died on May 5, 2013 after a short illness; her ashes are buried in the garden of her house in Tielenhemme.

After moving to the West in August 1977, Sarah published a collection of forty new poems under the title *Drachensteigen*, (Flying Kites, 1979). These poems reflect, among other things, her separation from the GDR and her happiness at being in Italy with a new lover. My translation into English of the first poem she wrote after leaving the GDR, "The End of the String" / "Der Rest des Fadens," appears below.

> Flying kites. Game
> For endless plains without trees and water. In the open sky
> A paper star
> Rises, unstoppable
> Drawn toward the light, higher, out of sight
> And onward, onward
> All we have left is the end of the string, and the fact that we
> knew you.

REINER KUNZE

I met Reiner Kunze in 1976 while I was on a sabbatical leave, living in Vienna and working on a project that would culminate in an 840-page book on GDR literature in the 1970s. In January 1976, I wrote to Kunze and asked him to participate in my project by permitting me to interview him and publish one or more of his recent texts in my book. His response came on a postcard dated January 23, 1976, which happened to be my 33rd birthday. Kunze indicated that he would be pleased to meet with me on March 22 and sent me his private telephone number. Before I describe that memorable encounter, let me provide some important background information on Kunze.

Kunze was a dissident writer, although he was not fond of the "dissident" label; he was a person of principle who stood up to the GDR's power elite and was harshly punished for doing so. To understand his unfortunate situation, one needs to know that in 1961 and 1962 he was living in Czechoslovakia, where he learned the Czech language, married a Czech medical doctor, and became friends with several Prague writers. His major confrontation with the GDR authorities was precipitated by the Soviet-led Warsaw Pact invasion of Czechoslovakia on August 20, 1968, which he protested publicly and vociferously. Thereafter, his writings—with the exception of one anthology, *Brief mit blauem Siegel* (Letter with a Blue Seal, 1973)—were no longer published in the GDR, and he was not allowed to read from his works or speak in public. This severe form of censorial repression, imposed and enforced by government officials, was just a step away from incarceration; the purpose was not only to discipline Kunze for his oppositional behavior and silence him, but also to prevent him from earning a living, the same punishment Sarah Kirsch received. Fortunately for Kunze and his family, his wife Elisabeth had a full-time job.

On the afternoon of March 22, 1976, I visited Kunze at his home in Greiz, a small city in Thuringia. My recollection of that visit is sketchy after all these years, but I do recall Kunze's passion, intensity, frustration, and anger as we discussed the Prague Spring and the 1968 invasion of Czechoslovakia, human rights issues in the GDR, and the ban on his publications and public appearances in his homeland. He also told me about the suffering of his Czech wife who worked at a nearby hospital and the mistreatment of his teen-age daughter at her school, due to his persistent opposition to repressive state policies and practices. As we conversed and while I tape recorded the interview,

Kunze mentioned that he was certain the secret police had bugged his house. Every so often he would make a comment he knew the state authorities and secret police would find offensive if they heard it, then he would look at a place in the living room where a bug might have been planted and say in a loud, defiant voice: "What do you think of that?!" Kunze answered all fifteen of my questions and, after an unforgettable visit that lasted several hours, I departed with the taped interview in hand. That interview, which appears in volume III of my book, *DDR-Literatur im Tauwetter* (GDR Literature During the Thaw), reveals above all Kunze's deep concern as a writer for human welfare, values, and dignity.

On March 23, 1976, the day after my visit with him, Kunze sent a note to me at my Vienna address, along with copies of the six short poems he had selected for publication in my book:

Dear Mr. Zipser,

six—so as not to push oneself forward, but also not to make oneself scarce, agreed? And then you mentioned a photo: as the situation requires. Hopefully, all is well with you. Our greetings to your wife and warm regards to you from my wife and me.

Yours, Reiner Kunze
Greiz, 3. 23. 76
PS: Confirmation of receipt requested, on account of restful sleep. . .

In the fall of 1976, following the unauthorized publication in West Germany of his controversial book of short prose, *Die wunderbaren Jahre* (The Wonderful Years), Kunze expected to be arrested. Instead, the GDR authorities expelled him from the Writers' Union, impounded his passport, and in April 1977 forced him into exile. He resettled with his family in West Germany, in Obernzell-Erlau, Bavaria, a municipality located close to the border of Czechoslovakia.

The Wonderful Years is a marvelous book, my favorite of Kunze's prose works. Cultural critic John Leonard reviewed the English edition of the book, translated by Joachim Neugroschel, for *The New York Times* on April 21, 1977. I want to share some passages from this insightful review with readers of this snapshot, so they will have a sense of Kunze's style of writing and the power of his words. Leonard begins by stating: "It will take you no more than an hour and a half to read this book the first time. The second time will take longer. The third time, you will probably pause at certain passages, having already memorized them, and look around for an ear into which to quote. For instance:

> On the morning of August 22, 1968, my wife nearly tripped:
> A bouquet of gladiolus lay at our door. An elderly couple of
> the neighborhood had a garden and would sometimes bring
> us flowers. 'They probably didn't want to disturb us last night,'
> said my wife.
>
> That afternoon, she came with three bouquets in her arms.
> 'These are only some of them,' she said. They had been left for
> her at the hospital where she works, and nobody but my wife was
> surprised. Everyone knows she's from Czechoslovkia.

"That's it," Leonard exclaims, "the whole of a two-paragraph story—vignette, anecdote, haiku?—called 'Behind the Front.' Nothing flashy, no rhetorical fatty tissue, just bone words. It helps to know, of course, that husband and wife are living in East Germany and that on Aug. 20, 1968, at night, East German, Bulgarian, Polish, Hungarian and Soviet troops marched into Czechoslovakia and got rid of Alexander Dubcek because 'he hadn't shown the necessary severity toward the class enemy.'"

Leonard also comments on Kunze's unusual literary style, marveling at his ability to craft powerful stories with ever so few words. "This book is more than economical: it is minimalist prose, moral pointillisme. By comparison, Hemingway was a chatterbox." Noting that Heinrich Böll had called this book 'the fist that weeps,' Leonard observes: "Astonishingly, it is also a fist that laughs. Yes, it reports on the politics, schools, stupidity and repression of East Germany the day before yesterday. But it also reports on raising a teen-age daughter in such an asylum."

Leonard elaborates:

Love of children—their logic, passion, curiosity and impatience—is the watermark and signature of this slim book about a system, anti-Semitic even now, that would turn them into obedient zombies; that would demand they wear "optimistic colors" in the classroom, that would label Pasternak and Solzhenitsyn "scoundrels"; that would outlaw a rock-music group because it hadn't caused a disturbance—"manipulations by the adversary"—and arrest and fine a boy for "Disturbance of Socialist Cooperation" (playing a guitar) and kick someone out of high school for "Theses unsettling to fellow students."

Nothing, we are told, is invented here. At what point has a society—in which the only organ is the state, for which even Bach is dangerous—lied to itself so crudely and systematically that to tell the truth is to appear satirical, that to record the quotidian is to be subversive? "Do you write what's in the newspaper," asks a drunken neighbor, "or what's in real life?" No wonder they had to get him out of there.

"The years may not have been wonderful," Leonard declares as he concludes, "but the book is." It certainly is!

Although Reiner Kunze's most famous book is *The Wonderful Years*, which contains critical insights into life behind the Iron Curtain, his literary output since the mid-1950s consists mostly of poetry. He is also an essayist, a translator of Czech poetry and prose, and the author of a book of children's stories. In this final section of my piece on Kunze, I want to comment on his poetry.

Haiku, a traditional form of Japanese unrhymed verse, emphasizes simplicity, intensity, and directness of expression. These are also characteristics of Kunze's poetic works, along with brevity and sensitivity. But he is not a haiku poet; he is a minimalist who manages to create powerful and often beautiful poetic images with few words. Take, for example, this poem which is about how a writer (presumably Kunze) sometimes has to wait patiently for inspiration and ideas:

REASONS FOR TAKING CARE OF THE CAR

You in the garage again!
(my daughter, looking at the abandoned desk)

Because
of the long distances, child

Because of the distances
between one word and the other

Kunze's most famous poem is *rudern zwei* (two rowing), which he wrote in 1956. It is a love poem that over the years has been popularized in the German-speaking world and is frequently read or recited on special occasions, such as marriage ceremonies and wedding anniversaries. Below is my translation of this poetic gem, which metaphorically presents a couple living and working together harmoniously, sharing important responsibilities, and thereby moving forward in life despite the trials and tribulations that are part of any romantic union:

TWO ROWING

Two rowing
a boat.
One

knows about stars,
the other one
knows about storms.
When one
navigates by the stars,
the other one
navigates through the storms.
And at the end, at the very end,
they will remember the sea
was blue.

In May 2013, I received a message from Andreas W. Mytze, editor-in-chief of a London-based literary magazine, *europäische ideen* (european ideas), which has literature and politics as its central focus. Mytze told me he was planning to commemorate Reiner Kunze's 80th birthday, upcoming on August 16, 2013, by publishing a special issue of his journal with short messages by friends of Kunze and other well-wishers, around twenty persons altogether. He invited me to contribute something (an anecdote, perhaps) and I readily accepted. The title of my contribution to Issue 155, *Reiner Kunze 80,* is "My Visit with *Dissident* East German Writer Reiner Kunze, Way Back Then."

Kunze received Issue 155 of Mytze's publication with an assortment of congratulatory messages in the second week of August. A week after his birthday, a mail packet from his home address arrived at my office at the University of Delaware. Inside I discovered a slim booklet with three short poems by Kunze printed on separate pages, a limited edition of 700 copies for booklovers, each numbered and signed by the author. Mine is number 410, and on the first inside page there is a nice message from the author: "Dear Mr. Zipser, Reiner Kunze thanks you very much, in August 2013." Reiner and his wife Elisabeth had this special booklet made to commemorate their 80th birthdays. The last page has a photo of the two of them, who had been together at that time for about fifty years. As I viewed the photo of them again while working on this piece, the love poem *two rowing* came instantly to mind.

GÜNTER KUNERT

Günter Kunert (1929-2019), poet, novelist, essayist, screenplay writer, and graphic artist is considered to be one of the most profound and prolific German writers of the post-war era. He was born in Berlin, where he spent five semesters studying at the Academy for Applied Arts following World War II. He turned to freelance writing in 1947 and in 1949 he joined the SED Party. His first volume of poetry, published in 1950, was seen as heralding the arrival of a fresh generation of writers whose works would celebrate the deeds and aspirations of the newly created GDR. Kunert's early writings supported the ideology and growth of the new socialist republic, but as political convictions and concerns began to influence his artistic expression in the 1960s, he became increasingly critical of socialism and pessimistic in his writings. Confrontations with East German government and cultural authorities led to his expulsion from the SED Party in 1977 and prompted his decision in 1979 to live in self-imposed "exile" in West Germany.

Kunert's sphere of influence as a writer extended beyond his homeland. His poetry volume, *Erinnerung an einen Planeten* (Memory of a Planet), was published in West Germany in 1963. From that time on an increasing proportion of his books appeared in West German editions. His published work includes numerous volumes of poetry, a novel, many books of short prose, a volume of essays on writing, and a number of screenplays, librettos, and radio plays. Several of his books, including *Der andere Planet: Ansichten von Amerika* (The Other Planet: Views about America, 1975) were printed simultaneously in both Germanys. This book in particular, which he began writing in 1972 while he was a visiting associate professor at the University of Texas at Austin, showcases his satirical sense of humor and his extraordinary ability as a prose writer to present a critical reflection of reality.

Americans, especially, will enjoy reading Günter Kunert's *Der andere Planet*, which is an unusual example of GDR travel writing. It presents Kunert's views on America and his insights into aspects of the American way of life, based on his personal experiences while living and travelling in the United States. He is a keen observer, not uncritical, who is unabashedly fascinated by many of the things he discovers in this country.

Der andere Planet enables us to accompany Günter Kunert and his wife Marianne as they explore Texas and various places in the United States, viewing and taking in America with East German eyes. The first GDR author to visit the United States, Kunert shares their experiences, impressions, and memories with us, making no effort to be objective, for—as he observes in the foreword—in spite of all our efforts, objectivity is not within our power. The book consists of forty-four short prose pieces, each one devoted to some aspect of Americana the author wants to highlight. Here are some of his topics: *Kennedy Airport, Austin (Texas), Campus, Padre Island, New Orleans, Santa Fe, Iowa City, In the White House, Impressions of Washington, Subway, Empire State Building, Wall Street,* and *Times Square.* Since this book has not been translated into English, possibly because of the complexity of Kunert's writing style, I decided to translate one of the pieces and present the complete text here for readers to enjoy.

Empire State Building

Tower of superlatives. The highest in the world. One hundred and two floors. From the tip of its antenna Mannix and Cannon (or whatever names the current heroes and detectives may have) are able to reach eight million televisions in four states. You can still see ships at sea that are more than sixty kilometers off in the distance. Seventy-two elevators. The express lifts race upwards at ninety kilometers an hour; their floor counters start working at number 72, and despite the speed they ascend in such a gentle way that, apart from the pressure on your eardrum due to the difference in altitude, you do not sense the upwards thrust.

65,000 windows: cleaned twice each month, a housewife's nightmare. 1860 stairs from street level up to the top floor: recommended for the training of mountain climbers who stayed home. 1600 employees work in this layered honeycomb, in this vertical small town, for which a term like "house" would sound like good-natured irony: that phenomenal structure weighs 365,000 tons; 14 tons of subflooring per person, not including cleaning personnel and the 35,000 daily visitors, among whom we also appear and help generate the numerical statistics, get on, get off, complete the tour, as the rules in force for world travelers have dictated.

But it turns out that the megalomania of the building produces the opposite effect. Not being overwhelmed by the sight of incomprehensible physical size. Instead of that (and related to the same feeling that is brought about by a suddenly unveiled secret) an encompassing of Manhattan, compellingly and affectionately: comprehending its small size for which its undeniably cosmic diversity compensates. The secret of this place is its resemblance to the universe, albeit limited by the inverse formula: limited, but infinite. How the sight of the nocturnal sky stimulates one's imagination (and has stimulated generations before us) to speculate about the possible and hidden, inconceivably divergent forms of life, just like that looking down from the Empire State Building triggers unclear visions, indefinite associations: as if one were standing on a pyramid of bodies, of human lives, of existences, each individual a resource never to be detected, each individual differing from each individually, under dissimilar circumstances present down there; the inestimable number of their dwellings, cellars, attics, backrooms, penthouses, basements, caverns, grottos, chambers, garages, hallways, stairs, sitting rooms, studios, stores, storage rooms, crammed with the vestiges of all epochs: a museum is situated at our feet, not at any time entirely fathomable, exactly like the realm at our heads to which we have just come twelve hundred and fifty feet closer. Up here one feels the allure of this exaggerated settlement, akin to that of other spaces in which the passion for discovery remains eternally unappeased, the farther it penetrates and presses forward, not deterred by any danger. Behind the thermoglass of the southern side darkish silhouettes: the setting sun casts a shadow across the facades facing the city; in return, the water from the Hudson and East Rivers at the confluence of the Upper Bay pure tin foil, slightly crinkled, a surface of dazzling reflection, and on this surface tiny among other tinies: Liberty Island with the freedom statue, clear cut in front of the marvelous background, a chess piece of the cosmic dwarfs, presumably: the Queen. (*Der andere Planet*. Munich and Vienna: Carl Hanser, 1975. 170-71)

Believe me, this is a terrific book! If you decide to read some of Kunert's works, start here!

As I mentioned at the beginning of this piece, Günter Kunert was a graphic artist as well as one of the most important German writers of the post-war period. Let me now add that Kunert was an extremely talented and accomplished artist whose artworks complemented his literary works. When I visited the Kunerts at their villa in Berlin-Buch in the 1970s, one of the first things I noticed was that their home resembled an art gallery. Works of art, presumably all or mostly by Kunert, were on prominent display, as were two of their many collections: original tin toys and blue cobalt glassware items of various sorts. Also and always present were the cats he and Marianne "collected" (six at that time) and loved so much. Later on, I would be introduced to some of their other collections—e.g., antique dolls and peaked (service) caps. Kunert enjoyed collecting and liked being in the company of objects, more so than people, for a reason. "Human beings lie," he explained, "objects never lie." I spent many pleasurable hours with the Kunerts in their beautiful home, which was decorated with uncommon good taste. Being with them in those surroundings gave me a sense of what a literary salon might have been like in pre-World War I Berlin. Looking back and remembering, I imagine that it must have been extremely difficult for the Kunerts to say goodbye to this elegant dwelling when in 1979 they moved in self-imposed "exile" to a remote village (Kaisborstel) in the northern state of Schleswig-Holstein, West Germany.

Let me conclude this snapshot in a different way and cite two book dedications I received from Günter Kunert back in the late 1970s. One is his amusing pen sketch of a "German democratic flower" on the first page of his 1967 novel, *Im Namen der Hüte* (In the Name of Hats). The second is on the inside title page of his volume of essays on writing, *Warum schreiben* (Why write, 1976). As an afterthought Kunert asks, "and why read?" Food for thought!

JOACHIM WALTHER

June 12, 2020, 9:20 AM. My East German friend and colleague, Heinz-Uwe Haus, sends me a link to an article that appeared in the "Cultural Enjoyment" section of the online *Berliner-Zeitung* (Berlin Newspaper). The article is entitled "Der Zuständige – zum Tod von Joachim Walther" ("The Person in Charge—upon the Death of Joachim Walther). Written by Ines Geipel on May 19, 2020, it announces the death on the previous day of former GDR author Joachim Walther and pays tribute to him. Geipel, an author and professor who spent the first thirty years of her life in the GDR, collaborated with Walther on various projects over a fifteen-year period. From 2001 to 2005, they set about collecting texts that 100 or so writers had been unable to publish in communist East Germany and established an Archive of Suppressed Literature in the GDR (Archiv unterdrückter Literatur in der DDR). They then began publishing some of the texts from the archive in a book series entitled *Die Verschwiegene Bibliothek* (The Concealed Library); ten volumes appeared in print between 2005 and 2009. The material in the archive led them to undertake yet another project, the publication of a co-edited book entitled *Die Gesperrte Ablage: Unterdrückte Literaturgeschichte in*

Ostdeutschland 1945-1989 (The Locked Repository: History of Suppressed Literature in East Germany 1945-1989, Düsseldorf: Lilienfeld Press, 2015).

Joachim Walther (b. 1943) had a distinguished and multifaceted career in East Germany initially, and later in unified Germany, as free-lance author, editor, scholar, researcher and chronicler of the relationship between GDR writers and the Stasi. In 1996, he published his landmark study, *Sicherungsbereich Literatur: Schriftsteller und Staatssicherheit in der Deutschen Demokratischen Republik* (Security Zone Literature: Writers and State Security in the German Democratic Republic, Berlin: Ch. Links). This 888-page book documents and analyzes how the Stasi went about implement-ing and enforcing the SED Party's cultural policies in the realm of literature, how it monitored and tried to influence and control GDR writers. Walther, who worked as an editor for the Berlin publishing house Buchverlag Der Morgen (Book Publishing of Tomorrow) from 1968 to 1983, had been forced to resign from that position due to his bold opposition to censorship and related issues. He began working on this meticulously researched documen-tary work shortly after the reunification of the two Germanys in 1990 and was given full access to the secret police files of all former GDR writers. His government-financed assignment was to use those documents to determine the nature of the relationship and level of collaboration between GDR writers and the state secret police agency commonly called the Stasi. He was the only author to have direct access to all of this highly confidential information; he was indeed the "person in charge."

One day, as I was thinking about *Sicherungsbereich Literatur* (Security Zone Literature) and what a magnificent contribution it makes to our knowl-edge and understanding of one of the darkest aspects of GDR history, it occurred to me that I should look for references to other US Germanists in the index to Walther's book, just out of curiosity. In the 1970s and 1980s, the number of US Germanists with a serious interest in GDR literature was not too large, and over the years I had become acquainted with most of them. With the help of US publications such as *Studies in GDR Culture and Society*, collections of papers presented at the annual New Hampshire symposia on the German Democratic Republic, *GDR Bulletin*, and *GDR Monitor*, I made a list of colleagues who had been active in the area of GDR studies in the 1970s and 1980s. When I completed that exercise, the list had more than thirty names on it. I then proceeded to look up each of those names in the index to Walther's book, hoping to find references to some of them. To my surprise and bewilderment, only one US Germanist is cited in that index: Richard Zipser. I have done a great deal of thinking about that and have come to this conclusion: There was only one US Germanist who had engaged in what the Stasi considered to be subversive activities in the GDR, and only one had been considered an enemy of the GDR state. Today, as before, I am proud of the fact that the vast majority of the GDR writers I knew and worked with on various book projects in the 1970s, 1980s, and 1990s viewed me and my work on East German literature in a very different—i.e., positive, light.

As early as April 1974, at the time when I first became interested in GDR literature, Joachim Walther had an important influence on my own work. His third book was a volume of conversations with East German writers which he published in 1973 under the title *Meinetwegen Schmetterlinge* (For All I Care, Butterflies). Christa and Gerhard Wolf, who were both in residence at Oberlin College that spring, had brought with them a small library of GDR literary works which they intended to use in their colloquium and then donate to the College upon their departure. Walther's book was one of the first they gave me to read and discuss with them, since his interviews with fourteen authors and his conversation with himself provide a splendid introduction to GDR literature from the perspective of insiders. Each interview has an informal tone and format, as Walther roams from one topic to the next. The writers respond to his questions directly and openly, presenting their views and convictions without being dogmatic. They talk about the craft of writing, how they actually go about it, what they hope to accomplish as writers, and they also mention some things that please and aggravate them. I read this book more than once, from cover to cover; the information in it was very useful to me when I began to design the project I would begin carrying out in 1975-1976 while on sabbatical leave. I decided that I wanted to do a project on GDR literature that would involve living writers who were active in the 1970s, with whom I would be able to interact in various ways. One way of interacting, reflecting Walther's influence, would be by conducting an interview with each author, something I hoped to do in person. I would also ask each interviewee to provide me with a literary text dealing with an issue in GDR society that was of current concern to him/her as a writer. These texts would supplement the information presented in the interviews, and together this material would give readers a comprehensive overview of GDR writing in the 1970s and the issues that were of concern to writers of different political persuasions. My ambitious project eventually culminated in a three-volume, 840-page book written entirely in German and published in 1985. The title is *DDR-Literatur im Tauwetter* (GDR Literature During the Thaw). I am indebted to Joachim Walther for inspiring me through his own work on "Butterflies" to undertake and bring this documentary book on an important period in GDR literary history to fruition.

I regret that I never had an opportunity to meet and converse at length with Joachim Walther, whose research interests and work as a scholar overlapped with mine in many areas. He was interested in documenting and exposing acts of suppression and repression by the GDR's SED regime. He actively opposed all forms of literary censorship, the banning of books, the harassment of intellectuals who dared to criticize governmental actions, and the harsher punishments that were meted out to dissident writers by government officials and the Stasi (e.g., house arrest, imprisonment, forced exile). He wanted to chronicle all of this for future generations, so what actually happened in communist eastern Germany between 1945 and 1990 would not be forgotten. In post-unification Germany, from 1990 to the present day, there have been many attempts by former GDR authorities and GDR loyalists to suppress the truth and rewrite history and literary history, to sugarcoat the indisputable historical record and present the criminality of the SED regime and its servants as understandable and acceptable. Joachim Walther was a person of extraordinary integrity and determination, who was unrelenting in his pursuit of the truth. For uncovering the truth and presenting it in an unvarnished, objective way—time and again during his fifty-year career as a writer—, we who are opposed to dictatorships are deeply indebted to him.

On June 12, 2020, I received a second announcement of Walther's death, this time from my publisher in Berlin, Christoph Links, who sent out a general message to persons associated with Ch. Links Publishing expressing his sorrow. (I should note that Links is a former East German citizen and the person who was responsible for the publication of Walther's monumental work, *Security Zone Literature*.) Although no response was expected, I immediately sent the following message to Links:

Dear Christoph Links,

I am also deeply saddened to learn that Joachim Walther has died at such a young age. In 1974 I read his book of interviews with writers, *For All I Care, Butterflies*, which prompted me to become involved intensively with GDR literature. I had great admiration for him and his standard book, *Security Zone Literature*. With this exhaustive documentary work he left behind something important for mankind. You too can be very proud of this permanent contribution to German history.

Kind regards,

Richard Zipser

On July 7, a Tuesday, I was pleasantly surprised to receive the following message from Christoph Links, who had been away on vacation during the second half of June:

Dear Richard Zipser,

Last Friday, on the occasion of the urn burial, we bid farewell to Joachim Walther with a dignified funeral service at the Luther-Cemetery here in Berlin. While doing that I tried to pay tribute to his lifetime achievements in a short speech at the end of which I quoted from your email. His wife and son were very interested in that and asked me to forward the email to them, which I have done in the meantime. So you were present after all at our ceremony.

With kind regards for old times' sake,

Yours,

Christoph Links

The remaining four of my favorite GDR writers—Christa Wolf, Ulrich Plenzdorf, Jurek Becker, and Stefan Heym—I have profiled in the previous section, VI GDR WRITERS IN OHIO.

CHRISTA WOLF

See above, VI GDR WRITERS IN OHIO

ULRICH PLENZDORF

See above, VI GDR WRITERS IN OHIO

JUREK BECKER

See above, VI GDR WRITERS IN OHIO

STEFAN HEYM

See above, VI GDR WRITERS IN OHIO

RECOMMENDED READINGS

For English-speaking readers who are not proficient in German, I have assembled a list of recommended East German literary works. The ten books on this list are personal favorites of mine and excellent examples of the high-quality, politically engaged literature that was produced in the German Democratic Republic (GDR), especially in the 1960s and 1970s. All of these books are available in English translation; specific information on the translated versions is available at the end of this piece.

The first three works are novels by Stefan Heym, Christa Wolf, and Jurek Becker, masterful storytellers whose prose fiction works brought them far-reaching international acclaim. The authors of the next two books—Stefan Heym and Ulrich Plenzdorf—make creative use of literary precedents to link the GDR of the early 1970s to England and Germany of the 18th century. They draw parallels to well-known prose works by Daniel Defoe and Johann Wolfgang von Goethe, in order to give readers a critical view of the contemporary GDR at that time. Sarah Kirsch, well known in Europe as a lyric poet and short story writer, is represented with both prose texts and poetry on my list. *The Panther Woman* presents her in-depth, tape-recorded interviews with five working women in the GDR, who offer us a glimpse into their personal and work lives. *Catlives* is a collection of poems that draws upon the poet's personal experience of the natural world and emphasizes subjective approaches to reality. In their works, Volker Braun and Reiner Kunze lay bare the harsh realities of daily life behind the Iron Curtain under the GDR's dictatorial brand of socialism. Kunze's minimalistic prose pieces in *The Wonderful Years* reveal what life was really like in the GDR for everyday people—school children, teachers, youth, writers—in common settings such as home, school, and workplace. Braun's novella, *Unfinished Story*, offers a realistic portrayal of an East German state inclined to distrust, restrict, and if need be ruin the lives of its young people for no good reason. Together, Braun and Kunze provide a devastating critique of a political system and society that is prepared to ruthlessly grind up basically innocent people.

Monika Maron's *Flight of Ashes*, her first novel, was born of her experiences as a serious investigative journalist, an unconventional and somewhat risky career choice for a free-lance writer in the GDR. This novel was completed in the late 1970s and lay for two years in the desk drawer, before being published in West Germany in 1981. Her novels could not be published in East Germany, where she lived, not because she attacked socialism but because the authorities thought her depictions of life under socialism were too negative.

Recommendations for Further Reading

5 Days in June
5 Tage im Juni (1956)
Stefan Heym (1913-2001)

Stefan Heym, one of the most significant German writers of the 20th century, settled in the GDR in 1952, moving back to the part of his native Germany where he was born after spending years in exile. As a result of his increasingly critical engagement with social and political conditions in that country, he quickly came into conflict with the ruling communist authorities. The first major altercation occurred in 1956 when his novel *5 Days in June* was rejected for publication in the GDR. This novel is a fictionalized account, based on firsthand or near-firsthand recollections of the workers' mass uprising in East Berlin against communist rule in 1953. The riots began among construction workers who took to the streets to protest an increase in work schedules by the communist government of East Germany. Soviet troops, supported by tanks and armored vehicles, quickly crushed the rebellion. Heym's novel humanizes this historical event by focusing on men and women who were caught up in the bloody demonstrations of June 16 and 17, 1953. The novel was banned in Soviet-occupied East Germany, but a German-language edition was published in West Germany in 1956. This work is the earliest and arguably the finest example of East German dissident literature during the communist era; it established Heym's reputation as both an advocate for human rights and a rebellious, fearless critic of the GDR's ruling SED Party.

He would remain a thorn in the side of the dictatorial government until the GDR was dissolved in 1990.

The Quest for Christa T.
Nachdenken über Christa T. (1968)
Christa Wolf (1929-2011)

Christa Wolf, one of the most accomplished German writers of the post-World War II period, spent her childhood years under Hitler and in time of war. In 1949 she began studying literature, first at the University of Jena, then at the University of Leipzig, receiving her diploma in 1953. She then worked as an editor and in the early 1960s published her first prose works, a novella and a novel, for which she was awarded prizes. Her third book, *The Quest for Christa T.* (1968), became a bestseller in its West German editions. When this novel was first published in East Germany, it immediately created a storm. It was viciously attacked at the 1968 meeting of the GDR Writers Congress, and it was condemned by government officials who eventually banned it. Even though it has nothing explicit to say about politics in the GDR, Wolf's *Christa T.*, its main character, and its author stirred up leaders of the ruling SED Party and made them apprehensive. On the surface it is a straightforward story of the unremarkable life of an introspective young woman growing up in Nazi Germany, then dying at age thirty-one in communist East Germany. Beneath the surface it is a firsthand, subjective account of everyday life in a repressive society that does not tolerate persons who question socialist beliefs and the way of living in a socialist state that expects all its citizens to conform. Christa T. is shown to be an unfortunate victim of this restrictive society.

Jacob the Liar
Jakob der Lügner (1969)
Jurek Becker (1937-1997)

Jurek Becker was a friend of mine. In addition to being an exceptional prose writer, he was a very likeable man, with a marvelous sense of humor, a great deal of personal warmth and charm, and a wonderful knack for telling stories. He was also candid, outspoken, and not afraid to express his views on controversial topics, such as problems in GDR society and his country's oppressive system of government.

International recognition came to Becker following the publication of his first book, *Jacob the Liar* (1969). This powerful Holocaust novel is set in an unnamed Jewish ghetto in German-occupied Poland, near the close of World War II. At the center of the story is a Jew, Jacob Heym, who accidentally overhears a German radio broadcast announcing that the Soviet Army is slowly advancing toward their town. The next day, when his comrade Mischa prepares to risk his life by stealing a few potatoes from the German commissary, Jacob tells him what he heard. He then lies to Mischa, telling him in confidence that he has a radio—in the ghetto a crime punishable by death. Word of Jacob's secret spreads quickly, and Jacob realizes that his lies give hope to his fellow Jews who now have the prospect of liberation to live for. Jacob finds himself in the uncomforting position of having to dream up more and more optimistic lies.

In November 1976, Becker became embroiled in a human rights conflict with the GDR authorities. In the ensuing months, he resigned from the GDR Writers' Union, was thrown out of the SED Party, and then barred from making public appearances and publishing his writing in the GDR. In December 1977, Becker moved from East to West Berlin.

The Queen against Defoe
Die Schmähschrift oder Königin gegen Defoe (1970)
Stefan Heym (1913-2001)

The Queen Against Defoe recounts English writer Daniel Defoe's clash with nobility and clergy during the reign of Queen Anne following the anonymous publication of his pamphlet, *The Shortest Way with the Dissenters* (1702). By appearing to support the English Establishment in the most exaggerated terms, Defoe satirized the extremist position of many high churchmen and Tories on the question of how to deal with religious dissent. The anonymous author was denounced as an enemy of Church and State. After Defoe's identity was discovered, he was eventually captured and made to stand trial. Defoe was persuaded to plead guilty. Subsequently, he was fined 200 marks, condemned to be pilloried three times, and sentenced to indefinite imprisonment. His exposure in the pillory, however, was more a triumph than a physical punishment or public humiliation, for the common people took his side and protected him from bodily harm. Heym's historical novella is concerned chiefly with the role of literature and the problems facing writers in states which attempt to restrict artistic freedom. Not only is Defoe portrayed as a pillar of strength in the battle against his oppressors, but he is also shown to achieve that elusive socialist goal—the solidarity of proletariat and intellectuals—through his courageous defiance of the Establishment. Like Defoe some three centuries earlier, Stefan Heym did not shy away from political conflict and controversy, and he, too, preferred to suffer the consequences rather than compromise himself as a writer. Fortunately, unlike Defoe, he was never imprisoned.

The New Sufferings of Young W.
Die neuen Leiden des jungen W. (1972)
Ulrich Plenzdorf (1934-2007)

Ulrich Plenzdorf, prose writer, playwright, and film scenarist, contributed greatly to the jeans mania that swept the GDR in the 1970s. His controversial novel, *The New Sufferings of Young W.* (1972), made its author famous overnight and became one of the most widely-read works ever published in the GDR. The story parallels and parodies Goethe's epistolary masterpiece, *The Sufferings of Young Werther* (1774).

The main character is 17-year-old Edgar Wibeau, a model all-GDR boy: disciplined, clean-cut, obedient. But all of a sudden he gets fed up with the restrictiveness of socialist society and the conformity it demands of every citizen. He drops out of school and flees to Berlin, where he lives alone in a garden house and proceeds to do all the things he always wanted to do previously but never could. In a long soliloquy, Edgar expounds on the topic of blue jeans, "the greatest pants in the world," which symbolize his rebellion and new-found freedom.

Edgar Wibeau, one of the most intriguing characters in all of GDR literature, is a frustrated teenager who rebels against the conformity that was so prevalent in every segment of GDR society. While he is not against socialism per se, he is in favor of almost everything the SED Party officials and others in positions of power were against. He wants to live a life without rigid constraints and picky regulations, opting instead for individualism and creative self-expression, while rejecting phoniness and stodginess in favor of that which is genuine and natural.

The Panther Woman: Five Tales from the Cassette Recorder
Die Pantherfrau: Fünf Frauen in der DDR (1973)
Sarah Kirsch (1935-2013)

Sarah Kirsch gained initial prominence in the 1960s as one of a group of GDR poets who challenged the official cultural-political dictate that literature should primarily reinforce the values and reflect the achievements of socialist society. In 1960 she joined a group of other aspiring poets who collectively charted a new direction in GDR poetry. Their poems emphasized subjective approaches to reality as opposed to ideological affirmations of socialist society. From 1965 until 1977 she lived as a free-lance writer in Halle and East Berlin. In August 1977, after the government authorities prohibited her from publishing and participating in public events in the GDR, she and her son Moritz moved without fanfare to West Berlin. Her published work in the GDR includes numerous volumes of poetry, a volume of short fiction, and a book containing portraits in prose of several East German women, *The Panther Woman*.

Kirsch's *Panther Woman* contains her in-depth, tape-recorded interviews with five contemporary East German women. These women offer us "uncombed" glimpses into their personal and work lives, and their intimate portraits enable us to enter into the experience of working and living in the GDR. The first to be interviewed is a tamer of circus panthers who speaks with surprising candor about everyday life in East Germany. The other voices are those of a bureaucrat, a historian, a businesswoman, and a factory worker. In the introduction to her translation of this work, Marion Faber writes: "Reading these five accounts, we learn much about the inner workings of circus life, the East German business world, the arduous nature of factory work. Furthermore, we gain a better idea of patterns of education in the GDR, work conditions, government controls, the demands made on personal life, and the range of individual aspirations within the socialist structure." (Lincoln and London: University of Nebraska Press, 1989. viii) Taken as a whole, these five interviews with women give us a better, fuller, and remarkably humane view of East German society.

Unfinished Story
Unvollendete Geschichte (1975)
Volker Braun (1939-)

In 1965, after studying philosophy at the University of Leipzig, Volker Braun moved to East Berlin where he earned his living as a free-lance writer and as a dramaturg with the famous Berlin Ensemble. His published work includes several volumes of poetry, a number of plays, volumes of notes and essays, and a highly controversial novella, *Unfinished Story*.

The plot of Braun's novella is not complicated. Karin, the eighteen-year-old daughter of a local official, is in love with Frank, a telecommunications worker. But Frank's family and personal background are somewhat suspect, with vague indications of criminality. While Frank is not a real troublemaker, he is also not an exemplary member of the socialist state. He has received letters from the West, enough to make him a suspicious figure in the minds of the authorities. Karin is pressured to stop seeing him, and she does for a while. But, true love prevails and she continues to be torn between her love for Frank and the demands of parents and society. Karin gets pregnant, Frank attempts suicide and winds up in a coma.

Basically, Karin and Frank are both victims of their innocence; they cannot survive because they are unable to comprehend the system. When

Karin is working as a volunteer for a newspaper, she learns the necessity of making compromises when she is told what is suitable to print and what is not; but, she neither understands nor accepts the reasoning behind these decisions which strike her as absurd. Both Karin and Frank are unable to adjust to the restrictive requirements of the system, as their parents and bosses have done. They are unable to adapt and therefore destined to succumb to a system that is cruel and corrupt.

Volker Braun's *Unfinished Story* provided a powerful critique of the mentality of persons in positions of authority in the GDR. Karin and her boyfriend Frank have their lives ruined by authorities who are unwilling to trust their loyalty, preferring suspicion and control to open dialogue. The story, which is based on a true story, is unfinished because it is not resolved whether the situation can be set right or not. Here, more forcefully than elsewhere, Braun is urging the GDR's leaders to make what he considers to be essential systemic changes that will lead to a more humane socialist society in their country. The collapse of the Berlin Wall in 1989 and the demise of the GDR in 1990 revealed that his public outcry for reforms had fallen on deaf ears.

The Wonderful Years
Die wunderbaren Jahre (1976)
Reiner Kunze (1933-)

Reiner Kunze was a dissident writer who stood up to the GDR's power elite and was harshly punished for doing so. His major confrontation with the GDR authorities was precipitated by the Soviet-led invasion of Czechoslovakia on August 20, 1968, which he protested publicly and vociferously. Thereafter, his writings—with one exception—were no longer published in the GDR and he was not allowed to read from his works or speak in public. This severe form of censorial repression, imposed by the government, was just a step away from incarceration. The purpose was to discipline Kunze for his oppositional behavior, silence him, and prevent him from earning a living.

Kunze's most famous book is *The Wonderful Years*, a volume of short fiction which contains critical insights into life behind the Iron Curtain.

In 1976, following its unauthorized publication in West Germany, Kunze expected to be arrested. Instead, the GDR authorities impounded his passport and in April 1977 forced him into exile.

New York Times cultural critic John Leonard comments on Kunze's unusual literary style, marveling at his ability to craft powerful stories with very few words: "This book is more than economical: it is minimalist prose, moral pointillisme." Leonard has this to say about the content: "Love of children—their logic, passion, curiosity and impatience—is the watermark and signature of this slim book about a system, anti-Semitic even now, that would turn them into obedient zombies." (April 21, 1977)

Those years were not wonderful, but this book certainly is!

Flight of Ashes
Flugasche (1981)
Monika Maron (1941-)

On the back side of this book's dust jacket, we learn that Monika Maron is a daughter of the East German political élite. Her father, Karl Maron, was involved in founding the German Democratic Republic and served as Minister of the Interior in the infancy of the new communist state. Although she was raised in a communist household, Maron's novel breaks decisively with the prescribed silences of her sociopolitical milieu—on censorship and self-censorship, the press, the SED Party, the position and exploitation of women, environmental problems and policies, and the real lives of workers in a Workers' State. In doing so, she gives us a thoughtful, passionate and completely candid view of one person's struggle to live and work honestly behind the Wall.

Completely new here is Maron's in-depth critical treatment of one of the most pressing environmental issues in her country—pollution from brown coal and its deadly impact on East Germans' health and quality of life, a topic GDR journalists and writers had hitherto avoided addressing directly in their writing. The main character is Josefa Nader, a 30-year-old newspaper journalist who leads a lonely life as a divorced working mother with a young son. A business trip to the filthy industrial city of B. (Bitterfeld) in the brown coal mining region of East Germany challenges her moral and political assumptions and precipitates a life-altering personal and professional crisis. Josefa tries to write a truthful feature article about an old, unsafe filth-spewing power plant in B. that should—but supposedly for economic reasons cannot—be shut down. A conflict with the Party leadership ensues when Josefa—unable to call attention to this problem in the press—sends the GDR's Supreme Council a letter informing them about "omissions in the building of socialism" (135) at the power plant. Her unwanted report on a serious problem the government already knows about but prefers to continue ignoring leads to a surprising conclusion.

Catlives
Katzenleben: Gedichte (1984)
Sarah Kirsch (1935-2013)

As noted in the introduction to *The Panther Woman*, Sarah Kirsch emigrated to West Berlin in August 1977. In 1978, thanks to a grant from the government, she was able to spend a half year as artist in residence at the German Academy in Rome at Villa Massimo. The stay at Villa Massimo enabled Sarah to devote herself to writing again, after several years of emotional and mental turmoil, and it marked the beginning of a new chapter in her personal and professional life. At the Villa she met and become romantically involved with a young German composer, Wolfgang von Schweinitz, who returned to Berlin with her. Sarah's life then went in a different direction. She and Wolfgang decided to move away from Berlin and its many distractions that made it very difficult for Sarah to write. They relocated and embraced a different style of life in the rural township of Bothel in Lower Saxony. Sarah craved the solitude of nature which stimulated her creativity more than anything else. While living in the peaceful countryside with Wolfgang, son Moritz, her mother, and their cats, she wrote the powerful collection of 86 poems that were published under the title *Catlives*. In her foreword to *Catlives*, Carolyn

Forché writes: "Kirsch begins with what is at hand, the sky coloring, snow in a field, and she follows the tenuous associative thread of her sensory intelligence, finding her concerns in things, rather than appropriating them to serve conscious intentions. Her work is whimsical and dramatic, but never degenerates into the idyllic meanderings of self-absorption." (Translated and edited by Marina Roscher and Charles Fishman. Lubbock: Texas Tech University Press, 1991. v)

In her translator's preface, Marina Roscher tells us the work of Sarah Kirsch is a "powerful poetic presence." (Ibid., 1) "In the present book," she says, "the course of four seasons experienced in a spare countryside provides the poet with opportunities for minute and intimate observations. She focuses on cats, cows, and dogs, on plants and leaves; she assigns to each grass and each weed its own place and its name. Overtly, the poems deal with nature, their environment is bucolic but, . . . they are far from idyllic. . . . The uncanny dwells beneath the surface, and existence is threatened." (Ibid., 1-2)

Sarah Kirsch's readers will see that her poetry is linguistically innovative, intense, and strikingly visual. There are few metaphors in her poems; mostly it is pictures, and concrete imagery conveys the message. The poet succeeds in painting with words to a remarkable degree.

East German Literary Works in English Translation

Becker, Jurek. *Jacob the Liar*, translated by Leila Vennewitz. New York: Plume, 1999.

Braun, Volker. *Unfinished Story*, translated by Richard Urmston. Madison, New Jersey: Drew University, 1979.

Heym, Stefan. *Five Days in June*. London: Hodder and Stoughton, 1977.

Heym, Stefan. *The Queen Against Defoe*. London: Hodder and Stoughton, 1975.

Kirsch, Sarah. *The Panther Woman: Five Tales from the Cassette Recorder*, translated by Marion Faber. Lincoln and London: University of Nebraska Press, 1989.

Kirsch, Sarah. *Catlives*, translated by Marina Roscher and Charles Fishman. Lubbock: Texas Tech University Press, 1991.

Kunze, Reiner. *The Wonderful Years*, translated by Joachim Neugroschel. New York: George Braziller, 1977.

Maron, Monika. *Flight of Ashes*, translated by David Marinelli. London and New York: Readers International, 1986.

Plenzdorf, Ulrich. *The New Sufferings of Young W.*, translated by Kenneth Wilcox. New York: Frederick Ungar, 1979.

Wolf, Christa. *The Quest for Christa T.*, translated by Christopher Middleton. New York: Farrar, Straus and Giroux, 1970.

VIII
EXPERIENCES

HOSPITAL STAY

According to the visa in my passport, I travelled to East Berlin from Vienna on March 22, 1976, to continue work on my book project on GDR literature during the thaw. For this visit, I had booked a room in Interhotel Berolina, where I had resided in November 1975. This hotel was centrally located and had convenient parking, which made it an ideal place to stay while carrying out the next stage of my project. However, due to illness I had to cancel most of my appointments with East German writers and return to Vienna prematurely.

I have very unpleasant memories of this visit to East Berlin. When I became ill, I foolishly continued working on my project, which caused my health problem to worsen rapidly. Eventually, the Plenzdorfs took me to the emergency room of the Friedrichshain Municipal Hospital for treatment. After examining me, the doctor recommended that I be admitted immediately to the hospital, since I needed an operation and was not strong enough to drive back to Vienna. What a situation! I had no choice in the matter, so

I entered the hospital without returning to my hotel and remained there for a week.

Three writers were especially kind to me in this time of need. Ulrich Plenzdorf let Christa Wolf and Jurek Becker know that I was in the hospital, and he also called all the writers I was scheduled to visit and cancelled the appointments. Christa Wolf went to Interhotel Berolina and was permitted to pack my clothes and belongings, which the hotel stored in a secure place. A week later, when I was feeling somewhat better, Jurek Becker came to the hospital and drove me to Hotel Berolina, where I settled my bill, retrieved my belongings, and then headed for West Berlin. In West Berlin, I stayed with a relative for a few days before driving back to Vienna, where I would soon undergo an operation.

Friedrichshain Municipal Hospital had been built in the nineteenth century and was Berlin's first municipal hospital. The construction began in 1868 and was finished in 1874, the year in which the first patients were admitted. It was more than a hundred years old when I was admitted as a patient, truly a relic, and it was in dreadful physical condition and filthy. The hospital had survived the passage of time and World War II, but when I saw it from the inside, I wondered if I would emerge from it alive. This was my first hospital experience since early childhood, and I was terrified. I have three memories of that one-week stay, which I have named isolation, sadism, and death.

Isolation: Friedrichshain Municipal Hospital had extremely limited visiting hours. Visitors were permitted to enter the hospital, as I recall, on Sundays only, and only during a two-hour period in the afternoon. There were no telephones, so direct communication with the outside world was not possible. I could not call my wife in Vienna to let her know what had transpired, so that she would not be trying to reach me at the Hotel Berolina. So there I was, very ill and trapped in the hospital, with an awful sense of isolation.

Sadism: My hospital stay, traumatic as it was, would have been even harder to endure if I had not had a roommate. His name was Siegfried and he had suffered a workplace accident that had led to major abdominal surgery. He had occupied our hospital room by himself for a couple of days before I arrived. The nurse who looked after us during the daytime was ill-tempered and sadistic, as Siegfried and I would discover, and we were at her mercy. One morning this nurse came to our room, said she had some free time and offered to give Siegfried a backrub with alcohol. As Siegfried was trying to sit up, she deliberately spilled alcohol on his incision, which was healing but still an open wound. As Siegfried screamed in pain, the nurse laughed and then left the room.

Death: There was a very frail old man on our floor who needed a gall bladder operation. But the doctors had determined that his heart was so weak that he probably would not survive the operation. They told him that they were not going to perform the surgery, and he related this to Siegfried in the corridor, as we were taking a short stroll. The next day we saw a hospital bed in the corridor, stripped of bed linen and mattress, just a metal bed. The old man had died the night before and it was his bed. Siegfried and I resolved to look after one another and not let them (the doctors, nurses, and hospital) do us in. Both of us were determined to leave that horrible place on our own two feet—and we did!

CARLOS AND THE COCKROACHES

In the fall of 1977, with the support of an IREX (International Research and Exchanges Board) grant I had been awarded in the spring of that year, I returned to East Berlin for a two-month period in order to continue work on a major book project I had initiated in the fall of 1975. The project involved interviewing GDR writers and gathering literary texts and other materials from them; hence, this phase had to be carried out in the GDR. My stay in East Berlin and work as an IREX scholar had the approval of the GDR Ministry of Higher Education and the sponsorship of the Humboldt

University. I was really excited about returning to East Germany and resuming work on the project that later on would become a three-volume book on GDR literature in the 1970s.

The Humboldt University provided me free of charge with a very modest studio apartment in a post-WW II high-rise building located in an area known at that time as the "Hans-Loch-Viertel" (Hans-Loch-Quarter). It was situated in the district of Friedrichsfelde, a good distance away from the center of East Berlin, "Mitte." But the Friedrichsfelde subway station was nearby and I had wisely purchased an older Volkswagen in West Berlin, to ensure that I would not be wholly dependent on public transportation.

The address of this drab concrete apartment house, which is called "Haus Friederieke" today, was and still is Volkradstrasse 8. It had seventeen floors with studio apartments that were occupied by retired individuals and couples, as well as some persons who were still working, and students from socialist and so-called (if I may use the politically incorrect Cold War term) third world countries. This building, erected in the mid-1960s, was an example of East German *Plattenbau* housing. A Plattenbau (Platte + Bau, literally 'panel/slab' + 'building') is a structure constructed of large, prefabricated concrete slabs. In the GDR, Plattenbau areas were designated as *Neubaugebiet* (new development area). Virtually all new residential buildings since the 1960s were built in this style, as it was a quick and relatively inexpensive way to curb the GDR's housing shortage, which had been caused by wartime bombing raids and the large influx of German refugees from countries farther to the east. After reunification, there was far less demand for housing in the communist-era Plattenbau buildings, due in part to their rapid deterioration as a result of cheap and quick construction methods. They were frequently derided as dreary and depressing, and many were demolished or reduced in size.

The students living in this apartment building were all housed on the top two floors. Most of them had full scholarships and were enrolled in graduate-level academic programs at a university or school of advanced studies in East Berlin. The East Germans referred to them as "Aspiranten," since they aspired to attain a doctoral degree. Soon after my arrival at Volkradstrasse 8, I got to know one of the aspirants, a Chilean by the name of Carlos who was a doctoral candidate at the Advanced School of Economics "Bruno Leuschner." He occupied a one-room apartment on the sixteenth floor, diagonally across the hall from mine. During the course of my two-month stay, Carlos and I became friends. We often would get together for a beer or a glass of wine in the evening and talk about life in Chile and the United States and our experiences in East Germany. Carlos felt very much like an outsider in East Berlin; he had not gotten to know any East Germans and was isolated. I enjoyed his company and our conversations, and I learned a lot from him. Indeed, it was Carlos who introduced me to the writings of Pablo Neruda, the Nobel Prize-winning Chilean poet.

I also learned some practical things from Carlos. For example, he told me to be careful around the middle-aged East German woman who occupied one of the apartments on our floor. "She is not a student," he said, "she is a watchdog whose job it is to observe and listen and make sure no one on the two top floors is doing or saying anything subversive." This woman was indeed a minder and probably a secret police informant as well, and—because she had a great deal of power—the foreign students were afraid of her. As aspirants with financial support from the GDR they were all at her mercy, whereas I was not. (I should mention here that, as an IREX scholar, I had been assigned a "Betreuer" or minder by the name of Anneliese Löffler, a professor of GDR literature at the Humboldt University and SED Party loyalist. Löffler was rumored to have close ties to the Stasi, and several East German writers warned me to be careful in conversations with her and not to trust her. I followed their advice and avoided her almost completely during my stay. When the Stasi archives were opened in the 1990s, it was confirmed that Löffler had collaborated extensively with the secret police in various ways.)

Carlos also taught me how to deal with cockroaches, a valuable lesson I remember well. As one entered my apartment there was a hall leading to the one main room where I worked, ate, and slept. On the left side there were two small rooms, first a kitchenette, and then a bathroom. Since I was out and about all day long, living in these cramped quarters didn't bother me much. What did disturb me, however, were the cockroaches that would start running for cover in the kitchen whenever I turned the light on. They were everywhere—on the counter and stove, on the floor, even in the cupboards. But they were not in the mini-refrigerator, so that was where I kept my food safe from the tiny predators.

I told Carlos about the cockroaches and asked him if his apartment was also infested with these filthy insects. He replied that it had been initially, but from his experience in Chile with similar creatures, he knew how to get rid of them. I asked Carlos to share the remedy with me and, mercifully, he did. We entered my apartment and Carlos turned the kitchen light on. This prompted the roaches to race helter-skelter in search of shelter. When all the roaches had disappeared from sight, Carlos told me this: "Cockroaches love darkness and hate the light. The way to get rid of them is to leave your kitchen light on <u>all</u> the time, during the day and night. That's what I do and I never see any roaches." And that's what I did from that day on, and I never saw any more roaches!

What else did I learn from Carlos? He was the first person who made me think seriously about what it means to be an American—and what a privilege that is. In one of our many conversations, Carlos noted that throughout the world everyone refers to US citizens as "Americans." This is not appropriate, he asserted, because in addition to North America we have South and Central America. As a citizen of Chile in South America, he too is an American. The use of the designation "American" should not be limited to citizens of the United States. I asked myself if we had managed, as the wealthiest and most powerful country in the Americas, to appropriate the "American" label for US citizens exclusively? And if so, did this signify that the other Americans on this continent are somehow inferior to us? Food for thought way back then and today as well.

More than forty years have gone by since I last saw Carlos. I'm glad that I got to know him and that he attended the farewell dinner party I had before returning to the US in mid-December, 1977. From time to time, and especially when Chile has been in the news for one reason or another, I have wondered what has become of Carlos. I'm confident that he was able to complete the doctoral program in East Berlin, but what does one do with an advanced degree in Marxian economics? More importantly, if he returned to Chile how did he fare under the brutal dictatorship of Augusto Pinochet with its inhumane practices? What's more, whenever I hear or read the word "cockroach," Carlos and his enlightened remedy come quickly to mind.

VINTAGE PHOTO POSTCARDS

In the hope of finding some then-and-now images of the Hans-Loch-Quarter in Berlin-Lichtenberg's Friedrichsfelde district and the apartment house at Volkradstrasse 8, where I lived for two months in the fall of 1977, I turn to Google Search for assistance. Happily, Google doesn't disappoint me! After a couple of clicks I find myself staring at a vintage postcard with a photo of that drab 17-story concrete "slab building" and a portion of the equally barren neighborhood that surrounded it. The somber black-and-white image dated 1967 comes from the collection of the DDR-Postkarten-Museum (GDR Postcard Museum). Eager to see what that neighborhood looks like today, I click a few more times and am able to view the same apartment house which is now called "Haus Friederieke." Nowadays it stands tall in a park-like setting surrounded by trees and shrubbery. What a difference a color photo and all the greenery make!

I continue clicking on the other postcard images that appeared when I Googled "Hans-Loch-Viertel." They depict numerous Plattenbau buildings of different sizes; most are flat roofed, multistoried, broader than they are tall, and placed within open spaces a good distance away from the sidewalk. I cannot find buildings that do not have a slab-covered façade, and the virtually non-existent landscaping reinforces the impression of monolithic standardization. One of the postcards depicts a small shopping center with a pedestrian zone that was adjacent to the apartment house located at Volkradstrasse 8, which can be seen looming in the background. It immediately triggers a memory.

Gazing at this postcard, I can see part of the entrance to the grocery store where my neighbors and I shopped now and then. It was run by Konsum, a cooperative retail chain that operated restaurants, grocery stores, retail outlets, and industrial plants in East Germany after WW II. This nearby grocery store was a convenient place for me to buy items such as bread, butter, yogurt, and preserves for my breakfast (except for coffee), also beer, which—unlike the East German substitute coffee—was really delicious in the GDR. Whenever I went shopping for groceries, I almost always had to wait in line—and often in a long line—before entering the store. The number of customers inside the store at any given point in time was determined by the number of shopping baskets in circulation at that time. Without a shopping basket, one could not enter the store; that was not permitted. The hand-held baskets were similar to the ones available in our super markets for customers who do not need a large shopping cart. When someone finished shopping and exited the store, s/he placed the basket in a bin beside the entrance. The person who was first in line would pick up the basket and then be admitted to the store. As I would eventually learn, the baskets had another very important function, in addition to regulating customer traffic. They also controlled the amount of food or other items any one individual could buy at one time. The store's shelves were never stocked fully, and some items—e.g., paper goods and especially toilet paper—were always in short supply. Hence, customers were not permitted to purchase a large quantity of any one item, nor could they purchase more items than the basket would hold. The Konsum employees monitored this carefully and enforced the rules strictly. So much for grocery shopping in the GDR!

I resume poring through the vintage postcards with images of the Hans-Loch-Viertel and Friedrichsfelde and come across several black-and-white photos of the Berlin Zoo (Tierpark Berlin). This sprawling landscape zoo is situated on a 400-acre tract of land, just a few hundred meters away from the apartment house I lived in at Volkradstrasse 8. Founded in 1955, it was established originally as a counterpart to the famous but much smaller Berlin Zoological Garden, which was located in what was then West Berlin and soon to be out of reach for residents of East Germany. My memory of the Tierpark in Friedrichsfelde, which I visited only once, is closely linked to what I remember about jogging in East Berlin.

In the 1970s my preferred form of exercise was jogging, and I would take a three-mile run almost every day. While living in the Hans-Loch-Viertel, I tried to go jogging as often as my schedule would permit, usually in the late afternoon. I would put on my jogging outfit and yellow Adidas running shoes, ride the elevator from the sixteenth floor to the lobby, and then jog over to the Berlin Zoo and along its perimeter on the sidewalk. I drew lots of stares inside and outside the apartment house. It was as if my neighbors and the pedestrians I passed by had never seen a jogger—and I think that might actually have been the case. For in the many months I spent in East Germany, I never saw another jogger. Obviously, I stuck out like a sore thumb or, as one reviewer of my memoir *Von Oberlin nach Ostberlin* (From Oberlin to East Berlin) put it, like a "green dog and bright-colored bird." And, perhaps some of the people who stared at me back then thought I belonged in the Zoo!

RESISTANCE AND SOLIDARITY

What do Germany, Vietnam and Korea have in common? In the post-WW II period each of these nations was split into two countries, one of which was **under communist control**, as follows: Germany (**East**-West), Vietnam (**North**-South), and Korea (**North**-South). The unification of Germany occurred in 1990, about one year after the fall of the Berlin Wall, and resulted in a democratic government for the reunified nation. The unification of Vietnam took place in 1975, after the Vietnam War had ended, and left the entire country under communist rule. The Vietnam War was a conflict between the communist Democratic Republic of Vietnam (DRV, also known as North Vietnam), allied with the National Liberation Front (NLF or "Viet Cong"), and the anti-communist Republic of Vietnam (also known as South Vietnam), allied with the United States. It began on November 1, 1955 and ended with a North Vietnamese victory on April 30, 1975. In today's communist-ruled Socialist Republic of Vietnam this conflict is commonly referred to as the American War or the Resistance War Against America. The military involvement of the United States in this conflict, in support of South Vietnam and democracy, commenced in the early 1960s and ended in 1973.

East Germany, officially known as the German Democratic Republic (GDR), was very much involved in the Vietnam War, but not as an active participant. There was some cooperation between the GDR Stasi and the Vietnamese Ministry of Public Security in the late 1950s, and this gained considerable momentum in 1965 after the US intervened in the conflict between North and South Vietnam. From this time on, the East German intelligence services assisted North Vietnam in the modernization of its security services. The GDR Ministry for State Security was asked to share its experience and technical expertise with its comrades in Hanoi—and it did so eagerly. The North Vietnamese came to rely on the support of their East German comrades in the common struggle against the "American imperialists." East German assistance, which came initially in the form of technical aid and training in how to use modern security and surveillance equipment, was viewed as a "solidarity" contribution. And beginning in 1966, the Stasi's Technical Operations Sector organized training courses in the GDR for high-ranking North Vietnamese security personnel. In the early 1970s, as the war was nearing its end, the GDR Ministry of State Security trained high-level specialists who later on assumed important positions in the Vietnamese Ministry of Public Security. The "solidarity" shipments that the GDR sent to North Vietnam included weapons and were meant to combat "US imperialism" and the so-called South Vietnamese "puppet government" in Saigon. [For the information presented above, I relied chiefly on Wilson Center Cold War International History Project Working Paper #71, "The East

German 'Stasi' and the Democratic Republic of Vietnam during the Vietnam War," by Martin Grossheim (September 2014)].

As Martin Grossheim explains in the working paper referenced above: "While the East German Stasi's technical assistance was instrumental in protecting high-level communist cadres in the south from being detected by the Saigon security forces and in facilitating their operational work, the modern technical equipment and training provided by the GDR also significantly enhanced the ability of their North Vietnamese colleagues to control and monitor the population—the second aspect of the German-Vietnamese intelligence alliance." (p. 14) In other words, through specialized training and other means the GDR helped the North Vietnamese security apparatus in Hanoi boost its ability to hunt down and suppress "enemies of the revolution" by conducting covert operations of various types during and after the war.

From time to time in East Germany, there were state-initiated organized events (Aktionen) designed to reinforce the international solidarity of socialist countries such as the GDR and Vietnam. I experienced one such event directly in November 1977, while I was living in a high-rise apartment house located in a new housing development in East Berlin known then as the "Hans-Loch-Viertel," located in the district of Friedrichsfelde. As I mentioned earlier, this building had seventeen floors with one-room apartments that were mostly occupied by retired individuals and couples, as well as some students from socialist and so-called third world countries. The students, most of whom had full scholarships and were pursuing a doctoral degree at an institution of higher learning in East Berlin, were all housed on the top two floors. My studio apartment was on the sixteenth floor. A middle-aged East German woman, who was not a student, occupied one of the apartments on the same floor. Her job was to observe and listen and make sure no one on the two top floors was doing or saying anything subversive. She was a watchdog and probably a Stasi informant as well, and—because she had a great deal of power—the foreign students were afraid of her. As doctoral "aspirants" with financial support from the GDR they were all at her mercy, whereas I was not.

My financial support came from an IREX (International Research and Exchanges Board) grant I had been awarded in the spring of 1977. This enabled me to return to East Berlin for a two-month period in order to continue work on a major book project I had initiated in the fall of 1975. My stay in East Berlin and work as an IREX scholar had the approval of the GDR Ministry of Higher Education and the sponsorship of the Humboldt University, which had agreed to provide me with lodging for the duration of my stay. That is how I came to occupy a very modest apartment, free of charge, in the high-rise building at Volkradstrasse 8.

Apart from diplomats, embassy personnel, and a few journalists from some countries in the West, there were virtually no Westerners living in East Berlin. I was the only Westerner residing in this apartment house. Not long after I moved in, the East German residents became aware that an American was living on the sixteenth floor and everyone knew who that person was. Dress and demeanor were distinguishing factors. Most East Germans had never met anyone from the US and were very curious about many aspects of our life. Still, no one ever said a word to me in the lobby or elevator, as I was coming and going each day, not even "good morning," and everyone was careful not to make eye contact. When in my presence the East German residents would look straight ahead and keep silent. They, like the foreign students on the top two floors, were afraid. Contact with Westerners could get someone in trouble, everyone knew that, so it made sense to play it safe and keep one's distance.

The international "solidarity" event I referred to above took place in November, about halfway through my two-month residency in East Berlin. One day, as I was walking through the lobby of our building, I saw a large poster on the bulletin board. It was an announcement of a campaign to raise funds for the GDR's socialist comrades in Vietnam, in order to help them recover from the war against the imperialists and reconstruct their country. Everyone in our building would be contacted by a designated campaign solicitor living on their floor and asked to contribute to this "Aktion." A donation of at least ten East German marks per adult resident was expected.

The goal of the campaign, which was scheduled to last for one week, was to have 100 percent participation from residents in our apartment house. The East Germans, who were accustomed to contributing on a "voluntary" basis to one cause or another, would of course all make the requested (read required) donation without much prompting. Here, too, no one wanted to get in trouble, so they were of a mind to pay up and be done with it—even if many resented being coerced in this way to do so.

One evening when I was finished with dinner and in my apartment, there was a knock at my door. When I opened the door, the East German watchdog was standing in front of me and asked if she could speak with me for a few moments. I politely asked her to come in and then listened to her appeal for a "solidarity" contribution to benefit Vietnam. She stressed the importance of 100 percent participation from those living in our building and told me I could give less than ten marks, if I so desired. When I told her that I would not be contributing, she asked me to explain why. I replied that while I had not been in favor of the US military involvement in the Vietnam War, I had never been a supporter of the communist North Vietnam regime or the Viet Cong. Hence, I could not in good conscience make a contribution. Disappointed, the watchdog disappeared.

A few days later, shortly after the solidarity campaign had concluded, I saw a new large poster attached to the bulletin board in our lobby as I was leaving the building. This one proclaimed proudly that **<u>everyone</u>** in our apartment house had supported solidarity with our comrades in the Socialist Republic of Vietnam and made a contribution—**<u>100 percent</u>**. Well, this prompted me to make a beeline to my apartment where I printed the following message in bold black letters on an 8.5" x 11" sheet of typewriter paper and posted it in the lobby.

> **This is untrue!**
> **The American in Apt. 1605**
> **did not contribute anything!**

That evening, when I returned to Volkradstrasse 8, I was in for a surprise. No, neither the secret police nor the civilian police nor the watchdog was waiting for me in the lobby. However, as I strolled through the lobby I noticed that my message had been removed from the bulletin board. I also noticed something else, something new and different. As I walked past East German residents, several of them made eye contact with me and even smiled. I entered the elevator and was treated to more smiles and even a few nods of approval. No one said a word to me about my message, not that evening, not later on. But from that time on, the GDR residents greeted me in the lobby and in the elevator and continued to make eye contact and smile at me. While I was the only voice of resistance in our building, there was apparently a great deal of solidarity with the American dissenter. I had taken a stand publicly on a political issue, and the fact of my refusal to contribute dissolved an invisible boundary between my neighbors and me.

STANDING IN LINE

Queue: a line or sequence of people or vehicles awaiting their turn to be attended to or to proceed. Standing in line was very common throughout East Germany, much more common than in West Germany or the United States. East Germans were trained beginning in early childhood to line up and wait patiently at public transit stops, at gas stations, outside grocery stores, butcher shops, bakeries, and bookstores, at the entrance to state-run restaurants and cafés, and at stores that had something special or unusual for sale—like much sought-after American blue jeans or wine from a Western European country. East Germans were very polite; they would form an orderly line and no one ever tried to cut in line or leap to the front. They were accustomed to awaiting their turn in line and accepted this as an inevitable part of everyday life in their country, which it assuredly was.

I have always disliked waiting in a line for anything. For that reason, I rarely dine at restaurants that do not take reservations. In my view, persons who cut in line are incredibly obnoxious and inconsiderate of others. So are those persons at the supermarket who blithely wheel their cart into the fast checkout lane with too many items in the basket. They come to the check-out point with more than the permitted number of items and pretend that everything is fine. To their credit, East Germans did not indulge in this type of rude behavior in stores or any other public setting. Everyone knew the rules and was expected to play by the rules, which meant that everyone was inconvenienced to the same extent.

The line I disliked the most in the GDR was the one that I occasionally had to negotiate at gas stations, which were few and far between and almost always crowded. I tried to fill up as often as possible at gas stations in West Berlin, even though that sometimes necessitated a special trip through Checkpoint Charlie. But that was not always possible, especially when I was travelling around parts of the GDR that were not close to Berlin. On those occasions, I had to get into a gas line at a state-owned filling station. There was usually a long line of vehicles stretching from the side of the street up to and into the station. Almost all East German automobiles had two-stroke engines that generated lots of black smoke and pollution. The noxious exhaust fumes in the air made it difficult to breathe, so drivers would turn off the engine for a while, leaving some space between vehicles, and then move forward in tandem. Some drivers of lighter cars like the Trabant would push their vehicle toward the gas pump. My Volkswagen, which had been manufactured in West Germany, would not operate on the special fuel the two- and three-cylinder East German cars used. It needed "super" gasoline, which had higher octane and could only be purchased with West German marks. An attendant would pump the gas and then take the customer's payment, cash only. How much time did one allot for a trip to the filling station in the GDR? As I recall, I tended to allot around two hours, but it did not always take that long.

My favorite standing-in-line story is based on an experience I had in June 1978. I had returned to East Berlin in May, with the support of an IREX fellowship, to complete the gathering of materials for what eventually would become a major book on GDR literature in the 1970s. My housing, provided by the Humboldt University, was a studio apartment in a low-rise building constructed after World War II. The most desirable feature of this apartment was its location in the central Mitte district of Berlin. It was just a few blocks away from Germany's biggest and most famous public square, the iconic Alexanderplatz, and within walking distance of writer Ulrich Plenzdorf's apartment, which I visited frequently. The Alexanderplatz has always been one of the liveliest places in Berlin, with shops of every sort and a department store, cinemas, restaurants, hotels and many tourist attractions. It was always bustling with activity, so when I had some free time I liked to go there and explore what it had to offer.

One afternoon, as I was strolling across "Alex," as Berliners often called their favorite public square, I saw off in the distance a long line of people waiting to enter a store. I could not see what type of store it was, but without hesitation I took my place at the end of the line. Everyone in that line seemed to be in a good mood and eager to chit-chat with their neighbors, which made the long wait seem shorter. I soon learned from persons standing nearby that we were making our way, at a snail's pace, toward a wine shop. This shop had apparently received a large shipment of Portuguese red wine that was being sold to raise funds to support the Communist-aligned People's Movement for the Liberation of Angola (MPLA) against US-backed interventions by South Africa and Zaire in support of two pro-Western independence movements competing for power in Angola.

Before proceeding to the wine store, let me provide a little background information that some readers might find helpful. Angola is a nation on the coast of southeastern Africa that the Portuguese colonized in various stages over a period of some 400 years. Following the decolonization of Portuguese Africa in the early 1970s, Portugal granted its former colony Angola independence in November 1975 and withdrew without handing over power to any movement or faction. Multiple Angolan nationalist forces began fighting among themselves to establish control over the newly liberated state. Angola became a one-party Marxist-Leninist system ruled by the People's Movement for the Liberation of Angola (MPLA), which had declared itself the government of independent Angola and become involved in a civil war.

In November 1975, Cuba sent combat troops to assist the MPLA in the struggle against enemy forces. In 1976, the number of Cuban military in Angola would reach 36,000 troops. Following the withdrawal of Zaire and South Africa (March 1976), Cuban forces remained in Angola to support the MPLA government throughout the 27-year-long civil war that began in 1975, immediately after Angola became independent from Portugal, and ended in 2002. Communist East Germany, like Communist Cuba and the Soviet Union, backed the Marxist-Leninist MPLA regime. The East Germans sought ties with African states which leaned ideologically towards the Soviet Union, such as Angola, Ethiopia, and Mozambique. German reunification in 1990 brought the era of East German military and political involvement with these African nations to an end.

The entrance to the wine shop moved closer to us and eventually came into view. It was an exciting moment, filled with anticipation as we approached two at a time, side by side. When we reached the entrance, I and the person beside me were permitted to enter the shop. Each person in the line was able to buy two bottles of inexpensive Portuguese red wine, that was the limit. I paid for my purchase with East German marks and walked straight back to my apartment. The wine was a special treat for the East Germans, since they never were able to buy wines from Western countries in the GDR's state-run stores. I could and did buy such wines on a regular basis, usually in West Berlin. Still, I had the feeling that my two bottles of wine from Portugal were something really special, perhaps worthy of a celebration.

From my apartment I called my friend Ulrich Plenzdorf and told him about my good fortune. My idea was to stop by his place in the evening and share the wine with him and his wife, Helga, who had kindly given me a standing invitation to have dinner with their family whenever I liked. Uli expanded on my idea right away and proposed that we invite some friends who lived nearby to join us, on short notice, for an impromptu party at 8:00 p.m. that evening. The gathering would be held in the Plenzdorfs' apartment, which was conveniently located for everybody. Uli said he would do the inviting, so all I had to do was show up with the wine at 7:30 p.m. or so.

Helga and Uli Plenzdorf did a lot of entertaining in their spacious, tastefully appointed pre-WW II apartment, which was a gathering place for their family members and their circle of friends. The guests arrived punctually at 8:00 p.m.; East Germans, just like West Germans, were sticklers for punctuality. And in Germany no one comes to a party empty-handed. Every person or couple brought a bottle of wine, some cheese or sliced meats from a foreign country, or a cold homemade dish, all destined for the buffet table. This was typical and expected in East Germany, where the hosts would have difficulty shopping for food and assembling a buffet on their own. All of our guests were in high spirits, delighted that we had organized a festive occasion around two bottles of "solidarity with Angola wine" from Portugal, which were prominently displayed. You might want to know who the guests were. Apart from a few of Plenzdorfs' relatives, all were friends of theirs from the GDR's cultural sphere—writers, actors, and persons from the film industry. On this occasion, there were no West Berliners or West Germans present. That meant the guests—who knew each other well—would be able to converse freely.

Social gatherings like this one had an important function in the GDR, where the pressing and frequently disturbing issues of the day were not discussed in the newspapers, in television or radio broadcasts, in movies, or in other public news forums. Such get-togethers provided a welcome escape from the humdrum of everyday life in the GDR, which prominent writer Volker Braun famously labelled "the most boring country in the world" ("das langweiligste Land der Welt") in his play *Die Kipper* (The Dumpers), 1965. There is much truth to that, I think, for it was not easy to find things to do in East Germany that were fun or entertaining. Indeed, some social thinkers have speculated that sheer boredom, along with the stifling confinement of all GDR citizens within the borders of that country, may have contributed to the notoriously high level of infidelity among East German couples. Be that as it may, the social gatherings of friends in private residences provided a sheltered environment where one could express repressed feelings, exchange ideas and views openly, release pent-up frustration and anger, and in so doing engage in a kind of group therapy that was not available elsewhere in the GDR. Conversations would focus on topics of immediate and ongoing concern to many of those present; there was no room or need for small talk so common at social gatherings and parties in West Germany.

Although the title of this piece is "Standing in Line," it is really about the nature, function, and importance of interpersonal communication in repressive dictatorships like the GDR and the Soviet Union. While East and West Germans spoke the same language, the exact same words in that language often came to connote something very different in the two Germanys. An East German writer who had embraced communism wholeheartedly used the example of a "social obligation" (*gesellschaftliche Verpflichtung*) to explain this to me. "In the GDR," he declared with an air of moral superiority, "we have socially-engaged citizens who have an obligation to contribute to society in positive ways. By contrast, a social obligation in the US or West Germany can mean that friends have invited you to a dinner or cocktail party and you now are obliged to reciprocate." There are many things I could have said in response, but I had learned that in this sort of situation it is best to bite one's tongue. My first rule of engagement when dealing with GDR authors was to listen and observe, rather than argue or aggravate them. This non-aggression strategy, which I deployed on numerous occasions, served me well.

LEIPZIG BOOK FAIR

Early in 1985, I received a telephone call from Cynthia Miller, USIA Public Affairs Officer at the US Embassy in East Berlin, who was serving as cultural attaché. (USIA is the acronym for the United States Information Agency, which existed from 1953 to 1999. It was an independent foreign affairs agency devoted to public diplomacy, much of which was carried out through US embassies.) Ms. Miller invited me to come to the renowned Leipzig Book Fair in March and preside over a special exhibit the embassy was putting together on "The Best Books in America: 1983-1984." This was the first time our embassy had participated in the Leipzig Book Fair and it wanted to make the exhibit as impressive as possible. Award-winning books in every conceivable category would be on display—fiction of all kinds, general non-fiction, poetry, biography and autobiography, history, philosophy, religion, science, contemporary affairs and contemporary thought, current interest, children's books (fiction and picture), documentaries of various sorts, photo essays, most original book, first novel, etc. Ms. Miller explained that my job would be to preside over the exhibit, which simply meant that I was to be present most of the time and prepared to converse with the attendees from the GDR in a friendly way. She wanted the presider to be someone who was fluent in German, knowledgeable about the GDR and its society, and not affiliated with the US embassy or the US government. The entire cost of my roundtrip flight, hotel rooms, meals, and even incidental expenses related to this assignment would be covered by the embassy. It sounded like it would be a terrific experience and—best of all—it would help to reconnect me with the GDR and many East German writers I knew. I accepted the invitation with great pleasure and anticipation. Almost seven years had passed since my last stay in the GDR, so I very much looked forward to this completely unexpected reunion.

I flew to West Berlin on March 5, 1985, and—according to the stamps in my passport—entered East Berlin on March 6 via the border crossing point known as Checkpoint Charlie, in a US Embassy automobile which picked me up at West Berlin's Tegel Airport. The embassy chauffeur, a GDR citizen, took me to the Hotel Metropol where I stayed for three nights before heading for Leipzig. I remember that day very well because I had a terrible bout of food poisoning that started not long after my lunch in the hotel restaurant, where I had foolishly ordered beef tartare. However, I recovered within 24 hours and was able to meet with Cynthia Miller on March 7, as planned.

Shortly before my departure for Berlin, Ms. Miller asked me to provide her with the names of some GDR writers I would like to see again before heading to Leipzig. She was planning to have a cocktail party and buffet dinner in my honor at her residence in Berlin Niederschönhausen, an upscale neighborhood where many diplomats lived. According to the formal invitation still in my possession, the social gathering was scheduled for 7:00 p.m. on Thursday, March 7, 1985. The party would not only give me an opportunity to reconnect with some writers I knew well, it would also give Ms. Miller an opportunity to expand her contacts with writers in an informal way. Invitations to events held at the US Embassy were viewed with suspicion in those Cold War days, so East German writers and artists were always hesitant to attend. I imagine that all the writers were surprised to receive Ms. Miller's invitation and, even more, to be invited to an event taking place in her private house. That was simply unheard-of!

Among the writers attending the party was my friend, Ulrich Plenzdorf, with his wife Helga and their son Morten; Fritz Rudolf Fries and his wife; Martin Stade and his wife; also, Eberhard Scheibner, a functionary from the GDR Writers' Union. Because the invitations were sent out only a short time before the event, several invitees were unable to attend. The reception lasted for about two hours and was an extremely awkward affair. The East German guests were obviously uncomfortable being in the residence of a diplomat from a Western and capitalist country, and I imagine they assumed they were under surveillance by the GDR's secret police. The conversations, including the ones I had with writers I knew well, were for the most part small talk, probably because none of the East Germans wanted to be overheard discussing anything of political or cultural importance with Cynthia Miller, her husband who was also a diplomat, or me. For everyone who attended, the party turned out to be a disappointment.

On March 8, 1985, Cynthia Miller and I were chauffeured in a US Embassy automobile to Leipzig, where arrangements for the exhibit of the best books published in the US during 1983-1984 were already underway. That evening I met US Ambassador to the GDR Rozanne Ridgway, who had kindly invited the book fair team from the embassy to a gala dinner. Ambassador Ridgway also invited Cynthia Miller and me to ride with her to the restaurant in her US Embassy vehicle. It was a black four-door Cadillac sedan, long and luxurious, with American flags fastened to the sides of the front headlights. As we drove around Leipzig's Ring Street with the flags fluttering proudly and attracting lots of attention, people stopped what they were doing and stared at the Cadillac. Undoubtedly, most of them had never seen an automobile like that. Another nice memory!

The next morning Ambassador Ridgway, Cynthia Miller, and I attended the book fair's opening ceremony and the reception that followed; there I met and chatted briefly with Klaus Höpcke, the powerful Deputy Minister of Culture in the GDR. Over the next several days, as I was 'working' at our stand in the multi-story building that housed the book fair, I would encounter many GDR writers I had first met in the 1970s, as they made their way through our exhibit area, and I would also meet some GDR writers I had known only by name. Most gratifying, however, were the conversations I had with the East German citizens who visited our large public display each day. Their level of curiosity and interest was extremely high, as this was for virtually all of them the first opportunity to experience the US in the way it wanted to present itself. Many persons spent several hours perusing the books, looking primarily at the cover designs, illustrations and photos, taking notes, asking questions, obviously delighted to be in attendance. They were not shy about asking me questions on topics that were not directly related to our book exhibit, e.g., about aspects of my life and our society in the US and what I thought about the GDR. The secret police were undoubtedly among the visitors to our display, but the likelihood of their presence and ongoing surveillance did not seem to disturb the other attendees.

For me, presiding over "The Best Books in America: 1983-1984" exhibit was a unique and very memorable experience, without question one of the highlights of my professional life. It was an honor to be invited to serve my country in that special role and I enjoyed every minute of it! Happily, the memory lingers on. . . .

IX
SHOPPING

INTERSHOP

Intershop was a chain of state-run retail stores in the GDR, in which only hard currencies like West German marks and US dollars could be used to purchase high-quality goods that had for the most part been imported from Western countries. The East German mark was not accepted as payment in these stores. Intershop was originally oriented toward visitors from Western countries; it later became an outlet where East Germans could purchase goods they could not otherwise obtain. The selection included food, alcohol, tobacco, brand-name clothing, blue jeans, toys, jewelry, cosmetics, watches, technical devices, musical recordings, appliances, and even Western-made automobiles, such as Volkswagen and Volvo. With the arrival of the first Interhotels, which were intended to house tourists from the capitalist West, Intershops began appearing in these Western-oriented hotels, the most upscale of which also had fancy restaurants that accepted payment in hard currencies only. Many East Germans came to view the Intershops as a key driver of inequality in the GDR.

While staying in the GDR, I made a point of shopping infrequently in the Intershops, so as not to support the regime's insatiable desire to secure hard currency by any means possible. Occasionally, East German friends would ask me to purchase an item or two for them in an Intershop. I usually complied, probably because I felt guilty about having plenty of hard currency and hence the ability to buy things in these state-run shops. When I bought something for someone, I paid for it with West German marks. I would then be reimbursed the amount of the purchase in East German marks. Although the black market exchange rate in East Germany ranged from 5 to 10 M (East) for I DM (West), I never charged a friend the black-market premium—probably because I felt guilty about the privileges I enjoyed as US citizen.

The oddest request I ever received to purchase something for someone in an Intershop came from a woman I met though the poet, Sarah Kirsch. Her name was Jutta W., and she worked as a Research Associate at the Academy of Arts in East Berlin. Jutta had a craving for cod liver filets, which—packaged in small tin containers like sardines and anchovies—were available in the Intershop in Hotel Metropol.

The two of us marched into the Intershop and there I purchased a few tins of the cod liver filets, along with a packet of German *Vollkorn* (full grain) bread, a dense rye bread that Jutta said complemented the cod liver perfectly. We then went to Jutta's apartment, located just a short distance from Hotel Metropol, and proceeded to have lunch. This was the first time I had eaten cod liver, so I was quite curious and eager to taste it. After a few bites I understood why Jutta liked it so much. It was really delicious, especially on the hearty full grain bread. I bought more of the same combination for myself and began eating it for breakfast. To this day I remain a fan of this unusual delicacy!

EAST GERMAN MARK

The East German mark (M) was officially valued by the East German government at parity with the West German mark (DM). However, because it was not readily convertible and because the GDR's export market was restricted, it was practically worthless outside East Germany. On the black market the exchange rate was about 5 to 10 M for 1 DM, depending on how eager the exchange partner was to acquire "hard currency." In the 1970s and 1980s, one could easily visit foreign currency exchange offices in West Berlin or Vienna and purchase East German banknotes at the rate of approximately 8 M (East) for 1 DM (West). However, the GDR forbade the import or export of GDR currency into or out of the GDR, in order to support their artificially high exchange rates for persons with hard currency, such as Western tourists. Penalties for violating this law ranged from confiscation of smuggled currency to imprisonment. The East German mark could not be spent in Intershops to acquire Western or luxury consumer goods; only hard currencies such as West German marks and US dollars were accepted. The only legal ways for East Germans to acquire hard currency were as gifts from relatives living in the West or from wages earned for work in Western countries.

In the summer of 1975, before travelling to East Berlin to begin work on a project that would in time give rise to the documentary book, *DDR-Literatur im Tauwetter* (GDR Literature During the Thaw), I purchased several hundred East German marks at the Creditanstalt bank in Vienna. The exchange rate for this transaction was approximately 8 M for 1 DM. Using a custom-made money belt, I carried a good number of one hundred mark bills into East Germany on my person. Once in East Berlin, I left them with an East German friend I visited frequently for safe keeping. If I needed money, I would stop by my friend's apartment and withdraw some bills from the envelope marked "ZIPSER". Hence, I did not have to exchange a significant amount of dollars or DM at an unfavorable rate. I only had to exchange the minimum required amount of 20 DM per day each time I entered the GDR. When I returned to East Berlin as an IREX scholar in the fall of 1977, I did the same thing. The additional money enabled me to frequently invite persons to dine with me as my guests at really good restaurants where I could pay with East German marks. Since I disliked (and still dislike) dining by myself, the extra cash made my stays in the GDR much more pleasant and interesting socially.

In retrospect, violating the GDR currency law was a reckless thing for me to do. From my two trips to that country in 1969 and 1973, I knew only too well that one should always play by their rules to avoid getting into trouble. But I took a chance and, as with the tape-recorded interviews with East German writers that I smuggled into West Berlin, I was fortunate not to get caught.

ANTIQUES AND ARTWORK

The dwellings of many GDR writers I visited had valuable antiques and artwork on display. Although I knew little about antique furniture, I could recognize top-quality pieces from the Baroque, Empire, Biedermeier, Art Nouveau, and other periods without difficulty. I also saw original works of art in these homes, paintings and drawings by twentieth- and nineteenth-century artists, some of them well known: e.g., Carl Spitzweg, Heinrich Zille, and George Grosz. Ulrich Plenzdorf collected original paintings by German artists and displayed them throughout his apartment. Playwright Peter Hacks's apartment was adorned with antiques and artwork of every kind; it was like a small museum. Also museum-like was the beautiful villa in Berlin-Buch that Günter Kunert and his wife Marianne occupied, along with their many cats. Kunert's own paintings and graphic art works were on display there, visual evidence of his extraordinary talent.

Works by contemporary GDR artists could be purchased at exhibits in art galleries or directly from the artist via a private transaction. Older art works by prominent artists such as the three mentioned above could only be purchased from private parties who were prepared to sell them. Nothing was available on the open market.

There were no antique stores open to the general public in East Germany, and art galleries were few and far between. Antiques and art works of value, such as pieces of old Meissen Porcelain, vintage sterling silver tableware, and old Baltic amber jewelry, were sold for hard Western currency in special state-owned shops located in newer, upscale Interhotels like the Hotel Metropol and Palasthotel in East Berlin. It was not possible to buy such items with East German marks.

In the spring of 1991, a short while after German reunification, the German news magazine *Der Spiegel* reported that East German officials from the ruling communist party (the Socialist Unity Party or SED) had systematically stolen from the country's art collectors and sold their possessions to Western clients to raise the hard currency it desperately needed. Between 1973 and 1989, according to a July 2014 report in SPIEGEL ONLINE (by Rainer Erices, Nicola Kuhrt, and Peter Wensierski), more than 200 GDR citizens had collections taken from them. Most often, the collectors were accused of having violated or evaded GDR tax laws. The confiscation of their valuable possessions was carried out by the secret police (the Stasi), tax officials, and regular police officers, usually in a surprise raid. The Stasi would lock the collectors away in pre-trial detention, then public prosecutors would sentence them to long prison terms. The confiscated property found its way to exclusive antique shops in large West German cities like Munich, Hamburg, Frankfurt, and Düsseldorf. Prominent actors, business persons, fashion designers, musicians, and companies were among the clients. The sale of the confiscated wares to wealthy clients in the West was done via the state-owned company Kunst & Antiquitäten Gmbh (Art & Antiques, LLC). During the 1970s and 1980s, SED Party spies would comb East Germany in search of treasures—such as antique furniture, paintings, porcelain, silver, and jewelry—for the regime to appropriate.

The systematic robbery perpetrated by government officials on GDR art and antique collectors is a particularly sordid chapter in the history of communist East Germany. Victimized families have been trying, for more than three decades now, to reclaim their property or obtain compensation for the treasures that were taken from them. Today, many victims of looting or their family members are still fighting with little or no success for the return of their valuable property.

In the late 1970s and early 1980s, I purchased a few pieces of old Meissen and Dresden Porcelain in the state-operated shop in Hotel Metropol and also in the antique shop located in West Berlin's famous department store, Kaufhaus des Westens (Department Store of the West). As I think about what I have written in this snapshot, I have to wonder if any of these antiques now in my possession were forcibly seized from an East German collector. That is a disconcerting thought.

BLUE JEANS

A pair of blue jeans made in the US was without question the most sought after item of clothing in the GDR during the 1970s and 1980s. However, not any brand of jeans would do; Levi's was considered to be the "genuine" brand, more desirable and prestigious than other historic brands like Lee and Wrangler—the ultimate status symbol. These blue jeans were invented in 1871 by Jacob Davis in partnership with Levi Strauss & Co. Levi Strauss was a Bavarian who emigrated to New York in 1847, then in 1853 made his way to San Francisco where he opened a dry goods business. Davis and Strauss patented the blue-colored denim trousers with copper rivets in 1873, and they went into business together to manufacture blue jeans. Originally designed as work clothes for miners and cowboys, jeans became popular in the 1950s among teenagers in the US. In the 1960s they were a common fashion garment worn by college students and members of the hippie subculture. They continued to be popular and fashionable as casual wear in the 1970s and 1980s, especially in the US.

Ulrich Plenzdorf, Berlin prose writer, playwright, and film scenarist, contributed greatly to the jeans mania that swept the GDR in the 1970s. His innovative novel, *The New Sufferings of Young W.* (1972), made its author famous overnight and became one of the most widely read, discussed, and reviewed works ever published in the GDR. The stage adaptation caused a sensation in the theaters of the GDR and was performed for many years to full houses in Eastern and Western Europe. The main character is 17-year-old Edgar Wibeau, a model all-GDR boy: disciplined, clean-cut, obedient. But all of a sudden he gets fed up with the restrictiveness of socialist society and the conformity it demands of every citizen. He drops out of school and runs away to Berlin, where he proceeds to do all the things he always wanted to do previously but never could. In a long soliloquy, Edgar expounds on the topic of jeans which symbolize his rebellion and new-found freedom.

> Jeans are the greatest pants in the world. For jeans I'd give up all of the synthetic rags in Jumo [a large department store in East Berlin] that always look squeaky clean. For jeans I would give up everything, except maybe for the *finest thing*. And except for music. I don't mean just an old Händelsohn Bacholdy. I mean genuine music, people. I didn't have anything against Bacholdy or the others, but they didn't exactly sweep me off my feet. Of course I mean real jeans. There's a whole pile of junk that just pretends to be jeans. If that's all I could get I'd rather not have any at all. Real jeans, for example, don't have a zipper in front. There is only one kind of real jeans. A real jeans wearer knows what I mean. That doesn't mean that everyone who wears real jeans is a real jeans wearer. Most of them don't even know what they're wearing. It always killed me when I saw some twenty-five-year-old fogy with jeans on that he's forced up over his bloated thighs and then belted up tight at the waist. Jeans are supposed to be hip pants. I mean they're pants that will slip down off your hips if you don't buy them small enough, and they stay up by friction. You naturally can't have fat hips and certainly not a fat ass, because otherwise they won't snap together. People over twenty-five are too dense to grasp that. That is, if they're card-carrying Communists and beat their wives. I mean, jeans are an attitude and not just pants. Sometimes I think that people shouldn't be allowed to get older than seventeen—or eighteen. After that

they get a job or go to college or join the army and then there's no reasoning with them anymore. At least I haven't known any. Maybe nobody understands me. Then you start wearing jeans that you don't any more have a right to. It's also great when you're retired and then wear jeans, with a belly and suspenders. That's also great. (Ulrich Plenzdorf, *The New Sufferings of Young W.*, translated by Kenneth P. Wilcox. New York: Frederick Ungar, 1973, 13-14.)

On Levi's official website, the company asserts: "We make the jeans. Jeans make the man." Nowhere was the latter statement truer than in the GDR, where brands of jeans from the US were not available. I wore Levi's much of the time when I was in the GDR, often together with a jeans jacket. Perhaps that explains why I was asked many times to purchase jeans for persons in East Berlin, either for them to wear themselves or give to someone else as a very special gift. They would tell me the size and sometimes even the name and location of the clothing store in West Berlin where I would find what they wanted. I already knew, of course, that they preferred the "genuine" brand endorsed by Edgar Wibeau.

CLOTHES AND SHOES

Clothes made in the GDR for its citizenry tended to be uninteresting and unattractive. The emphasis was on functionality, not fashion. Clothing items of every variety were not very stylish or colorful; I remember seeing men and women wearing drab gray, green, and beige clothes. Most fashion-conscious women had a special outfit for dress-up occasions like birthday parties, weddings, etc. More often than not, this was a gift from relatives or friends living in West Germany or West Berlin. Or, it might have been purchased in an *Exquisit-Laden*, special retail shops in the GDR with relatively high-priced clothing and cosmetics from Western European countries or made in the GDR specifically for export to the West. Such "exquisite" merchandise could only be purchased with Western currency in these luxury shops that were owned and operated by the State. Here GDR citizens could find name-brand clothing that was different from the commonplace items sold in the other stores, trendy clothing that would set someone apart from those persons wearing functional, unfashionable clothes.

Fashion-conscious women in the GDR would visit these stores on a regular basis, just to see what new merchandise had been put on display. As a result, it was easy for these women to recognize a dress or outfit that came from an *Exquisit* shop. Everyone also knew what was for sale in the ordinary clothing and shoe stores, and most people would have preferred to buy higher-quality, more attractive items.

Shoes made in the GDR were not a clothing item that was in high demand. They were sturdy and meant to last, but most of them were ugly, so East Germans preferred shoes that came from the West. Salamander was one of the most popular and recognizable brands. I wore shoes that were made or purchased in the US and generally not available in Germany. While strolling down a boulevard like Unter den Linden in East Berlin, I would often observe persons who were walking toward me looking down at my shoes. Everyone was aware that shoes like mine were not available anywhere in the GDR. An East German friend told me, "It's the shoes, that's how we can tell right away that you are not from here."

I should add that there were no clothing sales in the GDR, and individual items were always sold at the same fixed price from north to south and east to west. Sometimes, so-called *Exportrückläufe* (clothes that had been produced to be sold in the West, but for some reason had been rejected) were sold in regular stores. The trained East German eye could easily spot such items. Lines would form quickly outside the store. People would join the line and ask, "What are they selling?" Regardless of what it was, those in line would wait patiently in the hope that the items would not sell out before it was their turn. Even if someone did not need the item, one could use it to trade for something that another person had purchased and did not need. Or one could give the item to someone as a special gift. Attractive things were always rationed in the GDR. In other words, one could not buy ten T-shirts, just one per person. Couples would stand in the same line, pretending not to know each other, in order to be able to purchase two of the desired object.

TOILET PAPER

Shortages of food staples and basic goods we routinely need for everyday life were not uncommon in East Germany. Toilet paper and paper products in general (e.g., facial tissues, feminine hygiene products, disposable diapers, paper towels, wallpaper, and the list goes on) were always in short supply. East German toilet paper was gray and hard, but people would stand in line to buy it whenever it was available in drugstores; people in the GDR often had to rely on newspaper as a substitute. A friend of mine who grew up in East Germany recalls crumbling and massaging the newspaper to make it a little softer. I remember an instance, quite amusing in retrospect, when an extreme shortage of toilet paper in East Berlin and elsewhere in the GDR became a source of great concern to my writer-friend, Ulrich (Uli) Plenzdorf.

In the spring of 1978, I had returned to East Berlin in order to continue working on the project that would eventually culminate in a documentary book on GDR literature in the 1970s. During this one-month visit, from mid-May to mid-June, I stayed in a Humboldt University of Berlin studio apartment. The apartment was located a short distance from the Alexanderplatz, right in the heart of Berlin and within walking distance of the Plenzdorfs' (Uli and his wife, Helga) place in the artsy Prenzlauer Berg district. Helga Plenzdorf had kindly given me a standing invitation to join their family for the main meal of the day, which always began at 1:30 p.m., so I visited and dined with them frequently.

The Plenzdorfs also had a countryside cottage in Altrosenthal, a village in Brandenburg located about 36 miles east of Berlin. Their house was part of a farmstead consisting of several old buildings that had been abandoned. Uli Plenzdorf and some of his friends had leased the rundown buildings and were in the process of restoring and transforming them into weekend/vacation retreats, which were commonly called *Datschen* in the GDR. City dwellers who could afford year-round second homes were eager to acquire these obvious status symbols. On weekends during my stays in Berlin, I often would drive out to Altrosenthal and visit with the Plenzdorfs, usually spending Saturday night at their place. They frequently had visitors from West Berlin, friends who would arrive in time for a midday meal, stay until nighttime, and then drive back to the border crossing point to re-enter West Berlin before midnight when their one-day visas would expire. Since East Germans were prohibited from travelling to West Berlin or any Western countries, all such visits involved persons from the West coming to see East Germans in the GDR.

One day in June 1978, while I was having dinner with the Plenzdorf family in their Berlin apartment, Uli told me they were going to host some VIP visitors from West Berlin at their country house on the weekend. Coming for a visit on Saturday were the prominent German filmmaker, Volker Schlöndorff, and two of his colleagues. At that time, Schlöndorff was making the film version of Günter Grass's famous novel, *The Tin Drum*. Plenzdorf, who was also a filmmaker as well as a screenplay writer, was very excited by the prospect of this particular visit. There would be a festive midday meal in the Plenzdorfs' cottage, to which their Altrosenthal neighbors and I were invited. But, there was a big problem and the Plenzdorfs needed my help to solve it.

The problem was that the Plenzdorfs were almost out of toilet paper, both in their Berlin apartment and in the Altrosenthal cottage. Due to the toilet paper shortage in East Berlin and throughout the GDR, their efforts to find and purchase more of this essential product had proved futile. And now, in just a few days, they would have special guests from West Berlin and a group of friends to entertain. Uli asked me for a favor: Could I drive over to West Berlin that afternoon and buy a huge supply of toilet paper, as much as would fit into my Volkswagen Beetle? I was eager to help out, of course, and told the Plenzdorfs that there was a nearby supermarket on the western side of Checkpoint Charlie, the Berlin Wall crossing point between East and West Berlin that I used frequently.

The Plenzdorfs' teen-age son, Morten, was dining with us that afternoon and had been following our conversation closely. When we finished eating and I was about to leave for Checkpoint Charlie, Morten said with frustration and anger in his voice: "I'd like to drive over to West Berlin once, even if it's just to buy toilet paper!" But Morten would have to wait for more than eleven years, until November 1989 when the Berlin Wall collapsed, for an opportunity to visit West Berlin.

At the supermarket in West Berlin, I filled my shopping cart with toilet paper several times. I continued shopping until the front passenger side of the VW and the space behind the front seats were completely filled with packages of toilet paper. Then I drove back to Checkpoint Charlie, where East German border guards checked my passport and asked me with apparent amusement about the unusual cargo I had on board: "What are you going to do with all this toilet paper?" I told them the truth: "East German friends of mine are having a big party this coming weekend and are almost out of toilet paper. I'm invited to the party and want to help out." The border guards were well aware of the toilet paper shortage, of course, and kindly told me to be on my way.

This snapshot has a happy ending. The Plenzdorfs' dinner party was a great success! They shared the supply of toilet paper with their neighbors and friends in Altrosenthal, all of whom were grateful and thanked me as well as the Plenzdorfs for this unusual gift. And best of all, I got to meet and chat with the famous film director, Volker Schlöndorff!

X
THINGS

SOAP AND BANANAS

My East German friend Eva was a film actress who in the 1970s was best known for playing teen-age girls in coming-of-age movies. Featuring first-love, end-of-innocence and rite-of-passage themes, these movies were popular in East Germany, and so was Eva. When I met her in 1975, she was twenty-five years old, but looked like she was just sixteen or seventeen. She was also very attractive and had a natural, innocent look that made her the perfect choice for adolescent roles in these films focusing on the transition from youth to adulthood. But Eva was not innocent; she was married to a film director who was much older than she and had a one-year-old son. She and I had a mutual friend, the prominent GDR author, screenplay writer, and film-maker, Ulrich Plenzdorf, the person who introduced the two of us in Berlin.

Eva was well-connected and well-liked in the circles of GDR society that included writers, artists, and persons from the film industry. Because she had a young child, she was on an extended maternity leave when we met and had a lot of time on her hands. As we got to know one another, she took an interest in my project on GDR literature in the 1970s which involved interviewing GDR writers, and she offered to help me widen the circle of authors I might approach and ask to participate. She was happy to contact some writers she knew on my behalf and to arrange for us to pay them a visit. Once the connection was made, and making those connections was a lot of fun, the rest would be up to me and the writer.

When we began visiting people, I would receive invitations from some of them to social gatherings and dinner parties. In the GDR, most people preferred to entertain at home because of the difficulties associated with dining out—e.g., reserving a table, dealing with unfriendly waiters, driving after having consumed an alcoholic beverage—the GDR had a zero tolerance policy here. Eva let me know that she would be pleased to accompany me to any such social events and drive us back and forth. She had her own automobile, did not drink, and her husband would be happy to babysit. It was an ideal situation! Of course, I was delighted to have a movie actress accompany me to parties and Eva was good company. She was also more than welcome everywhere because of her celebrity status and effervescent personality. Her husband was not particularly interested in this type of socializing, so this was a convenient way for Eva to get out and about during her maternity leave. She and I got along very well and I think, in retrospect, that we made a good couple—the actress and her American friend.

At the private dinner parties there would usually be eight to ten people—our hosts, some of their family members or friends, and the two of us. Everyone was eager to know about my work on GDR literature and my contacts with prominent writers which many people viewed as remarkable, since I was a Westerner. They seemed flattered by the fact that I was so interested in GDR literature and the GDR itself. They were also very eager to hear about life in the US, so I always fielded lots of questions at these gatherings and did my best to answer them honestly, even if that involved being critical of certain things in the US. I tried to the best of my ability to discern and then answer the question behind the question, because the question being asked was often not the one that really required an answer. Understandably, many people were suspicious of me; they wondered if I was what I in fact claimed to be (and was!), an American Germanist with a keen interest in East German literature and writers.

I came to understand and appreciate that having a private dinner party in the GDR was a major and expensive undertaking that involved considerable planning and effort. One could not go to the butcher shop intent upon buying a beef or pork roast; you had to buy what was available. And you could not easily find fresh vegetables, other than white and red cabbage, in the grocery stores. The most difficult thing to find was fresh fruit. While apples were almost always available, it was nearly impossible to come by fruits like bananas and pineapples or melons and berries, fruits that were not grown in the GDR. Hence, having a dinner party for an East German film celebrity and an American visitor—probably the only ones you had ever met—was definitely going to be a stressful undertaking. Still, people were eager to do it for all sorts of reasons, the main one being exposure to something new and different. Life in East Germany was extremely monotonous, so stimulation of any kind was welcome.

Eva, my companion at many private parties in East Berlin, explained that such gatherings in someone's honor were uncommon in the GDR. Most East Germans limited their socializing to a small circle of family and friends, with whom they would celebrate special occasions. After I returned to East Berlin in the fall of 1977, she revealed that the persons who had invited us to dinner had concluded that I was not an operative working for the secret police, the opposite of what they had initially suspected. They had arrived at this conclusion by observing my behavior at dinner parties where I did two things an East German would never do.

Eva enlightened me. She reminded me that our hosts often served fresh fruit for dessert, exotic fruits that came from tropical and subtropical countries: bananas, for example. Bananas were of course not grown in the GDR, nor were they routinely for sale in East German grocery stores. Only someone with a good friend or relative in West Berlin would be able to come by bananas, figs, pineapples, fresh grapefruits or oranges. Apart from the considerable effort and expense involved in acquiring such fruit, one had to inconvenience a third party—a relative or friend—to do so. For East Germans, the opportunity to eat such fruits for dessert (or at any time) was a rare and delicious treat. But I have never been much of a dessert eater, preferring instead to fill up on "real food." As Eva and others had observed, I always declined the offer of fresh fruit for dessert, undoubtedly to their utter amazement.

Eva also explained that virtually every GDR household had a bar of finely milled soap, unused, which they would put on prominent display in the bathroom when entertaining special guests. Another bar of ordinary soap would also be available and within sight. Every East German knew not to use the fine soap that came from France or another Western country; it was for show only. But since I didn't know the code of correct conduct, I always did use the deluxe soap that was reserved for special occasions.

Eva went on to tell me that no one from the GDR would be able to resist the opportunity to eat exotic fresh fruit, especially bananas. And, no East German would dare wash his hands with the "special occasion" soap, since he would know and comply with the protocol. So my unusual behavior had led the people we visited to conclude that I was an authentic American after all and not someone secretly working for the Stasi. "We know you're for real," Eva exclaimed. "You use the deluxe soap and don't eat the bananas!"

In all honesty, I never suspected at the time that my hosts—at least some of them—doubted that I was what I claimed to be. But given the paranoid nature of GDR society, with its all-pervasive spying by the Stasi and their legions of unofficial collaborators, that certainly is understandable. Hence, it was not the careful way I answered the questions about my research that persuaded them, but rather my minor social infractions, my obvious ignorance of East German culture. Soap and bananas! Who knew?!

SECONDHAND SMOKE

Secondhand smoke is a mixture of the smoke that comes from the burning end of a cigarette, cigar, or pipe, and the smoke breathed out by the smoker. It contains more than 7,000 chemicals; hundreds of those chemicals are toxic and about 70 can cause cancer. There is no safe amount of secondhand smoke, even low levels of it can be harmful. The only way to fully protect nonsmokers from secondhand smoke is not to allow smoking indoors. While secondhand smoke is not worse than active smoking, despite reports to the contrary, exposure to it causes disease, disability, and death. (Source of the above information: National Institutes of Health) Passive smoking, the breathing in of other people's tobacco smoke, is a worldwide health problem, one I encountered in the US as well as in the GDR.

I have never been a smoker. That being said, I must admit that I did smoke a few cigarettes and several cigars while I was living in Ohio and teaching at Oberlin College (1969 to 1986). I enjoyed smoking a good cigar now and then, especially while playing poker with the guys, or while sipping fine cognac from a large snifter after a special meal such as Thanksgiving or Christmas dinner. It never occurred to me to smoke a cigar by myself; that act was always related to a social event of one sort or another. Once I went to an upscale cigar bar with a friend, but that was not a good experience. The air was filled with foul-smelling smoke, from which there was no escape. When smoking cigars, which I did infrequently, I took care not to inhale. In 1992, Bill Clinton famously admitted that he had attempted to smoke marijuana in the 1960s, but claimed he didn't know how to inhale. The last time I smoked anything was in 1986, before I moved from Ohio to Delaware.

My parents were both smokers, and so were all of their relatives and friends. It was the fashionable thing to do and a sign of sophistication. Actors and actresses were always smoking in the movies I watched in the 1950s and 1960s. One cannot imagine Humphrey Bogart without the cigarette he kept in the corner of his mouth, seemingly never drawing on it or smoking it. Nobody made the cigarette look more impressive than Bogie. He made smoking look cool and brought it to a new level of popularity. Bogart and his fourth wife, the very glamorous and always-sultry actress Lauren Bacall, helped make the cigarette the genre-defining prop of film noir movies throughout the 1940s and 1950s. In the end, however, it brought him a painful and early death at age 57.

Children ages 10 to 14 are much more likely to take up smoking if they have seen actors smoke in the movies. My father quit smoking in 1950 at age 35; my mother smoked all her life, although she halfheartedly attempted to stop on many occasions. Both of my parents were aware that smoking is bad for one's health and were determined to keep me from becoming a smoker. How were they going to do that? The answer is: through bribery. In 1954, when I was 11 years old and about to enter the 7th grade, my parents had a serious talk with me about the dangers of smoking, the addictive nature of cigarettes, and the importance of not starting to smoke in the first place. They proposed the following deal: If I would not smoke over the next ten years, they would give me either $500 or a gold watch worth more than that on my 21st birthday. $500 seemed like a fortune, so I was easily persuaded to accept this friendly bribe and promised to refrain from smoking. Every August, before I went back to school or college, my parents would remind me about our pact. I turned 21 on the 23rd of January during my senior year in college; the day of reckoning had finally arrived! When my parents asked, I told them that I had actually tried smoking a cigarette a few times in college, but really didn't like it. They said a few cigarettes didn't matter; I wasn't a smoker and clearly was not going to become a smoker. My reward was $500, which I used to finance travel in Germany, Austria, and Switzerland that fall. My parents said it was money well spent.

While I was not tempted to start smoking in junior high school or high school, college was another story. I was in a fraternity and everyone smoked—not just at our weekend parties, but every single day, throughout the day. At parties the room would quickly become filled with secondhand smoke, which would get thicker and thicker as time went on. Everyone's clothes reeked of cigarette smoke the next day. In classrooms, professors sometimes smoked while they were teaching, and most of them allowed their students to puff away during class sessions. Every classroom had a stack of aluminum ashtrays—hard to imagine today! I was an oddball of sorts, the only student who didn't smoke, or at least it seemed that way. But, determined to garner the $500 reward, I persevered.

In 1969, the year I started teaching at Oberlin College, the Public Health Smoking Act of 1969 required that all cigarette packaging contain this statement: **WARNING: THE SURGEON GENERAL HAS DETERMINED THAT CIGARETTE SMOKING IS DANGEROUS TO YOUR HEALTH.** In 1970, President Richard Nixon signed the Public Health Cigarette Smoking Act, which banned cigarette ads from airing on television and radio. Anti-smoking forces hailed the new law that banned cigarette advertising in the broadcasting media as a major victory. The expectation was that this legislation would reduce the percentage of smokers in the population and the number of young adults adopting the smoking habit. But the percentage of adult smokers actually rose slightly following the ban.

Since smoking habits didn't change right away, my personal battle against secondhand smoke was destined to continue. It was a problem in my own home when my wife and I entertained guests, also when we were invited to the homes of friends and colleagues who smoked. Most adults did smoke in those days, so whenever we had a dinner party at our place we needed to have ashtrays on hand. However, this frustrating situation began to come to an end in the spring of 1975, in a remarkable way. The person responsible was prominent East German writer and filmmaker, Ulrich Plenzdorf, who came to Oberlin as German Writer-in-Residence that spring. Uli (as all of us called him) was even more opposed to smoking than the Surgeon General and had a strict zero-tolerance smoking policy which he enforced resolutely—everywhere. Besides, he was our guest, so the polite thing to do was to totally refrain from smoking in his presence, which is precisely what everyone did.

Ulrich Plenzdorf set an example that I tried to follow, not only when he and his wife were in Oberlin, but after their departure as well. My efforts met with limited success in the beginning. I put away all of our ashtrays, hoping that guests would take the hint and not smoke. But that tactic was only partially successful, since the really addicted smokers would prowl through our living and dining areas, searching in vain for an ashtray—and then they would ask me for one. Guests were easily offended if I did not accommodate them immediately and cheerfully. In this transition period—transition to a NO SMOKING IN OUR HOUSE policy—I realized that Plenzdorf was right. A no smoking policy had to be enforced consistently and without exceptions. And that is exactly what we did. When we invited people to a party or reception, we let them know that our house was a "no smoking" zone. Most people accepted that, realizing that it was our house after all, and they visited with us. Plenzdorf, because of his celebrity status, was able to control the smoking situation in the houses of other persons and at public events involving him. It was very simple: if smoking was going to be permitted, he was not going to be present.

I first visited the Plenzdorfs at their spacious, beautifully appointed apartment in East Berlin in September 1975, at the beginning of my first sabbatical leave. This was the first of countless visits with them during the second half of that decade. Their apartment was on the third floor of a pre-WW II building with no lift, located at Wilhelm-Pieck-Str. 5 (renamed Torstrasse in the 1990s). The building had an ideal central location, right on the border of the popular districts of Mitte and Prenzlauer Berg, and just a short walking distance to the Alexanderplatz. In part because of its location and size, the Plenzdorfs' apartment was a gathering place for their family members and their circle of friends, which included writers, actors, persons from the film industry, some doctors, and occasionally a few West German journalists. The Plenzdorfs did a lot of entertaining in their Berlin apartment; it was more convenient than a restaurant and they did not need to drive anywhere. At these evening gatherings, I observed two things: everyone contributed something to the party, often something that was homemade or difficult to come by in the GDR, and no one smoked. There was a small balcony one could access from the living room, but it was off limits to smokers. They had to go down several flights of stairs to the ground floor, exit the building and walk to an adjacent courtyard. Understandably, when visiting the Plenzdorfs, most people simply refrained from smoking.

What explains Ulrich Plenzdorf's strong, lifelong aversion to cigarette smoking and secondhand smoke? I asked myself that very question in 1975 when he was our visiting German writer in Oberlin, and while visiting him in East Berlin in the fall of that year I found the answer. I discovered how widespread smoking was in the GDR, despite the efforts of government authorities to advance a campaign against it; it was permitted in most places of work, restaurants and bars, and other public places. Just as I had experienced as a college student in the 1960s, cigarette smokers were everywhere in East Germany and most adults smoked, especially men. For persons like Ulrich and Helga Plenzdorf, non-smokers who could not tolerate second-hand smoke, it was a dreadful situation.

East Germany's most popular cigarettes were Cabinets, which contained about 50% more nicotine than most Western cigarettes, and more tar as well. This made them more dangerous to smokers, of course, and to the innocent bystanders who were exposed to hazardous levels of toxic second-hand smoke. Also, the quality difference between Western cigarettes and East German brands like f6, Juwel, and KARO was extreme. The socialist countries, East Germany included, could never purchase the tobacco they wanted; they had to settle for low-grade plants from Pakistan, India and Bulgaria. The fact that only low-quality cigarettes were available in the GDR didn't matter to the smokers; they got used to smoking these cigarettes and didn't know the difference. They liked them because they were addicted to the high level of nicotine.

Western brands of cigarettes were not sold on the open market in East Germany, but smokers eager to try them could buy them on the black market. Other sources of such cigarettes were relatives visiting from West Germany, who might bring along a few packs, and the state-run Intershops, where various goods from the West could be purchased with hard currency.

The most popular Western brand was Marlboro, of course, then Lucky Strike and Camels. France's iconic cigarette brands, Gauloise and Gitanes, were also sought after by the GDR's elite, many of whom were in a position to acquire them with Western currency. Gauloise cigarettes were famous for their throat-stripping strength, especially in the original unfiltered version. The brand has always been linked to international celebrities like Pablo Picasso, Jean-Paul Sartre, Albert Camus, and George Orwell, which made it a favorite among a number of the GDR's writers and artists.

The GDR prided itself on being a nation of readers, referring to itself as "Leseland DDR" (literally: reading land GDR). While that was true and certainly something to be proud of, the GDR was also a nation of smokers. At least forty percent of East German adults had the habit, as compared to one third of West German adults. My documentary book on East German writing in the 1970s, *GDR Literature During the Thaw*, (DDR-Literatur im Tauwetter) contains literary texts by 45 GDR writers, interviews I conducted with them, and other pertinent information. There is also a full-page portrait photograph of each writer, most of which were taken by professional photographers in the 1970s. As I was writing this snapshot, I recalled that some of the authors were shown smoking in their photographs, so I took a closer look. To my surprise, four of the writers are pictured smoking a pipe; four others are shown smoking cigarettes, and one of those writers is crushing a cigarette butt in an ashtray. Only one of the smokers is a woman, Sarah Kirsch, who happens to be one of my favorite writers. Her appearance and pose make evident that she is an emancipated woman. Seated, she is looking straight at the camera with a serious expression on her face, a cigarette in her right hand, held high. For her, the cigarette clearly is a "torch of freedom" in a society where many people viewed smoking as socially unacceptable behavior for women.

In memoriam

Ulrich Plenzdorf was born in Berlin on October 26, 1934. He died in Berlin on August 9, 2007, shortly before his 71st birthday. He departed this world much too soon, leaving behind his wife Helga and three adult children. I wrote this piece not only to honor and remember him in a very personal way, but also to reveal a few interesting things about his person and life that not very many of his readers know. He and I had many things in common beyond our mutual, deep-seated aversion to smoking and secondhand smoke. Uli was one of the most creative and talented writers I have known. He was also a man of principle and my friend. I miss him.

BUCKET LIST

Many American retirees, knowing they will have plenty of time to do whatever they want and can afford, are inclined to create bucket lists. More often than not, travel is at the top of the list and is rarely the first item to be crossed off. Why travel? Travel exposes you to new cultures, broadens your mind, takes you out of your comfort zone, enables you to meet new people and experience the wonders of the world. Some other common bucket list items are: Learn a new language, try a profession in a different field, run a marathon, learn to ski or scuba dive, go horseback riding, try an extreme sport, learn a strategy game, perform an act of kindness without expecting anything in return, take adult education classes, be a mentor to someone, and the list goes on and on. If you have good health and adequate financial resources, the possibilities are virtually unlimited.

In the GDR, just the opposite was true. The possibilities were very limited, and everyone knew by early adulthood what was possible and also what was not possible. Young adults had their aspirations, of course, but by American standards these were modest and practical in nature. It was not always possible for bright young East Germans to attend the college preparatory high school (*Erweiterte Oberschule*), which started with 9th grade and finished with 12th grade, at which point students would have to pass the college entrance exam (*Abitur*) in order to be eligible to study at a university. In its constitution the GDR defined itself as "a socialist state of farmers and workers," so the previously exploited working classes were encouraged to ascend within GDR society and improve their lives via the socialist system. In the higher education admission process, preference was given to the children of working class families and members of the new privileged class—SED Party loyalists and functionaries. Young persons who were completing high school or vocational school were not always able to choose their preferred career path, nor could they decide not to work. A highly developed vocational training and guidance system helped them to find "the right job" and to negotiate the difficult transition from school to work. In East Germany's state-controlled and centrally planned economy, each person was assigned a job and not allowed to abandon that job without permission from the central planners. If someone did not have a job, that person could be declared "asocial;" asociality was a criminal offense in the GDR that could lead to imprisonment. Also, most GDR employees could not look forward to promotions and salary raises or other forms of career advancement, as we typically do in the US. They basically just marched in place.

East Germans, like West Germans and the rest of us, were eager to travel and see the world, but here too they had limited options and were subjected to many restrictions. The most fortunate GDR citizens would be able to take a group bus trip to the Soviet Union or to one of the communist countries in the Eastern Bloc—Poland, Czechoslovakia, Hungary, Romania, Bulgaria. Like the GDR, these Central and Eastern European countries were satellite-states of the USSR from the end of World War II until the collapse of the Soviet communist system in the early 1990s. The East German mark was not a convertible currency in Western countries, so from a financial viewpoint the East Germans were limited to traveling in Eastern Bloc countries that were under Soviet domination. The Berlin Wall, erected in 1961, would further restrict their ability to travel freely for almost three decades.

Young adults in the GDR did not have bucket lists, of course, but they did aspire to lead a good life and hoped to achieve certain things. Beyond travelling to foreign countries, here are some examples of items that in all likelihood would have appeared on most young GDR citizens' wish lists: obtaining a license to drive a car, purchasing an automobile, acquiring a comfortable apartment either for single occupancy or for a couple, landing an interesting and rewarding job, and in most cases starting a family. East Germany always had a negative birth rate, so the government encouraged GDR citizens to have children by offering various types of incentives, such as nicer living quarters.

At age eighteen East Germans could apply for a license to drive a car. As soon as they turned eighteen, most persons put their name on the waiting list, even if they had no intention of obtaining the driver's license. They did this because an application for a driver's license—just like an application to purchase a car—could be transferred to another person. After waiting for a period of four to six weeks, one could take the theoretical test and then begin practical driver training on a driving simulator. After successful completion of these two steps in driving school, as well as an eye exam and a first-aid course, students would be permitted to drive on the roads with a trainer. The cost of driving school was about 200 marks, which was not expensive, and it took about three months to complete. Upon successful completion of a road test, the student driver would receive a driver's license. But once someone had obtained a license, what was that person going to drive? That brings us to a related, much trickier issue—the purchase of an automobile.

In the period after WW II, two types of automobiles were manufactured and available for purchase in the GDR: the Trabant and the Wartburg. The Trabant was East Germany's answer to the Volkswagen Beetle—an affordable "no frills" car with room for four passengers and luggage despite its small size. It was made of Duroplast, a composite material similar to plastic, and had a noisy two-stroke engine that generated lots of black smoke and pollution. The first Trabant, a P 50, was produced in 1957; the production line closed in 1991, one year after the reunification of Germany.

Most East Germans first submitted an application to buy a car and then applied for a driver's license. Timing was a major issue, if the applicant wanted to receive the automobile and the license more or less at the same time. This is because one typically had to wait ten years or more from the time the car was ordered until the vehicle was ready to be picked up. And when the applicant received a letter indicating that the car was ready, s/he had to pick it up in person and pay for it with cash: the price was approximately 7,000 marks for a Trabant and 16,000 marks for a Wartburg. When submitting an application, one could choose between those two models. The long wait made it difficult to acquire a car, so it is easy to understand why the acquisition of an automobile was at or near the top of everyone's wish list.

Also high on the wish list of most young adults was obtaining a decent apartment in a good location, not an easy task. Housing was a huge problem in the GDR, one that went unresolved until the period following German reunification in the 1990s. There was an acute housing shortage throughout East Germany, especially in cities like Berlin, Leipzig, and Dresden which had suffered much destruction from bombing during WW II. The apartments that were available in damaged pre-WW II apartment buildings were for many reasons undesirable: These buildings did not have elevators, the plumbing and electricity were in bad shape, and the heating systems were problematic. Also, the toilet facilities were often located outside the apartment with access from the stairway landing between floors, so they could be shared by tenants on the floor above and the one below. In the assignment of living space, the post-WW II privileged class—SED Party loyalists and functionaries—would usually receive preferential treatment. Married couples with children came next, then single individuals who were in the workforce, and last of all retirees. Because of the housing shortage, married couples who shared an apartment often had to remain in that living space if they decided to separate or had gotten divorced. That could lead to a very awkward situation when one of the "separated" partners had a new lover and brought that person home. If both partners had new lovers, they would work out special arrangements for visitations that ensured privacy.

My East German friend Ida, who would occasionally assist me with various aspects of my book project on GDR literature, gave me much of the information provided above during our casual conversations. She was about thirty years old when we met by chance in a Berlin café in the fall of 1975.

Ida was single and did not want to get married, because—as she asserted firmly—that would just make life even more complicated. She worked in a Lutheran Church library, a boring job that nevertheless provided sufficient income to sustain her while enabling her to keep a very low profile, something she wanted. She lived in a tastefully decorated two-room apartment (plus kitchen and bathroom) in a plain but fairly modern building situated near the center of Berlin and close to a city railway station. She said on several occasions how fortunate she was to occupy this lodging and this amount of space by herself. As we got to know each other better over time, she told me a secret; she informed me that she had submitted an application for a permanent exit visa (*Ausreiseantrag*) which would enable her to leave the GDR forever and move to West Berlin, as her older sister had done some years earlier. This "hostile-negative" action had made her officially a persona non grata in the GDR and potentially put her at risk for harassment by government authorities.

For women especially, life in East Germany was very difficult. For women with children and a spouse or partner, it could be extremely demanding and tiring. Every able-bodied man and woman was needed in the labor force and therefore expected to work at an assigned job. Persons who refused to work or dropped out of the workforce could be declared "asocial" by the authorities and then possibly imprisoned. The typical daily routine for a woman with one young child might look something like this: arise at 4:30-5:00 a.m.; get child and herself ready for the day ahead; prepare and have breakfast; using public transportation take child to the pre-school nursery (*Kinderkrippe*); go to work from there, again using public transportation; work at assigned job all morning; if necessary, do some grocery shopping during lunch hour; pick up child in the late afternoon and go home; prepare and eat dinner; get child bathed and off to bed; go to bed at 9:00-9:30 p.m. Start all over again on the next weekday. Weekend activities would include doing laundry, cleaning house, shopping for groceries, etc., spending time with child, and more. Having a husband, as Ida told me, would just make life even more complicated. As I reflect on this while writing I am reminded of the saying, "a woman's work is never done." This certainly was true in the GDR!

One day, as Ida and I were discussing her plan to relocate to West Berlin, I asked her to tell me what had motivated her to apply for a permanent exit visa. Without hesitation and with considerable emotion, she said: "I'm in my early thirties and have done everything one can possibly do here in the GDR. I've taken trips to all the countries we are permitted to visit, including the Soviet Union, which I've visited twice; I've got my driver's license; I've also applied to purchase an automobile and have been waiting for years for my turn to do that; I've got as nice an apartment and as much living space as a single person could possibly hope for in East Berlin; I've got a job I don't like and can't look forward to finding a better one; and, I don't want to get married or have children. So, there's nothing left for me to do or accomplish here, I've done it all!"

(Note: The term "bucket list" and the notion of creating a list of things you want to do before you die or "kick the bucket" were made popular by a 2007 comedy-drama film starring Jack Nicholson and Morgan Freeman. In *The Bucket List* two terminally ill men break out of a cancer ward and head off on a road trip with an itinerary that includes skydiving, racing cars, flying over the North Pole, visiting Mt. Everest in Nepal, attending a lion safari in Tanzania, slinging poker chips in Monte Carlo, riding motorcycles on the Great Wall of China, visiting the Taj Mahal, and dining at a Michelin-starred restaurant in France. In the process the two men—a billionaire health care magnate and a mechanic—become unlikely friends and ultimately find joy in life, despite their illnesses.)

DEFENSIVE DRIVING

Consider this: If a GDR citizen submitted an application to purchase a car at age twenty, that person would be at least thirty years old when the automobile was ready to be picked up. Because of the decade-long wait between the time a car was ordered and when it became available, it is easy to understand why the acquisition of a car was so high on every young East German's wish list. Also, because of the long wait used vehicles were usually sold for more money than the owners had paid for a brand new one. People would not only sell their cars to friends, but also to strangers who would pay a premium to circumvent the long waiting period.

If you have to wait ten years or more to take possession of an automobile you ordered, you are in all likelihood going to take good care of it. That is precisely what East German car owners did, understandably, and they also did everything possible to avoid getting in an accident. They drove in a manner designed to protect their vehicle, consciously practicing what we commonly call "defensive driving." In the Safe and Responsible Driving guidelines from the Ontario Ministry of Transportation, defensive driving is summarized as three things: visibility, space, and communication. Visibility—be alert and actively checking what vehicles around you are doing. Space—maintain a safe following distance with sufficient room to stop without causing a collision if the vehicle in front stops suddenly. Communication—be sure to signal your intention to the vehicles around you.

Defensive drivers proceed at a safe speed and are cautious; they slow down at all intersections; they pay attention to what is going on all around them as well as directly in front of them; they try to anticipate other drivers' actions; they are tolerant of other drivers' mistakes; they minimize distractions; and they monitor their own driving performance. Moreover, they also do not drive while under the influence of alcohol or drugs, something that was strictly forbidden in the GDR. For a first DUI offense, one could have the driver's license taken away for as long as one year.

I am tempted to declare that East Germans were the best defensive drivers in the world, but since there are many countries in which I have not driven a car, I cannot do that. However, I can state with absolute certainty that they were the best defensive drivers I have ever encountered—out of necessity, to be sure. They obeyed the rules of the road assiduously, observed speed limits, and crossed through intersections with traffic lights only when the light was green. Yet, despite all their caution and precautions, GDR drivers occasionally had accidents and from time to time their vehicles needed replacement parts or repair. What did they do then?

For both Trabant and Wartburg automobiles, the two East German brands, there were repair centers that were authorized by the manufacturers. The repair work would be carried out in their shops, not at a dealership or gas station, but everything depended on the availability of replacement parts. Sometimes car owners had to wait for a long time because the parts were not readily available. There were also stores where you could buy a part your car needed—a new muffler, for example, and their mechanics would install the parts. Of course, it helped if you knew and/or bribed the store owner and the mechanic. Very few cars were totaled in East Germany, so trying to repair the damage was always the first option. But in the rare cases when the car was beyond repair, the owner would be provided after some time with a new vehicle, the cost of which would mostly be covered by insurance. All GDR car owners were required to purchase accident and liability insurance.

In the interest of full disclosure, I have to confess that I had an automobile accident in the GDR, a collision with a streetcar that was my fault. It happened in June 1976, while I was driving around the busy central district of East Berlin in my relatively new, conspicuously bright red/orange Volkswagen Rabbit. The streetcar or tram that hit me had two cars, no passengers (fortunately!), and an operator who was taking it for a midday practice run as part of her driver training. In East Berlin trams traveled on rails or tracks located alongside or in the public streets; some included segments of segregated right of way, which made driving a car in the urban environment more challenging. I collided with a tram that was moving on tracks in the street and about to negotiate a curve where I was about to drive my vehicle across the tracks. In these situations, trams always had the right of way so the driver pressed forward. For some reason, I was not driving defensively and did not observe the right of way. When I was crossing the tracks and almost on the other side, the tram rammed into the back of my Rabbit on the driver's side of the car.

I was not injured, but the rear chassis and body of my vehicle were seriously damaged by the collision. What happened next still amazes me when it comes to mind. The young tram operator and I discussed the accident and how to proceed. She was very frightened, and I was worried that the police would soon show up. Since neither of us was injured, and since the tram was not damaged in any way, we quickly agreed that it would be best not to report the accident and to simply go our separate ways. And that's just what we did—a stroke of luck after my misfortune! But unfortunately, my beloved Rabbit never recovered fully from that collision.

LITTLE TRAFFIC LIGHT MAN

The most popular man in East Germany wasn't actually a human being, but a symbol shown on pedestrian signals. His name was Little Traffic Light Man, *Ampelmännchen*, diminutive of *Ampelmann*. Today, thirty years after the collapse of the Berlin Wall, the Ampelmännchen remains a beloved symbol in eastern Germany. It has the distinction of being one of the few relics of the communistic German Democratic Republic to have survived the end of the Cold War, mainly because of its immense popularity. In post-Wall Germany, the "cute" little traffic light man gained cult status and became popular with tourists as souvenirs. The East German Ampelmännchen is a stout male figure in straight-legged stride; he is wearing a hat which always reminds me of the flat-topped hat Amish men wear. With his big head and short legs, he looks as if he just stepped out of a cartoon or comic strip. The more static-looking West German version, by contrast, has a traditional-shaped human figure and no hat or other accessories.

The father of the East Berlin Ampelmännchen was traffic psychologist Karl Peglau (1927-2009), who created it in 1961 as part of a proposal for a new traffic lights layout. Peglau was eager to design a pedestrian traffic light that would be comprehensible to everyone regardless of age or health—children, elderly people, the mentally and physically handicapped, and color-blind persons. His concept envisioned two little men: a side-facing green man in full stride, his arm stretched forward like an arrow, signaling permission to "GO AHEAD;" also, a frontal-standing red man with thick outstretched arms that had the function of a barrier, signaling "STOP." Peglau's ultimate goal was to create greater safety for pedestrians. The "walk/don't walk" symbols would make sense to all pedestrians, he reasoned, and would certainly help reduce traffic fatalities. He decided to give his clever creations noses and hands, to create a likeable effect in the hope of provoking the desired pedestrian behavior through an emotional response. And that is how the hatted Ampelmännchen, the purposeful-looking signalmen that have helped direct traffic in East Germany for more than fifty years, came into being.

The first Ampelmännchen was installed in 1969 at the corner of Unter den Linden and Friedrichstrasse, two major streets in East Berlin's central district. The little men were so popular that they were woven into comic strips and children's cartoons. Games with the Ampelmännchen were developed, as were stories for radio and television broadcasts. Partly animated Ampelmännchen stories were broadcast once a month as part of the East German children's bedtime program "Sandmännchen" (Little Sandman), which had one of the largest viewing audiences in the GDR. In the 1980s, parents and teachers spearheaded an initiative to make the symbol become part of road safety education for children. In the 1990s, however, the Ampelmännchen almost faced extinction. After the fall of the Berlin Wall in 1989, newly unified Germany decided to rid itself of some vestiges of the GDR, including its street and traffic signs as well as its pedestrian traffic signals. The East German safety education programs featuring the Ampelmännchen vanished. In 1997, the country prepared to switch to the more generic-looking West German traffic light man. East Germans, many of whom felt they had been treated like second-class German citizens during and following the reunification process, were outraged. They pushed back and their protests led to calls to save the East German version of the Ampelmännchen as a part of East German culture. A group rightfully called "Rescue the Ampelmännchen" successfully lobbied the government for their preservation, and the little traffic light men returned to pedestrian crossings.

Since that time, the Ampelmännchen has become a virtual mascot for the East German nostalgia movement, known as *Ostalgie.*

Ampelmann and Sandmann are two of the few cultural icons from the East that survived the change in direction that followed the collapse of the Berlin Wall. Today, Ampelmännchen are omnipresent throughout what once was the German Democratic Republic and have been embraced by East and West Germans alike. The Ampelmännchen are not only installed on pedestrian traffic signals in eastern Germany, but also in the eastern and some of the western districts of Berlin, as well as in some western German cities. In 2004, Joachim Rossberg invented the female counterpart to the Ampelmännchen, the *Ampelfrau,* which was installed on some traffic lights in eastern German cities, including Dresden and Zwickau. Ampelfrau is a squat, girlish figure with pigtails and a full skirt. There are three official Ampelmännchen variations in modern-day Germany—the much-revered East German version, the traditional West German version, and the pan-German Ampelmännchen that was introduced in 1992. Each German state has the right to determine the version it is going to use. East Germans have changed the look of Ampelmännchen traffic lights as a joke since the early 1980s. Some variations are Ampelmännchen with umbrella, with bicycle, and as warning light. But the best variation for sure is the one the West German city of Bad Nauheim created in Elvis Presley's honor in 2018. When Elvis was a soldier stationed in Germany, from October 1958 to March 1960, he lived in Bad Nauheim. The "King of Rock and Roll" Ampelmännchen shows a silhouette of Elvis, who gives the "WALK" signal when he starts his signature hip swinging. How clever!

Ampelmann has become a cult figure and an iconic brand with a flagship store in Berlin's Hackesche Höfe marketplace. There and on the Ampelmann website one can purchase all sorts of products—souvenirs, fashion accessories, clothing items, and more—featuring the East German Ampelmännchen logo. If you would like to see some of these innovative consumer goods and perhaps do a little shopping, go to this website: https:// www.ampelmannshop.com

[Note: For the information presented above, I relied primarily on the following online sources:

1. "Ampelmännchen," https://en.wikipedia.org/wiki/ Ampelmännchen. 8 pp.

2. "The Development of the East German Ampelmännchen," https://www.ampelmann.de/en/a-brand-with-a-history. 11 pp.

3. Olga Khazan, "The 'Little Traffic Light Man' That Could," https:// www.theatlantic.com/international. September 25, 2013. 7 pp.]

ERIKA, A GERMAN BEAUTY

Products made in East Germany had a reputation for shoddy quality and hideous styling, even if that wasn't always the case. One notable exception was the high-quality Erika Modell M typewriter which was first manufactured during the 1930s by Seidel & Naumann of Dresden, Germany. During WW II production of the Erikas was halted for a while, but it resumed in 1946 after the war ended and continued until 1991, when the GDR no longer existed. There were two major production phases of post-WW II Erikas: 1946-1965 and 1965-1991. GDR writers who used a typewriter during the 1940s, 1950s, 1960s, 1970s, and 1980s were more likely than not to have typed their texts on an Erika made after WW II. The Erika M was produced by Seidel & Naumann unchanged for some time after WW II, with production ending in 1949 following the creation of Seidel & Naumann VEB Dresden (nationally-owned company) by the new East German government.

The Erika M machine is a manual typewriter, with glass-covered QWERTY keys. All Erika model typewriters were designed to be portable, and this model came inside a leather case, with a cleaning brush attached to the interior of the lid. In an online typewriter review of the Erika M (1936), vintage typewriter enthusiast Daniel Marleau asserts that Erika is "in a class by herself." (December 22, 2015). Below are some passages from his tribute to Queen Erika, a magnificent machine.

By the 1930s, typewriters were firmly established in the workplace. While American portables were viewed as the less capable offspring of their office parent, it seems the German typewriter company Seidel & Naumann had focussed their efforts on perfecting the portable without an office standard looming over it.

And perhaps for this reason they named their typewriter Erika and made it the most visible label on the machine. Moreover, it's in a unique type style that speaks to the brand rather than the company. Most other typewriter companies made sure you knew who made their typewriter. And if their typewriters had names, they usually said more about their function than their form: Smith Corona Silent, Royal Quiet Deluxe, Remington Quiet-Riter.

Olympia didn't even bother to add a name label to most of their typewriters, since they were often obscure letter number combinations like SM3. Not exactly something that inspires. Olympia probably decided they'd let their typewriters do the talking. After all, they are superb machines.

But a name says much about what a company thinks of their product. The Teutonic roots of the name Erika suggests something that means noble. And among the Erika line of nobility, the model M is Queen, from her one-piece outer shell to her reinforced carriage rail and levers and silver-ringed glass top keys, she's not only pleasing to the eye, but has a firm touch that retains a lightening quickness. This is not a typewriter that lives in an ordinary office, she's meant to grace the desk of a writing aficionado.

[...]

[...]

Some have suggested the M, in the Erika M, stands for Meisterklasse, or Masterclass. While this seems appropriate, I like to think of her as Erika the Magnificent. She's also in a class by herself. There is no equal.

On December 17, 2014, Daniel Marleau posted an online typewriter review of the Erika Model 10 (1954). Model 10 is the one most people think about when they think of post-WW II Erikas. It was the second new model introduced after the war and was produced from 1952-1963. In his entertaining review, Marleau has high praise for the Erika 10 and the engineers, designers, and workers who crafted this top-of-the-line machine. As he points out, the Erika and similar German typewriters type like a dream; they are on a whole different level of class when it comes to typing actions and appearance.

> If you've ever used a high-end typewriter, such as an Olympia, Hermes or the versatile Smith-Corona and thought a typewriter couldn't get much better, think again. The Erika 10 takes the best these manufacturers have to offer and puts them into one of the finest typewriters ever made. It has the precise German engineering of an Olympia, the design flair of the Swiss Hermes and the simplicity of the All-American Smith-Corona. You'd think something produced in Soviet-controlled Eastern Germany would lack the refinement of its Western counterparts, but whoever was responsible for the Erika typewriter might have taken that as a challenge to beat the best that capitalism had to offer. Perhaps being behind the Iron Curtain afforded them a kind of free market exemption, allowing them to craft the ultimate weapon of words. For these workers, engineers and designers, the one allowed act of artistic expression in a life of grey oppression was when they stepped into the Erika factory. While other companies fretted over profit margins, Erika was under no such pressure and it seems they escaped the demands of Soviet-style quotas, where quantity trumped quality. Human

appetite for luxury exists in all societies and for the privileged nomenklatura in the Eastern Bloc that apparently extended to typewriters and Erika was there to fill that need.

This Erika is designed for writing, Marleau, himself an author, explains: "Lots of writing. Putting it on a shelf and looking at it would feel like an insult to this thoroughbred." He goes on to describe the experience of writing with an Erika 10, which he maintains is without equal:

> The keys seem to float on the wings of angels, where the merest whiff of thought moves your fingers to rapture. If a typewriter could be a muse, Erika would be her name. And if writing is your desire, she will inspire you to new highs. She's a beauty to look at, for sure, but not to the point of distraction. After all, she's there to work. And in the case of Erika, beauty runs in her bones.
>
> [...]
>
> There's nothing wrong with most other typewriters, they work, they get the job done, but when it comes to that elusive feel, the Erika has no equal. I've used dozens of typewriters, all in the quest for "The One." That journey just ended. If you're serious about writing and typewriters, stop looking. Get an Erika 10.

Now let me relate how I became acquainted with Erika, the German beauty, in the fall of 2012. It occurred in connection with a book I was in the process of publishing with the Ch. Links Verlag in Berlin, Germany. On November 20, 2012, I received via email graphic artist Nadja Caspar's cover design for my forthcoming memoir, *Von Oberlin nach Ostberlin. Als Amerikaner unterwegs in der DDR-Literaturszene* (From Oberlin to East Berlin. An American Travelling in the GDR Literary Scene). It featured a bright yellow Erika posing boldly on a bright blue background. The retro appearance of the typewriter appealed to me right away, as did the blue and yellow color combination, since these also happen to be the University of Delaware's school colors. Furthermore, I liked the depiction of a typewriter that had been so closely associated with East Germany and probably used by every GDR writer mentioned in my book. I could not have been more pleased!

In April 2013, not long after my book was published in Germany, two writer friends came to Newark and the University of Delaware for a visit. One was Fred Viebahn, a German-born writer I had met in East Berlin in the mid-1970s. The other was his wife Rita Dove, a prominent American writer who had received the Pulitzer Prize for Poetry in 1987 and served as Poet Laureate Consultant in Poetry to the Library of Congress from 1993 to 1995. I have known them since the late 1970s when the three of us were living and working in Oberlin, Ohio. Of course I gave them a copy of my new book, a few copies of which the publisher had just sent me. Fred took a look at the cover and fell in love with Erika at first sight. He expressed his affection immediately by locating a used yellow machine on eBay Germany and purchasing it. He arranged for it to be shipped to his mother's home in Germany. Fred has in the meantime transported the vintage Erika to their house in Charlottesville, Virginia.

For persons born during or soon after WW II, as I was, the clickety clack of a manual typewriter evokes pleasant memories. The joy of the feel and sound of the typewriter is something special, and persons of my generation who are now senior citizens never fell out of love with it. What's surprising though, according to an article in our local Wilmington, Delaware newspaper, is that the younger generation has begun taking a liking to typewriters once again. Carey Cranston, president of the American Writers Museum in Chicago, which features a popular section with seven manual typewriters and an electric machine that visitors can try out, is quoted as saying: "Typing for the first time is exciting, especially for younger people." He says he'll never forget the reaction of one fifth-grader discovering typewriters for the first time. "Wow, this is great! It's an instant printer!" he exclaimed. (Katherine Roth, "Feeling the love, typewriters return," *The News Journal*, July 4, 2019, p. 8A)

As I conclude this piece, I find myself wondering if the Erika typewriter is the finest machine ever manufactured in East Germany. Maybe, but who knows?

XI

IN RETROSPECT

FIRST VISIT TO EAST BERLIN

Three of my undergraduate student years were spent at Colby College in Maine, where in my sophomore year I decided to major in German. During that year I applied for admission to the Junior Year in Freiburg, an academic program in Germany sponsored by Wayne State University. Fortunately I was admitted, even though I was not a strong student at that time, and in September 1962 I sailed from New York to Rotterdam on a Holland America Line cruise ship with about 105 other students from various US colleges and universities. About 70 of these students would be spending the academic year as participants in Wayne State's Junior Year in Munich program, which was affiliated with the University of Munich; the other 35 students would be studying at the University of Freiburg, in a famous old university town located on the edge of the Black Forest in southwest Germany. At age nineteen, I was understandably very excited about the prospect of spending a year in Germany!

The year in Freiburg exceeded my expectations in every area and way. My German improved by leaps and bounds, as a result of the instruction that was conducted entirely in German in every course I took and also through my social contacts. Making connections to German students at the university was difficult at first, but eventually I was able to do so by participating in events and weekend excursions that the International Office (*Akademisches Auslandsamt*) offered, such as an overnight ski trip to the Black Forest resort, Titisee. These events were designed to bring the foreign students together with German students who were interested in meeting them. I got to know a number of Germans in this way and enjoyed socializing with them at what one could call "mixer" gatherings. By the spring semester, I had made friends with a female German student majoring in psychology who eventually became my girlfriend. This development made my life in Freiburg even more enjoyable and certainly helped improve my German.

Among the many special events in which I participated, the highlight of the year was without doubt a trip we took to Berlin, which was sponsored by both of the Junior Year programs and financed by the German government. The trip took place during Pentecost, a religious holiday celebrated in Germany and throughout Europe. The stamps in my passport from way back then indicate that it was a five-day excursion, from June 4 to June 9, 1963. I recall that our group made the journey on three large buses, each pulling a trailer filled with luggage. We drove north from Munich and crossed the border from West Germany into the GDR at Juchhöh (in Upper Franconia, Bavaria) and from there made the 194-mile journey on the GDR transit highway to Drewitz, the border crossing point from the GDR into West Berlin. The trip to West Berlin took all day, as would our return via the same route to Munich. The East German border guards kept us sitting in the buses for several hours as they looked through some pieces of our luggage in a leisurely manner. They obviously intended to delay and inconvenience us, to make our long journey even longer and as unpleasant as possible—and their hostile behavior did just that!

In West Berlin at last, we settled into a modest but comfortable hotel that was centrally located, just a block away from Kurfürstendamm, Berlin's most famous shopping boulevard. We were tired, but nothing could keep us from having our first taste of Berlin's free-swinging night life. Berlin was really *alive*!—especially at night, and it didn't shut down at midnight like other German cities. There were no fixed closing hours, so Berlin was known as the city that never sleeps. Night life like that was not to be found in Waterville, Maine, where I went to college, nor was there anything comparable in Munich or Freiburg. We twenty-year-olds, old enough to drink in Germany where the legal age for consumption of alcoholic beverages was sixteen, took full advantage of what Berlin had to offer. Of the clubs some of us visited, I can remember three: the Resi Bar, featuring private telephones fixed to tables with easily seen numbers so customers could contact patrons at other tables, the trendy Eden Saloon, and the Eierschale (Egg Shell), which was situated on a converted river barge.

During the four days we were in Berlin, we had considerable free time and therefore could explore the city as we liked. A guided bus tour of West Berlin and a few other group events had been scheduled, two of which left a lasting impression on me. The first was a bus trip to East Berlin, separated from West Berlin by a wall that had been constructed by the GDR, starting on August 13, 1961. This was a barrier that surrounded West Berlin and prevented access to it from East Berlin and adjacent areas of East Germany. Its purpose was to keep disaffected East Germans from fleeing to the West. Seeing and being inside the fortified and heavily guarded crossing point from West to East Berlin was a shock to us. We all stayed on the bus, taking everything in with fascination and fear. This was the front line of the Cold War between the US and the Soviet Union, and it was scary. Less scary but very sobering was our two-hour bus tour of East Berlin, as we saw for ourselves how the other Berliners were living under heavy-handed communist rule.

My recollection of our bus tour is hazy, as one might expect, but what I saw interested me enough to want to take a closer look on foot. So, together with a few other JY students, I made my way to border crossing point Checkpoint Charlie the next day and from there entered East Berlin. We strolled along the famous boulevard, Unter den Linden, attracting stares from the passersby. I still can remember a few things that made an impression on me. I recall the dreariness and colorlessness of East Berlin, especially in comparison to West Berlin. Also, how few automobiles there were on the main avenues and boulevards. Large propaganda signs and banners were everywhere, extolling the merits of socialism and the ruling SED Party. The showcases in front of stores presented few items one would want to purchase. A shop selling glassware and china had a few pieces of old Meissen on display, but a sign indicated that they were display items and not for sale. We went into a bookstore and found editions of Marx and Lenin alongside the literary works of Goethe and Schiller—communist Germany and classical Germany, side by side.

Another event that I have not forgotten, mainly because it has gained in significance over the years, was a special luncheon for our group in the cafeteria of the Technical University of Berlin. This took place on the fourth and last day of our visit. The guest speaker was the Mayor of Berlin, Willy Brandt, who in 1964 would become leader of the Social Democratic Party of Germany (1964 to 1967) and then serve as Chancellor of the Federal Republic of Germany from 1969 to 1974. In 1971 Brandt was awarded the Nobel Peace Prize for his effort to achieve reconciliation between West Germany and the countries of the Soviet bloc. After welcoming us and giving a short speech before lunch, Brandt walked from table to table and greeted us personally in small groups while we were dining. We, and perhaps he, had no idea that his political star was about to rise as high as it did.

The incident that made the biggest impression on me occurred on our first full day in Berlin. Our group had a bus tour of West Berlin in the morning, right after breakfast, then we were given the rest of the day off to explore the city on our own. It was lunchtime, so a couple of JY students and I decided to get a bite to eat in a pub right next door to our hotel. When we entered we saw immediately that no other Americans from our group were there. While we were eating the owner approached us from behind the bar and asked if we were Americans. We answered in the affirmative. In those days the Germans, and the Berliners in particular, loved Americans. They remembered the Berlin airlift (June 1948 to May 1949), carried out by the

Allies when the Soviet Union blocked their railway, road, and canal access to the sectors of Berlin under Western control. The Berlin Blockade was one of the first major crises of the post-World War II Cold War. The Western Allies organized the Berlin airlift to carry supplies of every sort to the people of West Berlin, so they could survive the chokehold. It was an incredible operation with cargo planes flying in and out of Berlin all day long—and thank goodness it was successful. The blockade of Berlin was finally lifted by the Soviet Union on May 12, 1949. The airlift demonstrated the ability and resolve of the US to stand up to the Soviet Union without being forced into a direct conflict. The West Berliners were immensely grateful for our intervention and assistance in this time of crisis; it was a different world back then!

When the pub owner learned that the three of us had not yet viewed the Berlin Wall or the Brandenburg Gate from close up, he called for a taxi and prepaid our ride to an elevated viewing platform that had been erected directly in front of the Brandenburg Gate, Berlin's most famous landmark. The gate is the monumental entry to Unter den Linden, the renowned boulevard in the central Mitte district of Berlin. Until the Berlin Wall was built in August 1961, pedestrians and vehicles could pass freely through the gate, which is located in East Berlin. From the tower-like platform, one could look over the wall and through the gate and have a clear view of Unter den Linden. We did that and saw, among other things, the East German soldiers who were assigned to guarding the gate from the East Berlin side. They, together with a mini-wall, made certain that no East Germans attempted to approach the gate, which as a result was situated in no man's land on the eastern side of Berlin. It was an eerie sight, one I will never forget.

Our group departed from Berlin on June 9, well aware of the long delays we would encounter at the border crossing points, the one from West Berlin into East Germany and then the one from East Germany into West Germany. Our mood on the trip back to Munich was somber and subdued, as we reflected on this first direct experience of the Cold War. In October 1962, just one month after arriving in Germany, we had experienced the Cuban Missile Crisis, but from thousands of miles away so it had less of an impact on us. In Berlin, however, one could see and almost feel the Cold War—and it was frightening! I am sure that reaction is just what the pub owner was hoping for, so that we Americans would be motivated to continue protecting Berlin against the ever-present Soviet threat.

On June 26, 1963, about two and a half weeks after we had left Berlin, US President John F. Kennedy gave his famous "*Ich bin ein Berliner*" ("I am a Berliner") speech in West Berlin. It is generally regarded as the best-known speech of the Cold War era and also the most famous anti-communist speech. Twenty-two months after Soviet-occupied East Germany erected the Berlin Wall to prevent mass emigration into the West, Kennedy wanted to underline US support for West Germany. The message was aimed as much at the Soviets as it was at Berliners and was a clear statement of US policy in the wake of the construction of the Berlin Wall.

FIRST TRIPS TO EAST GERMANY

Lead-up

My first two trips to East Germany, in the summer of 1969 right before I began teaching at Oberlin College and in the summer of 1973, were instrumental in bringing about my conversion in the later 1970s from a scholar specializing in nineteenth-century German literature to a specialist in GDR literature. As I look back over my career as a professor of German, I realize that these two trips to East Germany played a crucial role in my professional development. They helped me acquire some essential background knowledge that would enable me in a relatively short period of time to shift into an entirely new field comfortably. The transformation would require much more than these two learning experiences, of course, and—as luck would have it—additional decisive resources would soon be available to me in Oberlin. Put simply, one thing led to another and all the pieces of my career puzzle gradually fell into place. And, although I had learned nothing about

GDR literature while in graduate school, I was very eager to head off in an entirely new direction and embraced the change.

Summer of 1969

After four stressful years of graduate school in Johns Hopkins University's PhD program in German literature, I needed and deserved a vacation before starting my full-time job at Oberlin College in September, 1969. My then-wife Marjorie and I decided to take a long automobile trip to several countries in western, eastern, and southern Europe. Toward the end of the trip we planned to spend ten days in the GDR. Apart from a few half-day visits to East Berlin during my student days in Freiburg and Mainz, this would be my first experience of East Germany. A glance at my passport from way back then tells me that we were in the GDR from August 7 until August 17, 1969. The residence permit entered in my passport, part of which is hand-written, reveals that we stayed overnight in these East German cities: Weimar, Leipzig, Dresden, Erfurt, Potsdam, Schwerin, Rostock, and Greifswald.

It was not very easy to book a trip like this to a communist country like East Germany, which had sealed its borders and was not at all eager to have lots of visitors from the West. Lodging had to be arranged far in advance through the state-owned and –operated Travel Bureau of the GDR (*Reisebüro der DDR*), which controlled all hotels located throughout the GDR. The Travel Bureau had several functions, the most important of which was arranging travel for foreigners visiting the GDR. Their services included booking hotel rooms and providing confirmation documents used to justify the issuance of a GDR visa upon entering the GDR. I had contacted this agency a few months before our departure for Europe and given them an itinerary. The Travel Bureau selected the hotels for our stay in each city; about half of these were the more desirable Interhotels that had been built in the 1960s to accommodate tourists from Western countries. (Tourists from Eastern European and other communist countries were lodged in shabby pre-World War II hotels, which had primitive plumbing and were not clean.) When the hotel arrangements had been finalized, I had to pay for everything in advance, including the GDR Travel Bureau's fees, using US dollars. The East German travel agency then sent me a packet containing instructions on how to proceed and vouchers for each hotel stay. These I would have to present at the East German border, in order to get a tourist visa. When we arrived at a hotel on the specified date, I handed over the voucher for our stay there. After checking our passports, someone from the hotel would take them to the local police station, so they would know we had arrived. In this manner, the police were able to keep track of our whereabouts as we moved around the country.

My recollection of our activities during the first stay in the GDR is sketchy, not only because more than fifty years have passed since I was there, but also because all the photos I took on this trip were ruined due to a malfunctioning light meter in my camera. However, I do have a few memories that are worth sharing. I remember how excited I was when we arrived at the East German border on August 7, on our way to Weimar where we would spend the first two nights. I had really been looking forward to this final leg of our long journey that took us to more than ten European countries, including several communist ones. I had been looking forward to touring "the other Germany," but I didn't know what to expect.

I soon learned that East Germany was very different from West Germany in many ways. The Germans living there under fascism during the Third Reich and then under USSR-imposed communism after World War II, had never lived in a free society. Years of repression by dictatorial regimes had influenced their thinking, their view of the world, and various aspects of their social behavior. In public they were reticent, withdrawn, and well-behaved; for the most part they made a conscious effort not to draw attention to themselves. Everyone tried to blend in, so the dull colors of the clothing they wore—olive drab, beige, smoke gray, field brown—provided the desired camouflage. The East Germans were somewhat provincial, which is understandable given the fact that they lived in a country the size of Tennessee and were only able to travel in groups to some of the other USSR-controlled communist countries. GDR citizens were very eager to travel, especially to

Western countries that were off limits, but most had never gotten beyond the borders of the GDR.

The East Germans were wary of strangers and did not want to be seen interacting with persons from the West. Our clothing signaled to everyone that we were from the West, and we were travelling around the country in a West German Ford Taunus. I was eager to make contact with East Germans and had two strategies that enabled me to engage in conversations. The first involved picking up hitchhikers, who were to be found everywhere. We preferred to pick up young couples, who sometimes would do some sightseeing with us or join us for lunch or dinner as our guests, which was a lot of fun. The second strategy involved sitting with East Germans who were having lunch or dinner, which was easy to do in the restaurants that were for the general public—i.e., for persons who did not have hard currency. It was not unusual for two couples who did not know each other to sit together at a table for four. And, as one can imagine, this seating arrangement would quickly engender a conversation that usually began with the question "Where are you from, if I may ask?" when the other couple heard us speaking English. When I revealed that we were from the US, more questions would follow, including this one: "Why are you visiting the GDR?" It seemed that every East German we talked with knew everything about their country, and I learned so much from these informal conversations. As we drove through small towns and villages that had not been bombed during World War II, I frequently had the feeling that we were going back in time and seeing Germany as it was during the 1930s and earlier. In towns where no bombs had fallen, things were very much like they had been decades before, just older and in dire need of renovation. Damage from the war was evident mainly in larger cities like Dresden, Leipzig, Rostock, Halle, Chemnitz, Magdeburg, and of course Berlin. All of eastern Germany's major population and manufacturing centers had been subjected to strategic aerial bombing attacks by British and American air forces. Although the war had been over for twenty-four years, damage from the war was still to be seen everywhere in the GDR's largest cities. The physical condition of municipal and apartment buildings, roads, and the infrastructure was poor, since the GDR did not have the funds to repair and rebuild much of what had been destroyed.

During this ten-day tour, we immersed ourselves in East Germany and tried to absorb as much as possible of what that country had to offer. We would leave our hotel right after breakfast and follow the plan we had developed for that day until it was time for dinner. It was an exhausting routine, a very intensive learning experience. As I gained more knowledge about that eastern portion of Germany and its rich culture and history, the GDR became a country I desired to explore in greater depth. This first trip provided a valuable introduction to the GDR and its society; I came away from it with an awareness of what else I needed to see and learn about to really get to know East Germany.

Summer of 1973

An opportunity to take a second, much longer trip to East Germany did not materialize until 1973. In my third year at Oberlin College, I was assigned to serve as director of its German Semester Abroad Program (GSAP) which I had helped design and initiate two years earlier. As GSAP director, I would spend the spring 1973 semester in Germany and Austria with a group of fourteen Oberlin students. Since the expense of my international flight was covered by program funds, I planned to stay in Germany after the semester ended in late May and travel around the GDR. The GSAP was scheduled to spend most of April and May in Vienna, where I was able to book accommodations for my tour of East Germany through the Austrian Tourist Office (Österreichisches Verkehrsbüro AG). Again, I had to pay for everything in advance using hard currency. Since Oberlin College had awarded me an internal $1,000 H. H. Powers Travel Grant for this 30-day study trip through the GDR, most of my GDR-related travel expenses were covered. All communications with the Travel Bureau of the GDR went through the Austrian Tourist Office, which simplified things for me. In order to recreate my itinerary, I again turned to my passport for assistance. The tourist visa, part of which was handwritten onto a large official stamp, was valid from June 6 to

July 6, 1973. The visa was for travel to and within the following districts of the GDR: Berlin, Cottbus, Dresden, Leipzig, Halle, Rostock, Erfurt, Magdeburg, and Potsdam. I had vouchers for stays in hotels—Interhotels for the most part—located within each of those districts.

Today, as I look back on this trip and consider its importance, I realize that it turned out to be a total immersion in East Germany, the equivalent of a crash course on that country's culture, history, and society. It was an intense learning experience that was at once exhilarating and exhausting— exhilarating because I was seeing and learning so much that was totally new to me, exhausting because I was on the go all day long, every single day, as I struggled to adhere to the very ambitious schedule I had drawn up that took me into all regions and some remote corners of the GDR. I came away from this trip armed with considerable firsthand knowledge about East Germany, its citizens and their way of life under socialism, in-depth knowledge that could not have been acquired in any other way.

There were many memorable moments during my 30-day tour of the GDR, and fortunately almost all of them were positive in nature. Yet, the moment that stands out most was decidedly negative. It occurred unexpectedly on the first day of the trip while I was having dinner in the restaurant of the historic Interhotel Elephant in Weimar, where I was spending my first two nights in the GDR. In the small restaurant dining room, I had been seated at a table for four persons where two middle-aged women were sitting and about to order dinner. I was delighted to have their company, as I was eager to converse with East Germans and learn from them. They could see from my clothes that I was not from Eastern Europe, and I identified myself as an American right away. After a short while, the older of the two women told us that she was working for the SED Party (the governing Marxist-Leninist party of the GDR) as a political appointee. Her main job as a government official was to supervise and oversee the actions of Weimar's mayor. The other woman worked with her, as her staff assistant. They said I was the first American they had ever met, something I was told frequently in the isolated GDR. During the course of our conversation, they asked what I was planning to do the next day, what my first activity would be in classical Weimar. I indicated that I was going to visit the Buchenwald concentration camp the next morning.

Buchenwald (literally, beech forest) was one of the first and largest of the Nazi concentration camps situated on German soil. Established in 1937, it stood on wooded Ettersberg hill about 4.5 miles northwest of Weimar. Many actual or suspected communists, as well as antifascist resistance fighters, were among the first internees which explains why the GDR decided to transform the remains of Buchenwald into a memorial and permanent exhibition. However, as time went on prisoners came from all over Europe and the Soviet Union—Jews, Poles and other Slavs, the mentally ill and physically disabled, Roma and Sinti people, and prisoners of war. There were also ordinary criminals and sexual "deviants." All prisoners worked primarily as forced labor in local armaments factories. Poor living conditions, insufficient food, and deliberate executions led to 56,545 deaths at Buchenwald. The camp was liberated by the US Army in April 1945. [Note: For the information presented above on Buchenwald, I relied on the following online source: "Buchenwald concentration camp" – Wikipedia.]

At the dinner table, the SED Party functionary told me about the infamous "Blood Road" (*Blutstrasse*), a five-kilometer-long connecting road that runs out of Weimar and leads through the beech forest to the concentration camp. It had been constructed in 1938-1939 by inmates who were exploited as slave labor and cruelly goaded on by the SS (*Schutzstaffel*, literally: Protection Squad, a major paramilitary organization under Adolf Hitler and the Nazi Party during the Third Reich). For thousands and thousands of prisoners a trip on this thoroughfare was a one-way route from which there was no return. The staff assistant, who was silent while her boss told me about the blood road, suddenly had something she wanted to interject. She said that there was a wonderful restaurant in a tourist hotel located right on the Blood Road, where she went to dine now and then, especially on weekends so she would have time for a walk when she finished eating. I should be sure, she added emphatically, to time my trip to the death camp so that I would be able to have my midday meal at the Buchenwald restaurant. I was horrified by the staff assistant's insensitive remarks which under the circumstances struck me as utterly repulsive. That was a memorable moment, to be sure, and it has stayed with me in the foreground of my mind for over half a century.

Follow-up

Sometimes Lady Luck smiles on you, quite unexpectedly, and that is just what happened to me after I returned to Oberlin in the summer of 1973. Early in the fall 1973 semester, I learned at a meeting of the German faculty that the prominent West German author we had invited months earlier to be our writer-in-residence in spring 1974 had declined our invitation. This was a fairly regular occurrence, since we always aimed very high with the initial invitation and then, if necessary, lowered our sights and invited a second- or third-tier writer who would be likely to accept. Mindful that high-profile GDR writer Günter Kunert had just been visiting writer at the University of Texas, and eager for more rewarding East German experiences, I proposed that we invite Christa Wolf, a GDR author who had acquired celebrity status following the publication of her novel *The Quest for Christa T.* If we got lucky and Christa Wolf did come to Oberlin, it would be a major coup. With some hesitancy, since we realized that this was a long shot, we proceeded to issue the invitation—and to our amazement she accepted! I was delighted at our good fortune, of course, and so were all of my colleagues.

Emboldened by our successful attempt to bring Christa Wolf to Oberlin, members of the German faculty decided without hesitation to invite another famous GDR author to be our visiting writer in spring 1975. Our target this time was Ulrich Plenzdorf, Berlin prose writer, playwright, film director and scenarist. He had achieved widespread international acclaim for his controversial yet highly regarded short novel and screenplay, *Die neuen Leiden des jungen W.* (The New Sufferings of Young W.), which in 1972 propelled him to the top among young writers of the GDR. The German faculty, and I especially, got lucky once again when Plenzdorf accepted our invitation. Plenzdorf's residency at Oberlin College—like that of Christa Wolf the previous spring—was generally perceived as a prestigious coup. *The New Sufferings* became a phenomenal success, selling over four million copies in 30 languages. By the mid-1970s, mainly as a result of this work's extraordinary popularity, Ulrich Plenzdorf had become the most discussed, reviewed, and performed GDR writer since the death of Bertolt Brecht in 1956.

Christa Wolf spent six weeks in Oberlin as German Writer-in-Residence in spring 1974 and helped awaken my interest in GDR literature. Fortunately, she was accompanied by her husband Gerhard, a well-known literary scholar and editor with connections to many contemporary GDR authors and publishers. I spent a lot of time with the Wolfs that spring, and they introduced me to the GDR literary scene through carefully selected readings and instructive conversations that were truly fascinating. When I told the Wolfs that I would be taking a one-year sabbatical leave in 1975-1976, they encouraged me to think about doing a project on GDR writing in the 1970s and promised to assist me. During the course of our discussions, the outline of a possible project gradually emerged. The focus would be on new directions and trends in East German literature during the period of "thaw" that unfolded shortly after Erich Honecker became leader of the Socialist Unity Party in 1971. My interactions with the Wolfs were invaluable and enabled me to build and expand on what I had learned during my two trips inside the GDR.

When Ulrich Plenzdorf came to Oberlin as visiting writer in spring of 1975, my informal education in the area of contemporary GDR literature continued. Uli Plenzdorf and I became good friends that semester, and he too helped me shape and finalize plans for my first research leave, a good portion of which I intended to spend in the GDR. I remain ever so grateful for the advice, assistance, and encouragement he gave me in the period leading up to my sabbatical leave. Like Christa and Gerhard Wolf the year before, he helped me develop and shape the project I proposed to undertake involving GDR writing and writers who were active in the 1970s. Moreover, when I was working on the project inside East Germany, he continued to assist me in meaningful ways, as did both of the Wolfs. In retrospect, I realize that I could not have produced an 840-page book like *DDR-Literatur im Tauwetter* (GDR Literature During the Thaw), nor most of my other major publications on East German literature, without the strong and unwavering support of Plenzdorf and the Wolfs. I am forever indebted to them—but also to Lady Luck, for she guided them to Oberlin College at the perfect time!

(For more information on Christa Wolf and Ulrich Plenzdorf at Oberlin College, see the snapshots in VI GDR WRITERS IN OHIO.)

BORDER CROSSING

The opening report in my Stasi-file, dated June 6, 1973, amuses me. It begins with a one-sentence summary: "US-American, who has a doctorate in German studies, intends to spend four weeks as a tourist in the GDR, in order to become better informed in general." As I read through the report, the memory of that border crossing resurfaces from the depths of my mind. I am astonished by the level of detail it contains: factual information about me and my first wife, Marjorie, who accompanied me on this trip, our travel route, and plans to visit friends in Hannover after leaving the GDR. How did they know all of this? According to the report, the border guards gathered details in casual conversation with us, as I was switching license plates, replacing the oval international customs number from West Germany with a rectangular GDR plate.

The report concludes with information about my person: "Zipser speaks good German with a slight accent, makes an intelligent, bright impression, but appears to be somewhat helpless mechanically (inept performance while changing the license plates). He was clean and appropriately dressed for the trip. When asked questions, he provided information readily after a brief hesitation." "Somewhat helpless mechanically!" Should I feel insulted? On the contrary, I am delighted to read that I needed help switching license plates, for now I have written proof of my notoriously poor mechanical ability which has always been a joke among family members and friends.

FALL OF THE BERLIN WALL

From time to time we witness events of a historic and very public nature, and of such magnitude and importance that we remember forever exactly where we were when we experienced or learned of them. I have experienced four such events in my lifetime. The first was the assassination of President John F. Kennedy in November 1963. I was a senior in college, and I heard the devastating news while listening to the radio in my dormitory room. The second was Neil Armstrong's moonwalk in August 1969. I was vacationing in Athens and watched that unbelievable event through the window of a department store where countless televisions were broadcasting it to a large, fascinated sidewalk audience. The third was the fall of the Berlin Wall on November 9, 1989. I was in my office at the University of Delaware that afternoon, preparing for a department meeting, when my wife called and said excitedly "they are tearing down the wall." Incredible! I, like so many others, had thought the detested "Mauer" was there to stay at least through my lifetime, if not forever. Finally, I remember watching CNBC's daily business program on 9/11/2001 while getting dressed for work. It was approximately 9:40 a.m., and the New York Stock Exchange had just opened. As the co-anchors were puzzling over what had just happened to one of the World Trade Center towers that had been hit by an airplane, I saw another plane come out of nowhere and smash into the second tower, causing the huge explosion, death and destruction we all remember. Four colossal and unforgettable events, two of them horrifying, the other two uniquely uplifting.

The collapse of the Berlin Wall profoundly affected the lives of many Eastern Europeans, who had been living since the end of World War II behind the so-called iron curtain, sealed off from the West and non-communist countries. During this period, 1945 to 1989, Germany had been divided into two states, the pro-Western Federal Republic of Germany and the German Democratic Republic, a communistic socialist state occupied and controlled by the Soviet Union. In October 1990, the world witnessed the reunification of the two Germanys, another momentous historical event I never expected to see in my lifetime.

The period leading up to the Berlin Wall's collapse was one of unprecedented turmoil in the GDR, marked by mass demonstrations against the government and the system, first in Leipzig and then throughout the GDR. On August 23, 1989, Hungary opened its border to Austria, and thousands of East German tourists took advantage of this opportunity to escape to the West. The Socialist Unity Party (SED) leadership underestimated the seriousness of the situation and failed to make changes that might have calmed things down; nor, fortunately, did they use force to restore order. On October 18, 1989, Erich Honecker resigned unexpectedly as General Secretary of the SED Central Committee and was replaced that day by Egon Krenz. Krenz, a hard-liner like Honecker, was responsible at the time for security issues in the SED. He spoke vaguely of wanting to introduce a *Wende* or change in direction within the GDR, but did not initiate reforms or do anything else to improve the situation.

By sheer coincidence, GDR writer Helga Schütz was our house guest in October 1989, precisely when the change in the SED party leadership took place. She had come to the US to give lectures and readings at several universities, including the University of Delaware. We watched with fascination as events in the GDR unfolded, and it was incredibly interesting to hear Schütz's commentary. Her presentation to a German-speaking audience was a very special occasion, since she was able to give us an insider's perspective on what was occurring in the GDR.

On November 9, 1989, the Berlin Wall came down. It happened suddenly and took everyone by surprise. Thousands of East Berliners had gathered at the border crossings that day and demanded that the crossing points be opened. In the evening, the crossing at Bornholmer Strasse was opened peacefully and soon thereafter other border crossings were opened as well. East Germans from all over the GDR rushed to East Berlin, and from there they streamed into West Berlin. On TV one saw East Germans standing on top of the Wall and talking to border guards, who did nothing to stop what was happening. In the days and weeks that followed, the Wall would literally be torn down, and on TV I watched people from both Germanys chipping away at the Wall with pickaxes, eager to help tear it down and obtain a concrete piece of history. These people were commonly referred to as *Mauerspechte* (wall peckers), and some of them sold small pieces of the wall to souvenir seekers. A friend of mine, a former UD student from Berlin, bought a piece of the wall for me. What a nice present and memory!

The collapse of the Berlin Wall was not only the high point of Germany's "peaceful revolution," it was one of the greatest moments in German history! Another great moment would follow in October 1990 when the two Germanys were reunified and the GDR ceased to exist. A short while later, a colleague/friend of mine at the University of Delaware offered me his condolences: "I'm sorry, Richard, that your area of research has gone out of existence." How wrong he was!

LAST TRIP TO EAST BERLIN

In the 1970s and 1980s, I made countless trips to West Berlin and East Berlin, shuttling back and forth via Checkpoint Charlie. My last visit to East Berlin was in July of 1990, about eight months after the Berlin Wall had been opened. I spent a week in West Berlin, and from there I twice drove into East Berlin without the inconvenience of having to pass through Checkpoint Charlie. Yet, for some strange reason, I missed that border crossing and the inconvenience that was part of it. Perhaps I was feeling nostalgic for the extraordinary opportunity I had had in the 1970s to gain insight into the difficult and challenging experience of people in the GDR, mainly writers, and to share that experience to some extent through my publications. I spent some time just driving around East Berlin, surprised and pleased to see how much of the central Mitte district was still familiar. On my second visit, I met Ulrich Plenzdorf for lunch in a trendy new restaurant in the Nikolaiviertel, and he told me about some changes that had taken place in the GDR's literary scene and everyday life as well. The appearance of East Berlin had also begun to change as the two Berlins were gradually being forged into one gigantic city. Gone were the barriers that had rendered the Brandenburg Gate, the Reichstag Building, and the Wall inaccessible from East Berlin.

The Berlin I first visited as a student in June 1963 was already a divided city, and for me that contributed to its charm and allure. In the 1970s, I actually enjoyed the experience of shuttling back and forth between East and West Berlin, experiencing immediately the sharp contrast between the two cities, one bustling with life throughout the day and night, the other its polar opposite. I liked and was intrigued by both Berlins, and I relished the eerie tension that one felt in the two Berlins of the Cold War era, which John le Carré captured perfectly in spy thrillers like *The Spy Who Came in from the Cold* (1963). The memory of these very different Berlins and all the exciting experiences I had in both is one I will cherish forever. As it turns out, my last trip to East Berlin in the summer of 1990 was also my last visit to Berlin. I am sure that this final revelation will come as a surprise to most of my readers; in a strange way it even surprises me.

REUNIFICATION OF GERMANY

In 1990, the German Democratic Republic joined the Federal Republic of Germany, thereby creating a unified German state, and East and West Berlin were also reunited into a single city. The process of transforming the GDR into a democratic state and unifying the two Germanys began with the *Wende* (change in direction) in November 1989 and culminated in a Unification Treaty, which was signed by officials of both German states on August 31, 1990. This treaty, the result of intense negotiations between the GDR and the FRG, provided for the accession of the GDR to the FRG. The end of the unification process is officially called *Deutsche Einheit* (German Unity) and is celebrated annually on October 3, a national holiday in Germany.

In accordance with Article 23 of the Basic Law of the FRG, which took effect on October 3, 1990, five of the GDR's newly created federal states (*Bundesländer*)—Brandenburg, Mecklenburg-Western Pomerania, Saxony, Saxony-Anhalt, and Thuringia—became states of the FRG. The 23 boroughs of Berlin formed Land Berlin, which became one of Germany's 16 constituent states. Berlin was again designated as the capital of unified Germany and, after the establishment of German unity, it also became the seat of the parliament and government. The socialist German Democratic Republic, founded after World War II on October 7, 1949, was no longer a satellite state of the Soviet Union and no longer a nation by itself. It had ceased to exist.

Helmut Kohl, who died at age 87 on June 16, 2017, served as Chancellor of the Federal Republic of Germany from 1982 to 1993, then as Chancellor of unified Germany from 1993 to 1998. He witnessed the fall of the Berlin Wall and, following that momentous event, was a major force behind German reunification as the Cold War came to what many people thought was its end. He has been called, and he deserves to be called, the "architect of German unity." When he perceived the possibility of forging the two Germanys into one, he moved decisively and through skillful diplomatic negotiations helped press forward in that direction. Another leader, one with less courage and experience, might have hesitated and lost the opportunity to reunite Germany. But Kohl—like Otto von Bismarck who, after uniting all the states of Germany, became the first Chancellor of the German Empire in 1871—was determined to build a stable and prosperous German republic with a unified national identity. He succeeded and, in so doing, secured his place alongside Bismarck in German history. Today, over thirty years after the two Germanys became one, Germany is the most economically powerful and politically influential country in the European Union.

The reunification of Germany took me very much by surprise. I, like almost everyone else, did not see it coming. And as with the collapse of the Berlin Wall, I never thought an event of such momentous historical-political significance would ever happen or be permitted to happen in my lifetime. Many persons in the GDR, as well as in the governments and populations of

Western and Eastern European countries, were opposed to German reunification. But happen it did, to my utter amazement, and I am pleased that the German nation was reassembled and that it is once again intact!

I would like to make three additional observations on the subject of German reunification. First, one must acknowledge the important role that Soviet leader Mikhail Gorbachev played in reuniting the two Germanys after the Berlin Wall fell in 1989. Without his cooperation and goodwill, East and West Germany could not have come together. Second, it is important to understand the pivotal role US President George H. W. Bush played in the unification process, as he exercised his superior skills as diplomat and statesman. It was Bush, successor to President Ronald Reagan, who worked with Chancellor Helmut Kohl to harness the upheavals in the crumbling Soviet empire in order to deliver on the promise of German unification.

Third, the Unification Treaty was just the beginning of a long and difficult process of the two Germanys coming to a territorial and political union. There were many obstacles to overcome and no one, including Helmut Kohl, could possibly have foreseen what this process would entail. In order to achieve his goal Kohl hurried the East Germans into unification by promising them "blühende Landschaften" (blossoming landscapes), an unrealistic vision of the economic prosperity the West could provide. But today, more than thirty years later, wages and pensions in the eastern states of Germany still are not equal to those in the states of former West Germany; also, the rate of unemployment is much higher. Many of the former East Germans feel forgotten and, understandably, are resentful. For these reasons mainly, there is still a wide divide between the populations and states of former East and West Germany.

AFTERWORD

LEST WE FORGET: HISTORY AND MEMORY

Richard Zipser has written *Memories of Life in East Germany: Snapshots* as a companion piece to his recently published *Remembering East Germany. From Oberlin to East Berlin.* Both are rooted in the experiences of the author as a young associate professor from Oberlin College on sabbatical leave in communist East Germany, writing a book about GDR literature while dodging interference from state security officials. Like its predecessor, *Snapshots* offers us the unique perspective of an American who, as an outsider living in the GDR, gained unusual insider knowledge and experience of that totalitarian society. Nevertheless, the "sibling" memoirs are structured in very different, beautifully complementary, ways. The former is catalyzed by the documentary evidence of Zipser's secret police file, as he rediscovers his younger self through the eyes of the Stasi handlers and informants who spied on him. In the latter, however, it is his gaze, rather than theirs, that founds the memoir.

As the title *Snapshots* suggests, it is as if we are in a picture gallery. Before us are short prose pieces which, like the snapshots of a skilled photographer, capture telling moments, people, and experiences. These are word pictures, created by a meticulously engaged and insightful observer. Zipser explains that, in composing these, his memories were triggered by a list of topics—a word bank, so to speak—that he compiled as he read his secret police file and wrote *Remembering East Germany*. In fact, that earlier work may be seen as the first of a two-volume memoir, so utterly integral to his project is this second, snapshot volume. Having seen himself through the eyes of the Stasi—and having himself seen through the Stasi—in *Remembering East Germany*, he comes to *Snapshots* with a transformed perspective, his memories unleashed for a more personal, more subjective memoir of life in East Germany.

He seeks to "partially recreate this bygone world" he experienced at first hand in the 1970s and 1980s, for the benefit of English-speaking readers today; he includes a brief history of East Germany, 1949-1989, for readers too young to remember its 40-year existence. The snapshots are grouped, as in a gallery exhibition, into categories by theme—two series of snapshots focusing on the East German police state, two focusing on GDR writers, four focusing on various encounters with people and aspects of everyday life in the GDR, and a final series tracking watershed moments of East German history.

The book's epigraph starkly reminds us: "The German Democratic Republic was neither democratic nor a republic. It was a repressive dictatorship." The initial two series of snapshots ground us in that truth. These are also the closest "siblings" to the previous memoir. In the grouping POLICE AND SECRET POLICE, Zipser's snapshots provide an informative description of the police state and explanation of the role of the Stasi, with long shots and close-ups illuminating each other. State realities are translated into personal terms, the pervasive hierarchical state spy network crystallized in the specific acquaintances who informed on him. As we read the snapshot *In Search of My Stasi-File*, we see Zipser obtaining his file through a historic process created after the reunification of Germany—a law creating a new government agency responsible for preserving GDR State Security records and giving victims of Stasi surveillance the right to access their files. Like the files of hundreds of thousands of East Germans, Zipser's was classified as a victim's file ("Opferakte"). The informants' reports are not reproduced in this memoir, putting the focus even more squarely on the file's very existence and the memories stirred while reading it. Learning that the Stasi had classified him as "enemy of the state"—a person who from the State Security Service's point of view had given indications of hostile activity—put his scholarly work on East German literature into a new perspective.

Zipser had initially become interested in GDR literature during the visit to Oberlin of noted East German author Christa Wolf in spring 1974. A recent Johns Hopkins PhD in German, he had developed, with Wolf's encouragement, his first sabbatical project, focusing on contemporary literary trends in the GDR. He spent that sabbatical, and a subsequent 1977-78 stay in East Berlin as an International Research and Exchanges Board (IREX) grant recipient, meeting with many writers and collecting samples of their work for inclusion in a book to be published in the US. He became friends with a number of writers critical of the communist state, interacting with them professionally as well as at social gatherings, for which he occasionally made runs to West Berlin via Checkpoint Charlie to obtain items unavailable in East Berlin. The lives of these writers were made difficult by secret police surveillance, withholding of travel visas, Writers' Union censorship or ostracism, and even, in the case of famous writer/singer Wolf Biermann, expatriation. Zipser himself, given his work's potential impact on the GDR's image abroad, faced some heavy-handedness on the part of state Writers' Union officials. Despite obstacles, they all continued.

These early career experiences comprised a crucial part of Zipser's professional formation, as well as his personal growth. Indeed, this is a memoir interweaving his story with the story of a country not his native land, but which nevertheless significantly influenced the direction and meaning of his life. The memoir's *Bildungsroman* aspect serves as a reminder that study of another language, culture, and literature is a life-changing, coming-of-age sort of experience, enlarging one's world and expanding one's worldview. It is not at all a process of leaving behind one's native land, but of allowing one's native perspective and the perspective gained abroad to inform each other. Living in another country challenges and changes us in some way; as millions of study-abroad participants can attest, it is transformative and enriching. Still, how does that enriching experience play out in a totalitarian regime?

The two series of snapshots focusing on GDR writers are instructive. Just as the snapshot collections on police and state security revisit and refocus Zipser's *Remembering East Germany,* the collections on GDR writers recapture and refocus his *DDR-Literatur im Tauwetter* (GDR Literature During the Thaw), the book he wrote on contemporary GDR literature in the 1970s. The 840-page *DDR-Literatur im Tauwetter* included representative short works by some 45 GDR writers and a biographical sketch of each, as well as the transcript of a recorded interview with each writer discussing the evolving role of literature in the socialist state and the social problems of greatest concern to the writer during that Cold War time. *Snapshots* condenses the literary field to a representative photogenic essence: the author's eight favorite GDR writers and, with some overlap, the six GDR writers who were invited and eventually allowed to travel to Oberlin College as writers-in-residence. Their works are not anthologized here, but major works of each writer are discussed. The accompanying bios are not "traditional" biographies, but snapshots in a photo album of personal remembrances, compiled post-Cold War, post-Stasi file. These are close-ups of friends and professional colleagues, and the author is often included in the photo-shoot. Both in Oberlin and in East Berlin, Zipser's life was entwined with those of these writers, and with their works.

As we have seen, it was Christa Wolf, the first East German writer to come to Oberlin, who had inspired the 31-year-old Zipser's interest in GDR literature and helped design his first sabbatical project. Like all of the writers in *Snapshots,* Wolf had suffered literary persecution. Her third and most famous novel, *Nachdenken über Christa T.* (The Quest for Christa T., 1968), while a bestseller in West Germany, had been attacked by the East German Writers' Union and eventually banned by government officials who saw beneath the surface story of the young Christa T. a representation of life in a repressive, intolerant, conformist society. Zipser's presentation of Wolf's heroine captures both the immediacy and the universality of her quest: "[The] heroine searches with increasing awareness to find herself. The search, not so much for self as for the right way in life, is at the same time a search for truth. . . [T]he reconstruction of the past, even one's own past, gives rise to the question that concerns so many novelists: What really happened?"

This is a question worthily pursued by memoirist Zipser. It is not surprising that he notes the strong autobiographical component of the novel, pointing to "its insistence on finding oneself while at the same time serving society." It was an insistence he saw courageously shared by all the GDR writers he presents here, whose works testify to their crucial but dangerous quest for truth-telling in a society rife with repression and lies. Zipser's snapshot bios of these writers go beneath the banal surface of standard biographical profiles to try to reconstruct what actually happened, documenting their literary lives as well as the cost paid in a full gamut of persecutions endured—being banned from publishing in the GDR, expelled from the Writers' Union, denied other sources of income for livelihood, put under house arrest, assailed through harassment of family members, threatened with prison for protesting reprisals against fellow writers, forced into exile or self-exile.

As these dissident writers insisted on finding themselves while serving society, it must have been enormously heartening to discover at their side an American colleague who admired their personal courage and the honesty of their works, who was ready to stand by them and determined to bring their work to the international attention so feared by GDR officials. Zipser persevered in inviting these writers to Oberlin even when the GDR's creation of the "delegation principle" made that increasingly difficult. He joined their quest, with his boundary-crossing scholarship and friendships. Now in his memoirs he continues to seek the truth as he reconstructs the past—his own and that of the GDR he experienced.

Against the bleak backdrop of literary censorship and self-censorship in the GDR, he tells of brave unofficial and illegal publications, including one *samizdat* quietly entrusted to him by Luth Rathenow at the Leipzig

Book Fair in 1985 and an illegal anthology project, "Berliner Geschichten," planned by his friends Ulrich Plenzdorf, Klaus Schlesinger, and Martin Stade. He hails Joachim Walther's landmark 1996 study, *Sicherungsbereich Literatur: Schriftsteller und Staatssicherheit in der Deutschen Demokratischen Republik* (Security Zone Literature: Writers and State Security in the German Democratic Republic), which chronicles with painstaking documentation the countless acts of harsh literary repression committed by the GDR regime. Walther's work, writes Zipser, serves as a bulwark against attempts (by GDR loyalists even today) to suppress the truth and rewrite history—a bulwark further strengthened by the publication of previously suppressed literature, thanks to the efforts of Walther and his colleague Ines Geipel.

To fully honor the truth *about* the writers, it is necessary to read the truth *of* the writers. Zipser impels us to do that, following up *Tauwetter*'s anthology with an extensive, insistent annotated bibliography in his literary snapshots. In each snapshot of a GDR writer, Zipser gives an overview of that writer's oeuvre, discussing several works and their memorable protagonists—an army of witnesses. After Wolf's Christa T., he introduces us to blue-jeaned rebel Edgar Wibeau in (blue-jeaned) Ulrich Plenzdorf's famous Goethe parody, *Die neuen Leiden des jungen W.* (The New Sufferings of Young W., 1972); ghetto-bound Jacob in prose writer/filmmaker Jurek Becker's internationally renowned *Jakob der Lügner* (Jacob the Liar, 1969); rioting construction workers in Stefan Heym's *5 Tage im Juni* (5 Days in June, 1956) and a defiant Daniel Defoe in Heym's *Die Schmähschrift oder Königin gegen Defoe* (The Queen against Defoe, 1970); the teenage daughter of Reiner Kunze's minimalist masterpiece *Die wunderbaren Jahre* (The Wonderful Years, 1976); Wilhelm Blach, the fearful hero of Karl-Heinz Jacobs' *Wilhelmsburg* (1979); the disillusioned, displaced socialist idealist in Bernd Jentzsch's poetry volume, *Quartiermachen* (Securing Quarters, 1978); the distinctive "Sarah-Sound" of Sarah Kirsch in her lyric poetry collection *Landaufenthalt* (A Stay in the Country, 1967); the *Empire State Building* (translated by Zipser for this snapshot) in Günter Kunert's *Der andere Planet: Ansichten von Amerika* (The Other Planet: Views about America, 1975); the animal tamer in Sarah Kirsch's

Die Pantherfrau: Fünf Frauen in der DDR (The Panther Woman: Five Tales from the Cassette Recorder, 1973); the torn young lovers in Volker Braun's *Unvollendete Geschichte* (Unfinished Story, 1975); the brave environmental journalist Josefa in Monika Maron's *Flugasche* (Flight of Ashes, 1981); the cats, cows, dogs, and plants of Sarah Kirsch's poetry in *Katzenleben: Gedichte* (Catlives, 1984). Zipser's final literary snapshot of *Recommended Readings* includes many of these, available in English translation.

Snapshots also brings into focus scenes from Zipser's experience of everyday life in a country with an authoritarian regime—a transformative experience yielding valuable cross-cultural perspective. His snapshots in the collections PEOPLE, EXPERIENCES, SHOPPING, and THINGS are sometimes alarming, sometimes charming, always revealing. Anyone who has lived abroad will smile at Zipser's James Bond moment—using the hair-in-the-suitcase trick from a John le Carré spy novel to detect possible invasion of his hotel room—, or his stint as Marlboro Man in the eyes of East Germans taken with his shearling sheepskin coat, blue jeans, leather boots, and Burt Reynolds mustache, or—less flattering—his Maxwell Smart clumsiness while trying to switch license plates at an East German border crossing. We can identify with occasions on which he unwittingly gives himself away as a cultural outsider, as in *Soap and Bananas*, where using the luxury soap but eschewing the luxury bananas convinces his East German acquaintances that he is a clueless American, not a clever spy. He lives in a drab, cockroach-infested apartment supplied by the state, he joins long lines of people queueing for scarce goods, he experiences a frightening stay in a substandard hospital—while always aware that, for him, alternatives are available, that he has access to hotels for foreigners, to medical care abroad, to shopping at the exclusive Intershop. He enjoys trips across the border to West Berlin, often bringing back to friends coveted items such as blue jeans—or necessities in short supply, such as toilet paper (some fifty years before the American shortage). His one friend in his apartment building is another outsider, Chilean grad student Carlos, who offers him practical advice on dealing with the cockroaches. In *Resistance and Solidarity*, Zipser eventually wins the begrudging respect of the building's East German occupants when he posts a defiant sign announcing his refusal to make a "voluntary" donation to the communist cause in North Vietnam. In *The Inventor* he poignantly portrays an ambitious East German's eagerness to reveal his frustration to an American. While Zipser laments in *Bucket List* the severely limited prospects available to those living in the GDR, he does not fail to admire the brilliant photography of Roger Melis (whose portraits of many writers appeared in *Tauwetter*), nor to point out the enduring appeal of East Germany's *Little Traffic Light Man* and the wonderful ingenuity that created the beautiful *Erika* portable typewriter.

The cross-cultural perspective of the memoir is enhanced by the snapshots in which Zipser recounts experiences of the East Germans in Oberlin and their reactions to American culture—the counterpart to Zipser's experiences, and their own, in the GDR. He clearly enjoys recalling the visits of the writers-in-residence and the time spent together in the US. His office was always near the office assigned to the writer, conducive to daily back-and-forth. Zipser and his wife hosted many meals, just as Zipser had been a frequent dinner guest at the homes of friends in East Germany. Zipser's snapshot of Christa Wolf incorporates her delightful, insightful first-person account of her stay, in which she shows a good-natured accommodation to culture shock as she touches on topics ranging from American white bread to Midwestern tornadoes, from kitchen gadgets to bicycles, from Richard Nixon to medical care to the college classroom. Ulrich Plenzdorf, "even more opposed to smoking than the [US] Surgeon General," was in 1975 ahead of his time, inspiring Zipser to remove ashtrays and declare his home a no-smoking zone. Writers' reactions to life in the US are implicit in elements of Zipser's snapshots throughout: the Plenzdorfs' purchase of a car to "see the USA in their Chevrolet"; Jurek Becker's love of Baskin-Robbins ice cream and his defense of baseball; Stefan Heym's American citizenship, Bronze Star service in the US army in WW II and later return to discontent in East Germany. We have much to learn from looking at our society through their eyes.

Zipser's final collection of snapshots captures watershed moments of his shared history with the GDR, from his first visit to East Berlin—an undergraduate study-abroad excursion in 1963, just two weeks before President Kennedy's famous *"Ich bin ein Berliner"* speech in West Berlin—all the way to the fall of the Berlin Wall in 1989 and German reunification in 1990. The story of his early career intersects with the story of East Germany, and Zipser is deservedly recognized and celebrated today for the cultural and geopolitical significance of his groundbreaking scholarship, his courageous solidarity with dissident writers, and his career-long commitment to building community across boundaries. A signature legacy of his own formative experiences abroad may, indeed, be seen in the extraordinary panoply of study abroad programs and opportunities created for students of languages, literatures and cultures during his distinguished tenure as department chair at the University of Delaware.

The day in January 1999 on which Zipser's Stasi file arrived in his mailbox in Delaware was another watershed moment of shared history, as it was his reading of the file that inspired the writing of these memoirs. On the back cover of *Remembering East Germany*, Zipser quotes Timothy Garton Ash, another GDR memoirist: "But what a gift to memory is a Stasi file. Far better than a madeleine." The evocation of Proust's madeleine beautifully epitomizes the experience of rediscovering a lost time. The Stasi file was, indeed, a gift for Zipser, both triggering and transforming memories. While his younger self informed who he is today, his present self nevertheless sees through transformed eyes. Likewise, the Stasi file is a gift to us, via Zipser's memoirs, which put before us that "lost" time and place, offering us increased understanding that can inform—perhaps transform—our perspectives, as we strive to meet the challenges of free speech, disinformation, censorship, and surveillance today, and continue to face crises of oppression and aggression that threaten democratic society worldwide.

Bonnie Arden Robb

March 2022